Chronicles of Hope™

Chronicles of Hope™

The Collective

Book 2

Lois Hermann
with Gary Scott

*"Our vision is to shift humanity's course to be more positive
by sharing insights of the Collective."*

—Team Hope, those dedicated to *Chronicles of Hope*

For permissions, contact:
Lois Hermann & Associates, LLC
Email: Info@LoisHermann.com

Publisher:
Light Publishing
An imprint of Peter E. Randall Publisher LLC
Nashua, New Hampshire, USA

ISBN – Softcover: 978-0-9971567-5-1
ISBN – E-book: 978-0-9971567-6-8
ISBN – Audio Book: 978-0-9971567-7-5
Library of Congress Control Number: 2020913032

Chronicles of Hope™ is a registered trademark of
Lois Hermann & Associates, LLC
www.LoisHermann.com

Chronicles of Hope
www.ChroniclesOfHope.net

Cover illustration by Victoria Dry
Book design by Grace Peirce

Editors:
Christine B. Snyder
Lizabeth R. S. Fleenor

"Gaia never gives up.
She is the guiding force behind hope."
—Anquietas

"We are ever grateful to the Anquietas,
their Children, their Children's Children, and our precious Gaia,
for honoring us with their insight, wisdom, and sage advice.
We hope to bring humanity to a place of peace,
for our children and our children's children."
—Team Hope

Praise for *Chronicles of Hope*

"*Chronicles of Hope: The Collective* is your port in the storm. This book offers a solid format for fantastic intellectual, spiritual, and emotional growth. The structure of this book is brilliant. It is simple, not simplistic!" —Albert Marotta, MA, CHT, Transpersonal Hypnotherapist

"This book is so amazingly true. It is a truth I know in my body, mind, and spirit." —Linda M. Thunberg, MHT, Owner Transpersonal Power Hypnotherapy, President National Association of Transpersonal Hypnotherapists

"You will be guided to transform yourself and our conflicted world by the sacred messages that guide us to enlightenment. A masterful book to awaken the sleeping soul. A must read in this lifetime!" —Sheryl Glick, RMT, Author, Host of Healing from Within

"Inspiration and action. Lois Hermann's latest book provides the thirsty reader a greater understanding of how we as individuals can positively affect change for ourselves and our collective humanity." —Kelly Dwyer, Owner of Inner Balance Wellness Coaching, LLC

"I have studied many topics that Lois Hermann covers, and this critical information is a must read for all of us. It is time we wake up to live our true path, and this is the place to start." —Lisa Schermerhorn, CHT, RMT, Peak Performance Mindset Coach

"These profound, groundbreaking insights can guide us into a new era of safer times. We, the readers, will finish this story. The fate of humanity depends on the readers of *Chronicles of Hope*." —Caroline Snyder, Holistic Health Advocate, Teenage Blogger

Contents

Foreword

"By taking responsibility for your own spiritual awakening,
you impact humanity's awakening."
—Chantelle Renee

The greatest books are the books that change people's lives. They tell the world something it needs to hear, even if it challenges everything that was thought to be true. *Chronicles of Hope: The Collective* is exactly that book!

I had the pleasure of meeting Lois Hermann at the Heartland Hypnosis Conference in St. Louis, Missouri. I was instantly enamored by her compassionate heart and enthusiastic care and concern for humanity. Her vibrant and authentic energy is what allows the spirit of love to flow through her writing and into the heart of the reader. This genuine heart-centered connection between writer and reader invites you to delve deeply into each hypnosis session to connect with the Divine energy in everyone and everything. This book is a testament to the fact that there is nothing that love and hope cannot touch, not even our deepest wounds.

As an author myself, I've always believed the best books are those that truly make a difference. You know the ones, the books that lovingly tell you what you need to hear, and yet somehow manage to question beliefs that you have been taught. I invite you to a consciousness-expanding activation of your heart that will simultaneously awaken you, challenge you, and inspire you to join Team Hope. The information in *Chronicles of Hope* can only be described as a download of Divine proportions, a sacred tome. This series of messages provide insights to guide us through these transformational times.

Each session reveals gems of profound wisdom to help humanity usher in the age of unity consciousness. The ancient wisdom brought forth to these modern times takes you on an interstellar ride to new internal heights. Anyone who reads this book is sure to walk away with abundant resources that can serve them for the rest of their lives and beyond. The essential practices given by the Collective increase our vibrational energy and teach the world how to embody love and transcend fear.

As with any change, you will know the truth by the way you feel. With this in mind, I encourage you to feel your way through this book series. Keep your heart and mind open as you journey into an enlightened state of remembrance. I dare you to step into the magic of who you were born to be and allow the infinite possibilities to transform your life.

You can help save all generations to come by cultivating compassion and accountability for the energy you give and receive. Living the principles of the messages offered in *Chronicles of Hope* allows us to transform not only ourselves but humanity as well. Through the process of energetic purging and healing of our self-limiting programming, we neutralize destructive ideas that have rendered us powerless. Isn't it time to rid ourselves of those negative self-beliefs and heal the wounds we have carried for far too long?

Together, we can transform ourselves, one spirit at a time, from the inside out. We are no longer on the outside looking in, detached from our lives. Step into your Divine power now. As we focus on spiritual awareness, we usher in a new age in which we will live in tandem with our own Divinity and each other. We are here to transcend and anchor higher vibrational frequencies. When we build upon these foundational insights, we can birth peace in our hearts and bring hope to humanity. We are the new revolutionaries. Join the revolution!

Chantelle Renee
Certified Hypnotherapist, Intuitive Energy Healer
Golden Heart Hypnosis Center, Chatham, Illinois
Author of *Aligning with the Divine*

"The world is your garden from which you remove weeds of doubt and replace them with seeds of hope."

—Brahma Kumaris

Preface

"Our Mission is to save humanity for our children
and our children's children."

—Team Hope

When you look around at your world today, what do you see? Do you see hope, honesty, and respect? Or do you see fear, anger, and conflict? There is a noticeable lack of integrity in our political, financial, and corporate arenas, along with degradation of our entertainment and social systems. With record-breaking storms, fires, disease, and destruction of our planet, do you wonder how humanity can prevail?

Many of us watch the intense negativity of people in the spotlight with sad hearts and questioning minds. What is the truth? Who can we believe? With busy lives, we wonder if there is anything we could possibly do to avoid the negativity that surrounds us. What can be done to shift ourselves to a place of positive energy so we can make a difference in this compromised world? This book is intended to infuse you with hope and inspire you to make informed, proactive choices, right now.

In Book 1 of the *Chronicles of Hope*™ series, the Anquietas[1] shared their grave concerns about the direction humanity is headed and implored us to take action to stop the negativity that is so pervasive on Earth. In a series of hypnosis-based sessions, these Ancient Ones told us we may not have much time left. The Anquietas offered an understanding of the source of negative energy around us and gave us

---

1. Anquietas (ohn-kwee-A-tus) is ancient Greek for Ancient Ones. In *Chronicles of Hope: The Anquietas: Book 1,* they are the First Ones, the First Consciousness who say they are eight and they are one.

ways to clear our energy to be more positive. As professorial historians, they provided details on the creation of the Universe, the evolution of life, and the growth of humanity. They spoke of civilizations that flourished and others that have been lost. The Ancient Ones outlined fascinating details of the five mass extinctions Earth has experienced. They are alarmed that if we do not shift our energy to the positive now, we may be facing the sixth mass extinction. The Anquietas leaves us with a powerful desire to look closely at what is not working with our civilization and inspires us to do what we can to shift our energy to make things right before it is too late.

In *Chronicles of Hope: The Collective,* the second book in the series, we hear from individual spirits of the Collective.[2] This group of wise spiritual beings comprise the Anquietas, their Children, their Children's Children, along with other positive energetic beings who seek to assist our world in various ways.

These spiritual Guides in the unseen world help humanity with a watchful eye. Energetically close to life on Earth, they have been directly involved with the evolution of humanity. They speak with a unique wisdom from their experience with life on this planet since the beginning of time, sharing their passion to help us evolve to a peaceful existence.

You heard from the Anquietas in Book 1. In *Chronicles of Hope: The Collective*, you will hear from an ancient God, a beloved prophet, a little-known Goddess, and a misunderstood Archangel. The expansive Spirit of the Universe and the Spirit of the Earth, our Mother Gaia, share their insight. Whether you believe in many Gods, one God or no God, these spiritual beings of the Collective represent the positive energy that exists to assist us in our daily lives. They give specific information on what causes the intense negativity in our world and offer detailed instructions on what we can do to lift our individual energy. They encourage us to join together to shift the energy of our entire planet. If we each do our own part, we have the opportunity

---

2. The Collective is the group of spirits vibrating at extremely high levels that communicates in the sessions of this book. It consists of the Anquietas (the Ancient Ones), their Children, and their Children's Children.

to form a *human collective* that will make a definitive difference in the ultimate outcome for humanity. There is hope, and I hope you are inspired to embrace the teachings in this book to help yourselves, your family, your community, and your world.

The coronavirus disease (COVID-19) pandemic took over this world in early 2020. Writing this book, I observed the fear that pervaded our lives and affected our wellbeing on multiple levels: physical, mental, emotional, and financial. With the extended period of confinement, the world as we knew it came to an abrupt halt. How individuals respond to and emerge from this impactful change determines their fate. Will we see it as devastating and fall into the abyss of despair? Or, will we acknowledge the silver lining in this worldwide crisis as an opportunity for much-needed positive change that may ultimately save humanity and our beloved planet?

This timely compilation of wisdom from the Collective is designed to teach each of us how to shift our energy to be more positive, starting with ourselves. It is intended to bring hope in these uncertain times, giving us important information and specific instructions. Think of humanity as one collective organism, one being, made of many individuals on this planet we call home. This living planet, our Mother Earth, has a spirit known as Gaia. Currently, it's as if a cancer of negativity has infected humanity. As this negative energy spreads, it eats away at healthy lives and erodes the vital flesh of our precious Earth. What if we could neutralize this insidious disease and establish a strong, healthy civilization based on positive energy, respect, and hope? Can we create a paradise on this beautiful planet that is home to so many amazing creatures? It will take effort. Don't you think it is worth it to have a thriving civilization for ourselves, our children, and our grandchildren?

The intention of the *Chronicles of Hope* series is to share sacred messages that were given to assist humanity to shift their course in a more positive direction. As we evolve to a more enlightened way of relating to each other, we create a civilization based on respect, willingness, and hope for ourselves and our future. Please welcome this information into your minds and take it into your hearts as an offer of hope for everyone on Earth. You are invited to embark on a mesmerizing journey that will cause you to pause, to reflect, and to change the way you embrace life and others around you. *Chronicles of Hope* invites you to assist in the mission to save our precious planet and the life that lives in, on, and around her.

> *"We must protect the forests for*
> *our children, grandchildren, and children yet to be born.*
> *We must protect the forests for those who can't speak for themselves*
> *such as the birds, animals, fish, and trees."*
> —Qwatsinas (Hereditary Chief Edward Moody), Nuxalk Nation

Introduction

"Our vision is to shift humanity's course to be more positive
by sharing the insights of the Collective."
—Team Hope

Welcome to the *Chronicles of Hope*, a journey that began with the Anquietas, the Ancient Ones, who sounded the alarm for the troubling path of humanity in Book 1. We now continue this awe-inspiring adventure in Book 2, where I am honored to have received additional channeled insights from other High-Level Spirits. I am humbled to share these important messages, instructions, and valuable insights from individuals of the Collective. This group of Wise Beings came through in a series of hypnosis sessions to bring messages for you. Because you are reading these words, you are already an important part of this transformational journey. To gain a greater understanding of the Anquietas' concerns and the history of mankind, we encourage you to read Book 1. However, you will be able to grasp the concepts and messages shared by the Collective in Book 2, which builds on the foundational information from the Anquietas.

Much of what the Anquietas told us in the sessions compiled in Book 1 relates to negative energy, what it is, and how it affects humans. We received information on how to keep our energy clear and protected. These Ancient Ones are more distant to life on Earth and cannot comprehend how the negative became so pervasive in human culture. The Anquietas are 8 spirits, and they are one together. Many of their reference numbers are based on the number 8.

The Anquietas' Children experience closer contact with worlds, yet their energetic frequency, or "vibrational energy," is too high to incarnate or take physical form. Of their 512 Children, which is 8 to the third power, many are ancient Gods of mythology, some are Gods in polytheistic religions, and some we now call Archangels. There are 32,768 of the Anquietas' Children's Children, which is 8 to the fifth power. The Children's Children are able to incarnate, often as prophets of history such as Jesus, Buddha, Muhammad, Quan Yin, and Lao Tzu. When not in physical form, they assist as angels and Guides. Members of this "Collective" of spirits are the ones who reach out to connect with humanity in this book series.

These representatives of the Collective describe the root cause of fear, anger, and conflict in our civilization. They express concern at how it will be our own undoing if we do not shift our path toward the positive. These Wise Ones answer questions as to how these negative emotions came to be. They advise what we might do to make necessary changes to heal ourselves through choices we make and actions we take.

Join with me and listen to Rae, the Patron God of Atlantis, as he shares his advice on the mysteries of his civilization, as well as how it thrived on integrity, honesty, and truth. Walk the path with the prophet Jesus as he wants to know what happened to his messages of compassion, kindness, and brotherly love. He reiterates what he told us two thousand years ago: *"You are all one. Do unto others as you would have them do unto you."*

The Goddess Aurora is concerned there is so much hate and disregard for human life and the life of our planet. She encourages us to choose a path of acceptance, tolerance, and peace. Understand how the Archangel Samael brings discord and challenge so humanity may grow into strong, enlightened beings who choose to live a life of helpfulness. Meet the Spirit of the Universe, who reveals the message of our interconnectivity with all that is and encourages us to put aside differences that isolate, and instead seek commonality and togetherness. Welcome the spirit of our Mother Earth, Gaia, as she pleads with humanity, telling us exactly what we must do to help her return our world to the paradise it once was.

By listening to those who comprise the Collective, we will know it is possible to prevent the inevitable demise of our home. If we can shift the trend of negativity, these Wise Ones encourage us that humanity *does* have a chance to reverse the spiral and thrive. As each one of us makes choices every day that move us away from negativity and world destruction, we move toward positivity and inspire hope. Thank you sincerely for joining the journey with the Anquietas and the Collective, and for being an important part of the mission to save our precious planet and humanity.

While this book is not about hypnosis, it plays a large role as the information came through Gary while he was in a hypnotic state of awareness. Hypnosis is an altered state of consciousness where the subconscious part of the mind, the internal driver and storehouse of every memory, is in a place of focused awareness. A person in a hypnotic state is very relaxed, which allows them to tap into a place of inner knowing, become open to shifting old patterns, and receive positive thoughts for change.

I learned hypnosis in the mid-nineties to help myself and my children recover from intense personal trauma. Decades later, as a Board-Certified Hypnotist I help people find peace of mind in a variety of situations. Clients achieve goals, lower stress, get focused, change undesirable habits, and improve sleep. Coming from a place of non-judgment, I am privileged to have guided thousands of clients to resolve patterns of negativity with the influence of their amazing minds and powerful Guides. I love what I do and receive much satisfaction in helping people shift the negativity in their life to be more positive. While I am a private person and have little interest in being in the spotlight, I am committed to sharing the messages that were revealed to me through these hypnosis sessions.

Throughout this journey, I often wondered why I was selected to deliver these messages. Over time, it was unveiled to me why I may have been asked to be their messenger. I believe my background may have played a role. Having experienced extreme trauma and great loss, I learned to rise above personal challenges to a place of peace. As a seasoned medical professional, I witnessed extreme suffering. As a department manager, I was involved in acquisition of cutting-edge medical technologies. As a corporate director, I supported professional staff and patients in crisis. As a systems designer, I traveled the world experiencing medical care in many countries. As a single mother, I am incredibly proud of two remarkable young adults with whom I am blessed to share my life. I tend to be organized, am well-traveled, and unbiased. I have been on my own spiritual journey for dozens of years, have been fascinated by angels, have seen fairies, and have a deep connection with Mother Nature. I have fought my own intense battles with negativity and learned to embrace the powerful assistance from amazing Guides of the spirit world. These experiences helped to prepare me to bring this project to you.

Over the years, I have developed techniques to help people connect with the wisdom of their superconscious mind. This is the infinite part of the mind that communicates with higher sources of wisdom in different ways. It could be referred to as the wise mind, Divine wisdom, or higher power. This is the energy that connects with angelic beings, ascended masters, loved ones, and other spiritual Guides.

While connecting with their superconscious mind, people learn to ask for and receive messages and direction from their inner guidance system. Once they develop an ongoing relationship with their Guides, life is never the same. They feel safe and protected, gaining insight and awareness that allows for growth on all levels: mind, body, and spirit. Clients remember their hypnosis journeys and their personal connection with unseen helpers. They embrace the wisdom shared in their specific situation. As a facilitator in their empowerment process, I have learned much over the years. This has been an all-encompassing ascension journey for me.

One of the unique uses for hypnosis in my practice is to clear negative energies that are around clients. While in a trance state, clients can readily connect with their own wise mind and other helpful spirits. However, to communicate with higher vibrational beings, clients must first remove any negative interference from energies that are lowering their own vibrational rate.

Some spirits of people who died are stuck in the Earth's plane and are often attracted to and attach themselves to living humans. Because of the spirit's situation at the time of their death, be it from confusion, emotional attitude, or lack of belief, they did not go into the Light (many refer to the Light as heaven). Since these lost spirits often long to communicate with the living, they linger around friends, family members, or others for different reasons. As these earth-bound spirits have no energy source of their own, they unknowingly drain the energy of their living host. Often, they negatively influence the thoughts and behaviors of the one they are attracted to. With the assistance of spirit Guides, especially Archangel Michael, these lost spirits are taken to their appropriate place in the Light. As a result, the client's vibrational energy lifts, and they feel better, lighter. This shift allows them to resonate at a higher level where they can truly sense and receive answers from their own positive spiritual sources.

These higher sources of wisdom are ever here to assist. To communicate freely with them, we must raise our own vibrational rate to more closely match theirs. The techniques I have learned and developed over the years to help wayward spirits are gentle, much like helping a child lost in a store to find their parent. It is important to come from a place of non-judgment, compassion, and willingness to assist. Empowerment comes with knowing that the angelic realm truly does the work. I have learned to simply ask, believe, receive, and acknowledge their assistance with gratitude.

In Book 1, the Anquietas gave a more distant historical view of our world. Throughout the sessions in Book 2, you will hear from individuals of the Collective who have been more directly involved with the evolution of humanity from its inception. They share insights from their perspective on the specific origins of negative emotions humans exhibit and give detailed instruction on how to shift these toxic feelings. Low-level emotions such as hate, anger, greed, and fear cause great harm to individuals and humanity. Even emotional states of apathy and indifference generate distress, since they allow the negative to proliferate. These Wise Ones give us specific instructions as to what we can do to shift our emotions to be more positive. As a result, we discover ways of being calm, centered, uplifted, and enlightened, which is exactly what we need to do to save humanity.

Have you ever been around someone who is so positive you find yourself feeling uplifted and smiling as well? Energy is contagious. Even one person changing their energy has a ripple effect on others. A positive shift results in others around them experiencing an elevation in their vibration rate. People like the Dalai Lama and Mother Teresa resonate at very high levels and impact others in a positive way simply with their presence, be it physical or spiritual.

All beings across the Universe are made of vibrational energy. We vibrate at different levels based on our emotions, how old our spirit is, the number of lives (incarnations) we have had, and the type of spirit, i.e. animal or human. In his book *Power vs. Force: The Hidden Determinants of Human Behavior,* David R. Hawkins, MD, PhD, demonstrates the relative energy of emotions on a logarithmic scale of 20 to 1,000, with 700–1,000 being enlightenment or pure consciousness. Mother Theresa resonates at 750, the energy of peace is 600, love resonates at 500, and energies of acceptance and forgiveness are at 350. The mean value is 200, which is neutrality, empowerment, and courage. Emotions such as fear, anger, and hate are all extremely low-level emotions that resonate below 150. The lowest-level energies are shame and guilt, resonating at 20 and 30 on this scale. These low vibrational energies deplete our energy, restrict, constrict, and limit our mindset, which affect our choices, and can destroy our lives.

While a technical read, Dr. Hawkins' book is filled with insight as to the comparative values of emotional energy. In his research, he found that when we vibrate at the low-level energy of fear, for instance, everything we see through our lens of life will be fear-based. There may be other wonderful emotions and encouraging opportunities surrounding us, but our vision will be laser focused: we see only fear, think only fear, attract more fear, and sink into the heavy abyss of fear.

Dr. Hawkins suggests that raising our vibrational energy systematically allows us to experience higher-level emotions. For example, if we can lift ourselves from fear to courage, opportunities abound that were there all along; we just didn't see them because of the self-limiting lens of fear. He notes the energies of hope, willingness, optimism, and inspiration all resonate in the realm of 310. The messages in Book 2 are well above this vibrational level. We aspire to lift the energetic level of humanity, raising the energy one person at a time, so all of humanity ultimately prosper.

Many clients see me for issues related to low vibrational energies, especially those rooted in fear. This can lead to worry, stress, anger, insomnia, and addictive behavior, which often results in poor health. When individuals work to raise their vibrational energy through hope, they ultimately achieve a state of acceptance, contentment, and peace, which leads to joy and love. It is a relatively straightforward process to assist those who possess the courage to want to change themselves. With this book series, we are presented with an altogether different challenge as we aspire to collectively shift the energy of humanity. We are encouraged with numerous opportunities for change through the insightful messages of the Collective.

A few years ago, a quiet, science-minded client named Gary Scott (a pseudonym) came to me for help with sleep issues. His hypnosis sessions were surprisingly unique and different from others in that he remembered little of what transpired while he was in trance. Instead of angels, loved ones, or high-level Guides communicating in his mind, spirits of the Collective spontaneously conversed vocally with me using Gary's body as the means of communication. This phenomenon is often referred to as channeling, when a person allows the energy of a spiritual being to actively communicate through their body to speak with another person.

Starting as I usually do in hypnosis sessions with clearing negative energy, I surprisingly found myself conversing with the low-level energies that were draining Gary's energy. It was interesting to discover more about where they came from and why they were here. In the early sessions, they explained the different types of negative energies influencing people, animals, and places. I was given insight as to how to lift the energies in and around each person, place, and loved one.

Suddenly, High-Level Spirits started speaking to me through Gary. Calling themselves the Anquietas, these Ancient Ones sounded the alarm that humanity may not have much time left. They gave me insight into what we can do to shift ourselves toward a more positive and hopeful direction. The Anquietas offered incredible insight on civilization's history, the origin of conflict, the importance of spirituality, and gave humans hope for our future. They gave advice about what needs to change before it is too late for humanity to recover. These messages were given or channeled through Gary to me, with the request that I disseminate them to the world.

They shared that it is very unusual for members of the Collective to speak to humans directly, as it is difficult for them to match the energy of a human. Gary's purpose was to be the conduit for their direct communication. While in a meditative or prayerful state, we can all learn to readily communicate in our minds with members of the Collective. They share infinite wisdom from their expansive spiritual consciousness, which is incredibly valuable. The difference in this case was there was an actual two-way conversation. I am honored and humbled to experience these conversations, to receive their messages, and to share them with you.

While the Anquietas never offered unsolicited information, it was like listening to a lecturing history professor. They spoke slowly and methodically. Gary's body barely moved during these sessions, and his eyes usually remained closed. He reported being very stiff and a little sore when the sessions were finished. In the last session of Book 1, the Anquietas advised that we consult with one of their Children. Since their Children's vibrational energy was nearer to our physical realm, these Wise Ones could provide more details of life on Earth. This was the beginning of the amazingly insightful adventures in Book 2. These sessions were of a completely different nature than the more historical discourse from the Anquietas in the early sessions.

In Book 2, you meet some of the Children and Children's Children who have energies more closely matched to humans. Their conversations are more animated, expressive, and personal than the more professorial approach of the Anquietas (their parents). The spirits who came through Gary passed on things they had observed and learned. Some actually lived on Earth, and others have been closely associated with humanity for ages. The spirits with whom we communicated were of a vibrational energy level closer to Gary's own, thus were able to animate, to varying degrees, Gary's body. His eyes opened, he looked directly at me, gestured with his hands, and at times, even sat up and moved freely in the chair.

Most importantly, these spirits were not lecturing in response to a question; these were actual conversations with spirits who had distinct personalities. Although they, too, never offered unsolicited information, they waited to be asked like the Anquietas, yet would sometimes prompt the question. I capture their personas and convey the variety of their energy as the conversations unfold, but there is a striking difference in their communication and connection. Although the theme of their messages is similar, their distinctive personalities influenced their attitude, perspective, and delivery style. I am determined to present these messages to you exactly as they were provided to me by these ancient sources of wisdom.

Not only were the interactions in these sessions different, but so was the manner in which the spirits told their stories. Being vibrationally closer to the physical realm, they were more connected to us. Since the Anquietas only knew of humanity's existence through their Children, they told stories based on what they had learned from their Children. Since most of the spirits in Book 2 were more connected with Earth, or had experienced life with humans, they were able to interact with us more naturally during the sessions. This became clearer as I conversed with the Children's Children. The Children and Children's Children offered more personal and passionate advice. In every instance, their messages were fascinating and complex.

Although each of the spiritual beings of the Collective disclosed similar messages in their individual sessions, they added clarity through each conversation. These Wise Ones request that we pay attention to their advice and accept their messages into our hearts. As we take whatever action we can to make a difference, to be more understanding and compassionate, we become uplifted and transformed. Consistently, they tell us *we are all one species* and we need to honor our connection with Gaia, our Mother Earth.

What they deliver in these conversations is a precious example of how deeply vested they are in helping humanity to succeed. Throughout all of our conversations in Book 1 and now in Book 2,

∞   *Chronicles of Hope: The Collective*   xxv

the Collective has been concerned about an approaching apocalypse if humans do not change. They share their knowledge and wisdom with the goal of helping civilization and humanity to survive and thrive. The teachings from the *Chronicles of Hope* series provide a powerful resource for everyone who is sensitive to energies, helps shift energy, or those on a quest to help humankind and our planet evolve. I am grateful there are others around the world who are receiving similar messages in an effort to guide humanity at a very difficult time.

I acknowledge these same messages have been communicated many times from and through different messengers over the course of history. The Collective reinforces and clarifies the messages that were forgotten, misunderstood, or misinterpreted in the past. This time they share more detail with us in a more "human" tone. These insights are vitally important for humanity to hear. Perhaps some of them are clearer in this presentation and quite possibly more current.

In my holistic practice, I work with many healing practitioners who assist clients to achieve their fullest potential. Some of my closest associates are my energy-clearing consultants. These are spiritually-aware individuals who, while in a guided trance state, have developed the skill of seeing, sensing, or feeling another's energy. They can observe and clear energy disturbances in another's auric field. We work together as a team with the incredible guidance and assistance of the Collective to clear negative energy from around clients and gain insight as to what the person should do to keep themselves healthy.

My spiritual team includes Jesus and the Archangels, some of whom you may know and will learn about later: Michael for protection, Raphael for healing, and Jophiel for illumination. Many years ago, I was encouraged to call on Archangel Michael as a protector for my family during a time of intense negative influence and have since developed a strong relationship with him. When asked, the Archangels and others of the Collective are always here to lift our spirits, share their comforting insight, and encourage growth in our own spiritual awareness.

Keeping our team's energy clear of negativity and boosted positively was vital to the creation of this book series. Together, with my valued clearing consultants, we connected with individuals of the Collective to gain additional advice, confirm the accuracy of information, and acknowledge that what they want to be shared was from the highest sources of wisdom. Several of these consultants, including Paul, Denise, and Zeke (all pseudonyms), were present during the sessions and are referenced throughout the sessions.

While my clearing consultants and I regularly clear the energy in and around a person's auric field, it is up to the individual to actively keep their energy clear and positive. They do this by thinking uplifting thoughts, calling on positive energy through prayer and meditation, and asking for assistance from the Collective. There are infinite numbers of physical and spiritual practices that resonate with individuals to enhance their energy. An essential part of the healing process is for a person to take responsibility for their healing. Over time and with consistent effort, people can sustain a lasting change in healthy energy, a transformation that is so needed across all of humanity right now.

An extremely valuable part of this mission is the gratitude I have for my etheric team and my human team who have each played a unique and important role in sharing this work. I could have only produced *Chronicles of Hope* with their encouragement, loving support, and spiritual embrace. It has been an intriguing, life-changing experience for me, and I know it has been for others in a positive, learning, and healing way. These extensive experiences and challenges have shaped my life and coalesced to help me present this work. I am ever grateful to my dedicated Team Hope who support me on this journey.

The intention of *Chronicles of Hope* is to share the words of the Collective without bias. To enhance understanding, each chapter (or hypnosis session) includes an Intention, Conversation, and Reflection section. The Intention section begins each hypnosis session as we set our intention and goals. These capture the essence of the pre-session discussions where Gary, one or more of my clearing consultants, and I consider what we might like to know and what questions would be best to ask.

The Conversation section allows the reader to experience the actual dialogue of the session with the questions I asked, along with detailed answers from the spirits who communicated through Gary. You may notice some inconsistencies with modern grammar in this section as I honor each individual of the Collective, preserving their exact speaking style and unique personality. Some of the Spirits paused frequently to reflect on or search for the appropriate words to say. These pauses are indicated in the text by isolated ellipses (. . .). Brackets [ ] are used to describe behaviors and emotions. Parentheses ( ) are used for clarifying comments. Certain words have been capitalized in this work to acknowledge the importance of their spiritual essence: Earth, Universe, Archangels, Wise Ones, Wise Beings, Guides, High-Level Spirits, Collective, God, Goddess, Divine, and Light.

As a professional hypnotist, I ask open-ended questions to avoid leading clients. I use the same approach in these sessions. In the conversations, I aspire to capture their unique personalities and attitudes by sharing their gestures and expressions in brackets for you to readily experience the session as it transpired. Occasionally, I inter-ject some information or context on topics that might need further explanation. The chapters are purposefully presented in the order of the actual hypnosis sessions, an important element as each session reinforces and expands on the next. I believe the information was methodically provided to us as necessary, and unveiled as intended by the Collective, one spirit at a time.

The Reflection section offers my insight on what transpired in the session based on decades of professional and personal experience. Just as each of the individuals of the Collective who came through were different, each of the ways I interacted with and related to that spirit was unique. Many of my personal and private insights and emotions are captured in this section to offer explanations that may add more insight for the reader.

The Resources section includes lists, guidelines, and specific instructions for living to be used as reference tools. The Highlights section features an outline format for those who would like a recap of the concepts presented. It provides a cohesive summary of the key points from each conversation and is organized in categories for continuity and rapid review. Use these as a reference to reflect on the many deep concepts that are shared. Refer to the Glossary for definitions and expanded versions of the footnotes when you need further clarification.

Through the ages, religion, creed, and faith have played an important role in spiritual growth and connection. People around the world connect with God in diverse ways based on their belief systems. The concepts in *Chronicles of Hope* are spiritually based, though this is not a religious book, nor does it denounce organized religion. One of the important lessons is to feel and act on what resonates within yourself, whether it is going to church, praying on a mountaintop, or meditating on the beach. While visiting mosques, temples, cathedrals, and sacred spaces around the world, I was always fascinated by the similarities between worship methods and prayer offerings among belief systems. All were focused on offering gratitude and requests for assistance, no matter the country, language, or culture.

I will always remember standing on the steps of the Tōdai-ji Temple in front of the Great Buddha at Nara Park, Japan, where the deer roam freely. Visiting on the day of a spring festival, I was taking in the delightful vista of a sea of schoolchildren wearing different-colored beanies. Quite unexpectedly, I heard a strong voice say: "Take care of my children." Having no idea who it was or where it came from, I turned around and no one was there. I shrugged it off and continued to enjoy watching the children when suddenly the voice boomed in my mind even louder: "Take care of my children!" I had to listen, to take notice. Interestingly, I had just received my Reiki Master-Teacher attunement. As one who could now teach the healing modality of Reiki[1] to others, my intuitive connection with the infinite had been awakened. This was the first of many powerful messages from spirit I was to receive over the years to come. I took a moment to wonder if I was supposed to do something specific to take care of children. However, I now understand we are all God's children on

---

1. Reiki (ray-key) is a form of energy balancing and healing that involves a Reiki practitioner placing their hands on or over parts of the receiver's body and can be sent energetically. It is passed to a student through attunements.

this life-giving planet, and I am asked to do what I can to help the children of humanity.

In recent years, people across all demographics have moved away from organized religion for different reasons. In so doing, many of these individuals have lost sight of the importance in the power of prayer, of asking, and expressing gratitude. We are communal beings and thrive on being connected with one another, as well as to higher sources of wisdom. Prayer should be an invitation to commune with helpful energies of our own choosing, whose connection should be comforting, loving, and above all, positive. When you define how you pray, you assist in your own spiritual health and growth. Many consider meditation, chanting, singing, drumming, or dreaming to be forms of prayer. Whether you vocalize your thoughts out loud or have a quiet conversation in your mind, it need not be robotic or memorized.

Spiritual connection could be as simple as a mindful walk in the woods, thanking nature for the air we breathe, acknowledging the trees that give us oxygen, and appreciating the birds who share their songs. When people reconnect with the power of prayer in their own way, they feel less alone, more safe, and experience magical and miraculous healing. Embracing nature is one of the strongest themes emphasized in the teachings of the Collective.

Time and again, these messengers encourage us to pay attention to the native or indigenous cultures' way of living, with their deep respect, prayer, and honor for Mother Earth and all who live in and on her. Their traditions and beliefs should be upheld as a model for living our lives.

I invite you to explore the healing messages shared in this body of work from the Collective. Though some of their directives may surprise you, they are eternally positive, uplifting, and delivered with the intent of bringing hope to humanity. As you experience these conversations, some may challenge your beliefs and undoubtedly fuel much thought from within. As you assimilate their call to action, the objective for you is to understand more about yourself as well as the seen and unseen world around you. Their words may cause you to question what you have been taught, or what you currently believe, which is part of the lesson. Rather than accept everything as absolute, we should open our minds, ask the questions, and explore possibilities in order to learn and grow.

Ultimately, the messages from the Collective give us great insight to help us live happier, healthier, more positive lives. This work is also meant as a guide to help you understand how energies affect us without even being aware of them. Please take the necessary time to notice what resonates within you and integrate what you learn into your daily life. To be more positive, it is imperative to shift negative energies, harmful thoughts, and draining emotions.

We must change our perspective of each other to come from a place of acceptance, harmony, and peace, to shift our world to be more positive. We must heal ourselves to heal our planet . . . individually and together. We need to honor our Earth and show respect for nature. Since we don't know what the future holds, we should focus on doing our best in the present to create the potential for a positive future.

At this moment in time, the foundation of our world is being shaken to cause us to take inventory and appreciate what is important. As we learn to listen to our own hearts instead of the noise so prevalent around us, we will come to know what is true. Let us come together as one civilization to help each other through our world crisis to create a better place for humanity. The intention of this book is to spark your own path toward living a positive life filled with healing Light.

I have taken these sage words from the Collective into my mind, heart, and life. Through my commitment and honoring my promise to these amazingly Wise Beings whom I now consider trusted friends, I humbly share these words with you. Welcome to this most healing journey—one filled with hope!

"The world doesn't belong to leaders.
The world belongs to humanity."
—Dalai Lama

Session 1 ~
I Am Rae
Patron God of Atlantis

"No world is at such a tipping point right now as Earth."
—Rae

Intention

Gary and I were committed to gather insights that these Wise Ones were intent on sharing. In Book 1, our questions prompted the Anquietas to suggest we may want to speak with a Spirit[1] who had been to Earth, one of their Children[2] or Children's Children.[3] These high-level beings would have been among the mythological Gods, Archangels,[4] or other helpful spirits that have a vibrational energy[5] level that allow them to be more closely matched to the Earth's energy.

---

1. Spirit is the immortal part of a living being that continues on when the physical body expires. Sometimes defined as a supernatural being, or a nonphysical entity such as a ghost, fairy, or angel.
2. The Children of the Anquietas have closer contact with worlds, yet their vibrational energy is too high to incarnate. We might know them as Gods of mythology or what we call Archangels.
3. The Anquietas' Children's Children are able to incarnate, often as prophets.
4. An Archangel is an angel of high rank, usually associated with Abrahamic religions. Derived from the Greek ἀρχάγγελος, the word literally means "chief angel." The names and number of Archangels differ by religion.
5. Beings across the Universe are made of vibrational energy. Living things vibrate at different energy levels based on how old the spirit is, the number of lives they have had, and the type of spirit, i.e., animal or human.

We learned much about the different vibrational energy levels of spiritual beings from the Anquietas. Their Children would have been more directly involved in humanity's daily existence and could be able to give more specific details as to what has transpired over time, as well as share their concerns for our future and how we may be able to help.

We were intrigued by the possibilities of communicating with and hearing insights from one of these High-Level Spirits. Perhaps an ancient God or Goddess would come through? We were eager to begin. One of my spiritually-aware clearing consultants,[6] Paul, joined us this day to observe and help to keep the energy strong around us while we embarked on another journey.

Session 1 participants are: Lois, the hypnotist[7] guiding the session; Paul, the clearing consultant observing the session and protecting the energy; Gary, the client channeling the High-Level Spirit; and Rae, the Patron God of Atlantis being channeled through Gary.

---

6. Clearing consultants are spiritually-aware individuals who have developed the skill of seeing, sensing, or feeling another's energy while in a guided trance state. They assist in remotely clearing negative energies around clients.

7. A hypnotist is a person trained in the art of hypnosis who guides others on their journey of self-discovery to change patterns, habits, and attitudes by connecting with the power of the subconscious and superconscious mind.

Conversation

I guide Gary into a gentle hypnotic trance. When he is ready, I proceed.

Lois: We ask for an advanced teacher to come through and speak with us today. It could be Archangel Michael;[8] it could be the Ancient Ones.[9] We are ready, and welcome whomever the Anquietas wants to send to us to answer questions and give us guidance. We are here to listen and be of service.

Rae: Hmmm . . . [Stirs as he takes a deep breath. Opens his eyes, looks at hands, and moves his fingers around as he leans forward in the chair.] *En corporo. Gi estu aeonoy.* [Sits up and looks curiously at Lois, then at Paul.] *Que es tas tee?*[10]

When Rae first speaks, it is in an unknown language. We assume he was speaking an ancient language and have spelled the words phonetically, as they sounded to us in English.

Lois: And, who are you?

Rae: Ah . . . English.

Lois: Yes, English, please. We don't understand many other languages.

Rae: [Smiles as he speaks in a soft, pleasant voice.] I am Rae.

His tone is very different from the more strained and somber dialogue with the Ancient Ones. He pronounced his name "ray," not "rah" like the Egyptian Sun-God Ra.

Lois: Hello, Rae. We are honored to have you here with us.

---

8. Archangel Michael, sometimes referred to as Saint Michael, is considered the great protector. He is often called on to protect humans from evil and help lost souls find their way into the Light.

9. The Ancient Ones, who call themselves the Anquietas, are the "First Ones" in "The Collective" of spirits that we meet in this book. They were coalesced out of Universal Energy when the Universe was formed.

10. Spelled as we heard, we assume this is an Atlantean language spoken by Rae.

Rae: Thank you.

Lois: Please tell us about yourself.

Rae: It has been a long time since I have been in a body.

Lois: Oh really . . . how long?

Rae: [Pauses to consider.] Fourteen thousand of your years.

Lois: Oh my, that is quite a while.

Rae: There are few bodies that can handle my presence. [Looks again at his hands with fascination, as he moves them about.] This one seems remarkably well adapted.

Lois: Yet he has a hard time in this life with this body.

Rae: That is not uncommon for corporeal[11] beings. [Smiles knowingly.]

Lois: Yes, especially those of higher-level vibrations, I understand.

Rae: I do not know you. [Looks at Paul.]

Paul: I am Paul.

Rae: Pleasure to meet you. [Nods with a smile.]

Paul: Nice to meet you.

Rae: I do know you. [Looks quizzically at Lois.]

Lois: I am told my name was Arianya.

Rae: It is a pleasure! [His expression brightens. He smiles broadly, places his right hand over his heart, and bows slightly.]

Lois: Well, thank you.

---

11. Corporeal (kor-por-ee-uhl) means having, consisting of, or relating to a physical, material body; having a physical, material existence. The Ancient Ones often refer to physical life forms (including humans) in this way.

Rae: Your highness . . . it has been so long. I knew one day our paths would cross again.

Lois: I have some vague memories of Atlantis, but I don't really know who I was.

Memories from past lives are typically blocked from us when we are born, though some do have spontaneous prior life recall from when their spirit was in a previous body. I do have several personal recollections from my past lives, some spontaneous, others through prior guided hypnosis sessions.

Rae: That is entirely understandable. The destruction of the city of Muir[12] and the rest of the Atlantean Realm[13] was a force the Earth had never seen before.

Lois: I understand.

Rae: It took a great deal of effort to put your spirit back together after the accident, and some of the memory was lost . . . some of it deliberately excised to protect you.

Lois: I remember being in a crystal room . . . some sort of room with a huge crystal . . . and there was . . .

Rae: Yes, you were the last High Priestess[14] of Atlantis.[15] You were also its greatest High Priestess. You served for 126 of your years at the time. Which would be . . . 147 current years.

Lois: Really? As High Priestess, what would I have done? What would be my role?

---

12. In this book, Muir is the capital city of Atlantis, located in the Altiplano region of Peru.
13. Atlantean Realm refers to the mainland and twelve islands that comprised the civilization of Atlantis.
14. The High Priestess was the spiritual leader of Atlantis, who received messages from the Patron God, Rae. She brought peace and balance to the realm.
15. Atlantis was an ancient land believed to have been the home of a great civilization circa 12,000 BC. Its capital city, Muir, was located in the Altiplano region in South America.

Rae: Atlantis was broken into four parts . . . ruled in four parts (called the Council[16]). There was the hereditary King and Queen; Titus and Thea were the last. They set the course for the Atlantean Realm. The ruling body was the Thirteen.[17] There was one representative from each of the twelve islands, elected, and one representative from the capital city, Muir. They ran the day-to-day business of the realm. There was the military: the army and the navy. The First Prime,[18] which was chosen by the military, always came up through the ranks. The fourth was the priestess. There was a temple of priestesses, and the High Priestess was always chosen by me. You were an exceptional individual. Do you know what your name means?

Lois: No. Can you tell me?

Rae: It means golden eye. You had golden eyes . . . such has never been seen before or since. That is why you were put into the community of priestesses. And, it was why I selected you . . . partly why I selected you to become High Priestess. You were seven feet tall by today's measurements. You had hair as black as a raven's wing and extraordinary golden eyes. The queen herself was deeply jealous. [Smiles playfully.] Those four groups ruled the Atlantean Realm.

Lois: Interesting. I do have memory of being in a temple, an open-air healing temple with other sisters, priestesses, anointing one another. There were flowers and music and oils and laughter . . . such pure joy. I feel as if some of the holistic health providers I work with today go back with me to that time. I have a deep knowing, a connection with some of

---

16. The Council was an Atlantean governing body comprised of the Thirteen Representatives, the King and Queen, the First Prime of the military, and the High Priestess.

17. The Thirteen were the elected representatives from each of the islands and mainland of the Atlantean Realm who ran the day-to-day business of the realm.

18. The First Prime was the military leader of Atlantis, who rose through the ranks and governed the army and navy.

the women I work with. When I experienced Shirodhara,[19] I traveled in my mind to a time with this type of an open-air temple. I thought it might have been Egyptian or Greek, but maybe it was truly Atlantean.

Rae: You were the opposing force to the military.

Lois: Okay, the balance.

Rae: Yes, so your job was . . .

Lois: To keep the peace.

Rae: Yes, to keep the peace. Not that Atlanteans were particularly warlike. It was a federation, a confederation of states. Atlanteans were at peace with all of their neighbors, except for those neighbors who wanted no peace. And that's why there was an army.

Lois: I was going to ask why there would be a military.

Rae: Purely defensive. Few dared to actually attack Atlantis. They might make raids here and there, but there was no civilization, then or now, that could rival what Atlantis was capable of.

Lois: I understand it was large. Where was the seat of Atlantis? Many times, we think of it as being in the Atlantic Ocean, and then it disappeared near the Bermuda Triangle.[20]

Rae: That's a story.

Lois: Is that all myth?

---

19. Shirodhara (she-row-dar-ah) is a sacred form of Ayurvedic therapy that involves gently pouring warm oils onto the forehead.

20. Also known as the Devil's Triangle or Hurricane Alley, the Bermuda Triangle is a location in the western part of the North Atlantic Ocean where many ships and aircraft have disappeared under mysterious circumstances.

Rae: Yes. The capital city, Muir, was in what you now call the Altiplano,[21] a region high in the mountains mostly in the country now known as Peru.

Lois: Near Machu Picchu.[22] Did that have something to do with . . .

Rae: No, no. Machu Picchu was a later civilization. Atlantis is quite old. There were twelve islands also part of the Atlantean Realm. Several of them were in what you now call the Bermuda Triangle. When the accident occurred, all of the crystal generators exploded in the capital city. The same occurred in all the crystal chambers in all of the islands. There were a cluster of islands (in the Bermuda area) . . . the confluence of forces . . . the magnetic nature of that particular piece of space combined to tear open a rift[23] in reality. We and our parents required much of our energy to *patch* the rift. [Sits up and gestures with his hands as he speaks.] It was too great to completely close. We sealed it as best we could, but there are still traces of it (the rift).

Most of the rumors around the Bermuda Triangle are simply accidents that occur. It's a heavily travelled area. *Some* of them are not. Some of them . . . if you hit the right space, at the right time, with the planet in the proper alignment . . . the rift does allow passage in both directions. There are things that do come in through that point, and there are things, sadly, that are lost through that point. There is a similar point . . . if you draw a line through the Bermuda Triangle area through the center of the Earth . . . in the Sea of Japan region, there is a similar opening. It was never as bad, but the shape of the magnetic field of the earth caused a rift in two places. The one near Japan we were able to patch

---

21. Altiplano (al-tuh-plah-noh) is Spanish for "high plain." The Altiplano is a region in west-central South America, where the Andes are at their widest. It is the most extensive area of high plateau outside of Tibet.

22. Machu Picchu (1438–1472) is an Incan citadel located on a mountain ridge in southern Peru.

23. Geologically, a rift is a linear tearing apart of the Earth's crust. Esoterically, it is a tear in the energetic layers surrounding the Earth.

almost completely. This one, where the crystal generators exploded, was too great.

Lois: Why did the crystal generators explode? What was it that the people were doing? Were they wanting something bigger, more power? Or was it simply an accident?

Rae: Accident and hubris. The Atlanteans controlled energy that your civilization today still does not truly understand. They wanted to . . . control time. They believed they could control the ability to pass forward and backward through time. That *cannot be done* at the macroscopic level. It can be done at what I believe you call the quantum level.[24] But they wanted to be able to move their bodies between timelines, and the Universe[25] forbids that.

The amount of power they tried to put in to open a portal . . . completely overloaded all of the crystal generators, and they exploded. In fact, I had told you to warn them that this was the likely outcome. But we could only warn them.

Lois: I do remember . . . I remember being in the room. I remember trying to stop them.

Rae: You *were* in the room when the detonation occurred.

Lois: Yes, I *was* in the room.

Rae: It was strong enough to tear even your spirit apart. But I put you back together. [Nods to Lois with a smile.]

Lois: Thank you. I appreciate that. [Returning his smile.]

Rae: You were always my favorite priestess. [Looks fondly at Lois.]

---

24. In physics, quantum level describes a system of particles that are confined spatially and can only take on certain specific energy levels.

25. The Universe is the expansive cosmos that comprises space and time including planets, stars, galaxies, and all other forms of matter and energy.

Lois: Thank you. I aspire to do well for the people and for the planet. We get a little frustrated with humanity. Did you have the frustration back then?

Rae: Yes and no. [Pauses to consider.] There was a much lower population back then. The people were simpler. The reason that we encouraged the belief in Gods was to encourage them to follow a path which was less self-destructive. By making people think there was reward and punishment in an afterlife, we could make them behave, even if they weren't so inclined on their own.

Of course, there is no reward and punishment in reality, except that which your spirit carries with you. When you pass on from a mortal form, you bring with you the memories, all of the memories of the actions that occurred when you were in physical form. And you can see your life with much more clarity than you possibly could when you were in physical form. All of the rationalizations, all of the reasons you think "This is a good thing" disappear, and you see everything for what it truly is. Not that there are any absolutes. There is no "good" and "bad." Everything is entirely relative. But you see your life with great clarity once it ends.

Many spirits that pass on linger for some period of time, still within the physical dimension while they sort through their lives, and that can determine what they will do after. Some will want to atone for things they've done and might immediately reincarnate to try and start again. Others believe they led a just life and move on or come back because they enjoyed themselves. It is entirely up to the spirit what happens to it.

There are those who realize that . . . the human language does not contain all of the words that I would like to use . . . realize that their life has been so hurtful to others that they . . . lose so much energy through the negative thought, that they sink down to a dimension from which they cannot reincarnate. It can take an amount of time, assuming they ever recover, to bring themselves back.

Lois: That is one of the things that Paul and I work on. We help
those that are low-level energies into the Light,[26] where they
have an opportunity for healing. When we identify them
. . . working with Archangel Michael and Jesus . . . we help
transfer and transport them to a place of healing. That seems
to be part of my mission in this life.

Rae: Several of my kin do that sort of work, and particularly for this
planet. There are many other worlds with corporeal life. Some
. . . I don't like the word *advanced* . . . are more evolved, an
older civilization. Some progressed in such a way that they
never went through a competitive stage. If you're on a world
that . . . easily provides for everything that you need, if there
is never need for conflict, then the conflict never develops,
and you wind up with a very different type of civilization.

Earth, of course, has had many civilizations. Life on Earth
spawned in three separate places at roughly the same time.
Each civilization grew in areas of Earth that were prosperous
at the time. Earth provided everything they needed. But,
when each of these civilizations grew and contacted them
(each other), that produced a problem. Each believed that
they were the center of the Universe . . . that there were no
other living things . . . no other intelligent living things.

It is a shock to the ego to discover you are not special,
that there are others. At each point of contact . . . that
produced conflict. While humanity survived those conflicts,
these small civilizations learned to live together. As the
populations grew, they hesitated to spread out any farther
for fear that they might meet yet more people and stayed as
one group in common areas. That led to a reduction in the
sustenance that they needed. You can over-live an area of
your world to the point that there is not enough food.

You can spread from that point, migrate from that point;
many do. Or, those who live there can fight over the limited

---

26. The Light is a human understanding of the higher vibrational and greater
energy level that exists between corporeal existences. Some consider the Light to
be what many refer to as heaven.

resources. Sadly, this is what happened in most of those civilizations.

Lois: So, three civilizations . . . could you identify the ones who started at the same time? Are they civilizations we're aware of now?

Rae: Yes. The way in which they found each other has not been recorded in history, but it is just simple migration. The Asian culture was the most isolated for the longest period of time. The African culture met with the North American culture more quickly. That seems a little odd given the ocean in between, but it was not so impassible at one point, when the Earth was much younger. It was . . . the African civilization that migrated north, as did the North American civilization. They met through what you now call the Bering Sea,[27] which at the time was not a sea; there was a land bridge, more of an ice bridge. The civilizations met in that area. But, having traveled that far, the traveling groups had almost formed their own civilization different from their original parent group.

Humans actually evolve much more quickly than many other species . . . non-terrestrial species. They have a great capacity for imagination. They are, in general, more willing to accept . . . [pauses to consider his words] . . . the groups that were willing to make the change . . . to leave . . . were more willing to accept that they would meet other groups. Those meetings were generally very peaceful, and those groups formed other communities of their own. But again, having traveled far, they decided this is where they wanted to stay and overstayed the land's ability to provide. Some, remembering their ancestry, traveled on; others stayed and fought.

It is a curious piece of human nature that the capacity for love and the capacity for war are equally great. It's difficult

---

27. The Bering Sea connects the continents of America and Asia in the area of Alaska. On a world map, the Africans would have traveled up through Asia to get to this location.

to explain, even for us who have watched humanity grow for . . . fourteen thousand years. We still observe.

Lois: So, the three separate places of initial growth of humanity . . . do these predate Atlantis?

Rae: Oh yes. This is a time when . . . [Speaks thoughtfully.] This is a time of *Homo sapiens* Neanderthalensis. Modern scientists now believe that the Neanderthal, the Cro-Magnon, and modern man were not the separate species that had long been thought, but were merely subspecies . . . not Neanderthal, Cro-Magnon, and *Homo sapiens*, but *Homo sapiens* Neanderthalensis, *Homo sapiens* Cro-Magnon, and *Homo sapiens* Sapiens.[28] Much as two breeds of cat are the same species.

 The Neanderthal were the first species truly recognizable as human, by today's definition of human. They were hunters and gatherers. They migrated far and wide. The reason the Earth is as populated as it is, is because they were willing to travel.

 Life was not quite the hardship that modern people think that it must have been at that time. Certainly, there are areas of the planet that were less hospitable, but as a whole, the climate was stable. There were glaciations, but between the glaciations, Earth was very fertile. Earth has always been an amazingly productive planet. There is an ideal balance between the amount of radiation that causes mutation and the amount of radiation that would be dangerous. The mutation rate is just right to spread life quickly. Even though the original spark of life was not from Earth, it was . . . a hospitable area for which life could come. Eventually that spark would have happened. Mars just got there first. It has no cosmic significance.

Lois: Is there any truth to the idea that it was beings from other galaxies that came—those we sometimes refer to as aliens—

---

28. *Homo sapiens* is the name for primitive man. The Collective says we are all descendants of the same ancestor, we are all one species with different subsets.

to help perpetuate or expand the *Homo sapiens* species? Was there some interaction with otherworldly beings that caused the evolution to change?

Rae: There are a great many species on many worlds that develop into intelligent life. Not quite as many as some of your scientists think there might be, but enough. However, the physical distances are so vast that it is almost impossible to travel between worlds populated by intelligent species. The ability to cross greater distances at what would be perceived as faster than light travel is possible. Very, very few species develop it. Partly because it is a difficult process; mostly, sadly, because species who develop that level of technology tend to exterminate themselves before they get that far.

What you perceive as alien visitation is not a physical visitation, but a spiritual one. It is possible to project your spirit . . . a part of your spirit . . . enough is always left behind to keep the body going . . . project part of your spirit and part of your consciousness to any point. Humans have that ability. Some develop it and some do not, but the process is known as astral projection.[29]

It's not strictly necessary to project only into the astral plane;[30] you can project within your own physical dimension. There is no speed-of-light limitation on that process. You can be anywhere at any time. Present time . . . travel to the past and the future . . . *is* sometimes possible with the right thought and the right control . . . and the right reason. Why you want to do a thing is always more important than what you are actually doing. So while you physically cannot move freely through time, mentally, it is actually possible.

---

29. Astral projection is an intentional out-of-body experience in which the astral body or spiritual consciousness of a person travels outside of the physical body. Astral travel is associated with dreams, meditation, or trance states.

30. The astral plane comprises the entire existence of spiritual life. It describes where all spirits go to live out their non-physical life, and where all consciousness resides across all existences, encompassing all worlds.

Lois: Therefore, could someone project their spirit into a human body that might be perceived as an alien?

Rae: That is very difficult. When a physical body is born, a spirit is either chosen or created to take that body, and they're matched. That match exists for the life of the combination. When the physical body dies, then the bond is broken. It is . . . almost impossible for another spirit to enter someone's body. Partly because the body can only barely hold the spirit that it holds; partly because the vibrational match won't be precise enough.

    The match that occurs at the moment of birth . . . is a magical thing, and it is very difficult to replicate on a conscious . . . by conscious effort. It can be done . . . I'm here [gestures to himself] . . . but I have no physical form. I have never been matched to a body. For me to try to incorporate as a physical entity would destroy the body within moments. The amount of energy is too great. Even to do what I do now, I have not done since you [smiles as he looks at Lois] . . . fourteen thousand years ago. You were the last body that I was ever able to . . . [Pauses to think.] There is no English word for this . . .

Lois: Say it in your language. I would love to hear it in your language.

Rae: *Kumo'a*[31] (spelled to match Rae's pronunciation). We . . . what is happening now, we could do. [Motions to Gary's body.] It was slightly different because the spirit of this body is one of my kin. I have more access to this body than I otherwise might. Even if we could take this type of form more often, we would not. We want races to develop on their own.

    In the case you mentioned . . . aliens . . . what typically happens is the projection can appear as solid form. It's possible to take local material and form a temporary body

---

31. The Collective offered the term *Kumo'a* for direct communion between a high-level being and an incarnated human, where the human allows the high-level being to physically use their body to communicate through.

held together by the energy. That's extremely difficult. There are very few races that have evolved to that point. Humans are not there yet. But typically, we see them project themselves into the minds of others, and all that humans see . . . all that any corporeal form sees . . . is a function of how its mind processes the sensory apparatus that it contains. If you introduce into someone's mind . . . a vision . . . they will think they see it. In other words, it is possible to make yourself appear to really be there. This is what alien encounters typically are.

Lois: So, it's like a hologram.[32] It's an imaginary vision that the person is able to see?

Rae: No . . . A hologram is a trick of the light. It is still something seen by the eye and processed by the brain. This occurs entirely within the brain. There is literally nothing there. If I were to project myself into you to see something, you would see something [looks at Lois], and you would not [looks at Paul], while you are looking at the same space.

There are races who do share their information. They want to see other races evolve to their level. They want to be visited in return.

Many of the mysteries of ancient artifacts are actually not alien projections. Humans today do not give humans of the past sufficient credit for their abilities. They tend to think of everything they learn as having been learned by civilization for the first time. Much was known by ancient humans and was forgotten or destroyed, and that is why there are races that have evolved higher. Even though most corporeal races have existed for more or less the same period of time, the Universe had to be in a certain state for this type of life to develop. So, the differences between the different races are caused by how the race developed, not by how long they had actually been a race.

---

32. A hologram is a three-dimensional image created by a system of light diffraction that can appear to be real.

Chronicles of Hope: The Collective ∞

The Atlantean culture was, by some measurements, more advanced than anything you have today. Even if there is technological improvement, there are things today that could not have been conceived of by the Atlanteans. But their system of government, their democracy, preceded the creation of the word "democracy" by over ten thousand years.

Sadly, all that was known of Atlantis was destroyed. The failure of the experiment obliterated everything. Only those few Atlanteans who happened to be out elsewhere in the world survived. What little culture they had was carefully preserved, and then lost when the Library at Alexandria[33] was destroyed. That was truly the end of the Atlantean civilization. Even their genetic makeup has been lost by seven thousand generations; there would be no trace of it.

We try not to take favorites. Some of us do have worlds we prefer to visit. Some of us do have civilizations that we have preferred on any given world. Atlantis was always very special to me. I was the Patron God of Atlantis.

Lois: Were you in corporeal form at that time?

Rae: No, no. I cannot take corporeal form. Even this is a great strain and will have to end soon. [Motions to Gary's body.]

Lois: Yes. I want to honor that.

Rae: I could not be born in corporeal form, but it was an enormous honor for me to be able to share your form with you, even for such short periods as we did. I always tried to give you information that would balance what the other sections of Atlantis were trying to do.

The King and Queen were good people; they made a mistake. The Thirteen were good and just people; they made a mistake. That is the nature of all life. We are not perfect; [indicates self] we make mistakes. We are sometimes

---

33. Located in Alexandria, Egypt, the Great Library of Alexandria was one of the largest and most significant libraries of the ancient world. It contained massive amounts of scrolls and was the greatest source of literary knowledge.

overcautious. I could have made myself appear before the Council, without burning their eyes out, and told them to stop. It probably wouldn't have helped. You were one of the most respected citizens of the realm and they didn't listen to you [looks kindly at Lois] . . . knowing your words came from me. Sometimes children can only learn from their mistakes. It doesn't mean that the parent has failed, but that makes it no less painful.

Lois: Exactly. We're being guided to do something . . . you're here for a reason now. The Anquietas is imploring *us* to do something . . . to help create change. From what I understand, we're facing a similar situation with humanity now.

Rae: My kin have conveyed that information. That this world . . . in a sense it is one civilization now on Earth. [Sighs deeply.] In another, there is still . . . tribalism. We would like to see humans outgrow this (tribalism). It is such a deeply engrained piece of humanity. Coupled with the fact that . . . this world is . . . infamous among the Universe for the nature of life here. It attracts new spirits that seek to learn by doing. They can do so much more on this world than on most others. That they come here . . . this is their first choice . . . *that* can destabilize a world. We cannot intervene; we can recommend. But, we believe there are enough old souls[34] *here* to make Earth the paradise that it once was.

I believe my . . . it's so funny to call them *parents,* the word doesn't even begin to apply, but . . . when you speak to our *creators* [motions to self and above] . . . the information *they* give you is to . . . try to return people to the beliefs that we wanted them to have when we said: "Yes, we are your Gods. We make thunder, we make lightning, we make it rain." We recognized that humans, more than most intelligent species, seem to need the ability . . . seem to need to believe

---

34. The concepts of a person's spirit and soul are actually the same. The term "soul" carries more of a religious connotation. This is the immortal part of the being that survives bodily death.

in something greater than themselves. [Speaks slowly and considers every word.] It doesn't get much greater than to be human, if you're corporeal. When a human body dies and its spirit is released, even if that was its first incarnation,[35] it will have grown more than older spirits who are leaving an incorporation in other species. Partly, it's the nature of Earth.

Gaia[36] is alive; not all planets are. The spirit of the Earth, suffering though it is in modern times, still strives to spur evolution. Gaia is a good mother. She has nothing but love for her children . . . nothing but the best intentions for them. Humans seem to have lost the ability to *hear her*. If you want to convey information to help humanity, that is the most important thing. My parents (the Anquietas) wouldn't tell you that. We (of the Collective) have more of a free hand because we have the ability, at some level, to interact with the physical world. They have become too detached. They have infinite wisdom and knowledge, but no heart. We learn to have heart, even though we have no hearts. [Smiles with a nod.] We feel the suffering of the races that suffer, and humanity, for all of its . . . ability, almost seems to enjoy suffering. And in some ways that's not a bad thing. Suffering and conflict promote growth and strength, but that growth can take many paths. You want to choose a path that promotes . . . harmony between people, as opposed to a path that promotes yet more conflict.

On Earth, there has always been more or less a balance. It may swing like a pendulum. [Sweeps his arms like a pendulum.] Today, the pendulum has been pinned too far to the wrong side for too long. If some sort of balance does not begin to restore itself, it will reach a point where it will not be possible (to achieve balance) anymore. The nature of the

---

35. Literally meaning embodied in flesh, "incarnation" refers to a particular corporeal existence of a spirit. When a body is born, the spirit that motivates that body is living out an incarnation.

36. Gaia (gai-eh), from the Greek Γαῖα, is the primordial Goddess "Mother Earth," from whom all life springs. During the dialogues in this book, Gaia refers to the living spirit of Earth, while Terra refers to the physical Earth itself.

spirits that Earth will begin to attract are such that they won't even *permit* that to happen.

Lois: Is that what we are encountering in the work Paul and I do? Part of what we are called to do is to identify what I'm calling "nasties." I prefer to avoid calling them "demons."[37] Sometimes, they're just low-level energies, other times they're lost human souls, but some seem to be malevolent. They appear to be decidedly, to use a word, evil. They want to manipulate; they want to make people suffer. When we encounter them, we call on your brethren to help them. But we're in a unique position to identify that they are here. I know better than to do battle with them myself, because they are not at my level. I understand they are at a different dimensional level. Archangel Michael, Jesus, or their Legions of Light[38] will come to take care of the low-level entities.[39] Is this what you're referring to by attracting these energies that will cause more destruction and chaos?

Rae: That is a large part of it, yes. It is the balance of energies within a vibrational dimension that defines the dimension. As the balance changes . . . in this case, as the vibrational energy lowers, it becomes harder for higher vibrational beings . . . what you would think of as "angels"[40] . . . to come in because the vibrational difference is too great. At the same time, it becomes easier for lower vibrational energies . . . what you would call "demons" . . . to get in. This is an accelerating

---

37. A demon is a supernatural being or spirit with divine power. The term historically did not carry negative connotations. In some religions, they are considered harmful entities that can take possession of humans.

38. The Legions of Light are angelic helpers who assist the Archangels, especially Archangel Michael.

39. Low-level entities are dark spirits with a low vibrational energy. They come from a dimension that has a lower vibrational energy level than our physical dimension and seek to feed on people with higher and lower energy.

40. An angel is any spirit who is dedicated to helping others. They may be found in the physical and spiritual realms.

curve. It hasn't reached the point yet that it cannot be corrected. *That point is very near.*

Even *we* don't see the future. We predict, based on what we see happen and what we have seen happen, we know the time is close. The message to get out to people is the message that my Child (Jesus) delivered two thousand years ago. You must cooperate. You must harmonize. We hesitate to use the word *love*; it has so many meanings.

Lois: Yes, we understand.

Rae: We . . . Those who have too much need to give. Those who have too little must be willing to accept. The balance has got to be brought back before it's too late.

I failed Atlantis, and a civilization died. Many of my kin spend more time here than on many of the other worlds. No world is at such a tipping point right now as Earth. We have lost some (worlds). As I said, there are races that evolved . . . their technology outstripped the evolution of their wisdom.

Greed comes from a belief that there isn't enough; it comes from insufficiency. If you believe there isn't enough for everyone, then you will hoard it, and it becomes a self-fulfilling prophecy. Now there isn't enough for everyone.

Even given Earth's population, there is still enough for everyone. There is nothing that needs to be hoarded. Humans have the technology to fix even the problems that Gaia cannot fix. [Speaks now with some urgency.] There are places which are arid; they could be watered. There are trees that can be replanted. The rainforests *are not gone yet*, they can be brought back; once they are gone, they cannot be brought back. The system is such that it needs the proper environment in which to grow. Once the environment has been destroyed, you *cannot* bring it back. It's not simply a matter of planned genetics. The system as a whole has a hysteretic[41] ability. But just as you can bend a piece of wood so far . . . if you bend it too far, it breaks. You can't put it

---

41. Hysteresis is a lag in response based on change.

back together again. These are the messages that they (the Collective) want passed along.

Lois: I know right now one of my personal missions is to teach other people to do the clearing and energy alignment work that I do, because in my own small way, I am making a difference. With Paul's assistance, we bring in the Archangels to help release the dark energies, the shadows, whatever we want to call them. We help bring some balance back at a small level, but I'm only one person and feel compelled to teach. I'm having a hard time finding those who are willing to learn. Can you help to send those who I may teach? I have three people interested, and three is enough to start with. I want to spread these simple, valuable techniques that I have learned from my teachers, and developed with your guidance, with other people who work in this realm.

Rae: If you teach two people, and they teach two people, it doesn't take very long to reach everyone. I do not have the ability to send people to you. However, if the message you put out is the right message . . . there is a lot of despair in the world today . . . a message of hope is all most people need to want to listen.

The problem is that there are people whose intent is questionable . . . who are offering what they call hope. The reason that Hitler[42] was able to create the most powerful and efficient civilization in modern history was because, after World War I,[43] hope was stripped from Germany. What most people never stop to realize is the first country the Nazis[44]

---

42. Adolf Hitler was a German politician and the leader of the Nazi Party in 1933. His aggression was the primary cause of World War II. He was responsible for the genocide of millions of Jews and others considered socially undesirable.

43. World War I (1914–1918) was also known as the First World War or the Great War. This global war originated in Europe and was one of the largest wars in history.

44. The Nazis (1920–1945) were a German political party under Adolf Hitler that established the ideology of National Socialism. Nazis implemented a system of genocide, murdering millions of people in what is called the Holocaust.

took over was Germany. This can still happen again today. There are so many people in need of hope that they will believe the wrong message . . . as well as the right message. You have to reach them first.

The book you are writing is good . . . a good idea. It is sufficiently controversial that it will attract attention. There will be many people who will speak out against it, and that will drive more people to it. Never be afraid to publish your thoughts; say what you want to say. The words that we have given you are good words. Make them your own, and you will succeed. Let opposition strengthen you. Don't be afraid. Don't back down. We are here. [Motions to self.] We are behind you.

Lois: Thank you. You have mentioned your kin who are here. Are you speaking of our friend Archangel Michael? Is he one of your kin who you've referred to who is here with us? Because we have a great deal of honor and respect for all that he's done for us.

Rae: The name Archangel Michael takes credit for a lot of the work that my kin do. [Smiles knowingly.] We are not . . . individuals in the sense that corporeal beings are. It's not so much a shared consciousness, but . . . a joint consciousness . . . Despite being the most prolific language in the creation of new words, English is missing quite a few . . . [Shakes his head.] We each know what the other does. We each are a part of what the other does. When you ask for (Archangel) Michael, you're asking for an image of a being that has a certain task that it can perform. Just as each of the Archangels has always been associated with different activities, they are all equal. Any one of us can do any of those things. It is in human nature to want to put labels on things.

Lois: We understand.

Rae: Jesus was my kin in that we were part of his creation. He is capable of incorporating in physical form, as all of his siblings are. But the same rule applies . . . when not in physical form, any one of the 32,768[45] of his siblings can at any time be Jesus to somebody who seeks his name. He got rather a larger reputation than we generally like to get when we appear on worlds. Those who can incorporate, try to help from a quiet distance. He hit a sore spot at just the right time. He's not the first, and he won't be the last.

Lois: I know that we are taxing you. [Rae's energy starts to look strained.]

Rae: This body is starting to hurt.

Lois: I want to honor your time here. Are you able to answer one last question?

Rae: Yes. Go on.

Lois: The angelic energy, the vibration of an angel, is that what Jesus would be when he's not in corporeal form?

Rae: That is a fair description. [Takes a deep breath.] He . . . his spirit, all of our spirits, exist in a higher-dimensional plain. We can, to one degree or another, lower ourselves . . . lower our energies . . . to enter the physical. It is easier for my Children than for us. We can only do this temporarily, and only under very special circumstances, which I'm pushing to the limit right now. [Strains uncomfortably.]

Most of the spirits that people consider to be *angels* are my Children. Many of the spirits that people think to be demons are also my Children. The imposition of "good" and "evil" is a corporeal thing. When you see something that you agree with, you think of that as good. When you see something you disagree with, you think of that as evil. But those are *your* definitions. And you have yours and everybody has theirs. Good and evil are not absolutes. They are relative.

---

45. 32,768 is the number of Anquietas' Children's Children, which is 8 to the fifth power. Rae states that about half are incorporated on a planet, and the other half are in spirit form across the Universe.

Something can only be good in comparison to something that isn't. But make no mistake . . . there *are* spirits which *do not* have the best interests of corporeal life in mind . . . and a lot of times it is hard to tell the difference. It's what's in their hearts, not what comes out of their mouths (that matters).

The people . . . who put the greatest good for the greatest number ahead of themselves . . . those are the people you can trust. [Speaks very slowly.] There are a lot of them on Earth. Their activities go largely unnoticed. It is much easier to attract attention when you do something that is perceived as being wrong, than it is when you do something that is perceived as being right. That's sad. And . . . if you can find a way to fix that, you'll go a long way toward making this a much better place.

I wish I had an answer for you; I wish I could tell you how to do it . . . It would be nice if I could simply appear in the sky and tell people what I'm telling you. It doesn't work that way. I depend on you to take these words and put them out where everyone can see them. Some will believe; some will not. Some will follow; some will not. But I will tell you what my Child (Jesus) said two thousand years ago . . . "I am not God. Don't follow me." [Indicates himself.] You are the Gods. [Motions to Lois and Paul.] Follow each other. Learn to love each other. That will solve all your problems."

I have to leave.

Lois: Thank you so much, Rae.

Rae: It was so good to see you again. [Smiles kindly at Lois.]

Lois: It was so good to see you, too.

Rae: It was nice to meet you. [Nods to Paul.]

Paul: It was nice to meet you.

Gary's body takes a deep breath as Rae departs.

After a few moments, Gary breathes deeply as Lois guides him to fill his body with glowing light, fully reintegrating his body, mind, and spirit. As he returns to present awareness, Gary states this session felt different than the others. He said, "I don't remember a thing. In the last few sessions, there was a moment of overlap where we were together. Not this time, something came in and put me to the side, and I don't remember a thing."

Paul expressed amazement at the session and was bewildered by the experience. He noted that when Gary looked directly at him as Rae, his eyes seemed to be a different color. Although we had been holding the sessions with the Anquietas to thirty minutes, this session with Rae was over an hour. Because Rae's vibrational energy was more closely matched to Gary's body, he was more comfortable staying in the body longer.

Reflection

In the final session of Book 1, the Anquietas spoke of a civilization called Atlantis. They stated there has never been any civilization on Earth that truly rivaled the Atlantean civilization in terms of ethics and understanding. The Atlanteans had a good grasp of the true nature of the Universe, which was in part due to one of the Anquietas' Children, Rae, who was the Patron God of Atlantis. Since Rae had much knowledge of events in the physical world, the Anquietas suggested that we might want to speak with him. We could have expected Rae would be the one to come through next.

In this amazing session, Rae (ray) corrected our pronunciation, to not be confused with the Egyptian Sun-God, Ra (rah). Unlike the more lecture-based conversations with the Anquietas in the first eleven sessions of Book 1, this was a very engaging, animated two-way conversation with a tenderly personable being. As one of the Anquietas' Children, Rae's energy was more closely matched to Gary's, so he was able to more readily animate Gary's body. He sat up, moved his hands for emphasis, made eye contact, and sustained a sixty-minute visit, which was much longer than the Anquietas was able to stay.

As a transpersonal hypnotist, I have extensive experience with past life and other metaphysical-based memories with my own personal recall of multiple lives from different times and places, some more memorable than others. Holding a long-held fascination with Atlantis, I have memories of being in beautiful open-air temples that felt Atlantean. More disturbingly, I remember being very upset about something that was happening as I walked down a set of stairs into a large circular open room. I did not remember the details of what was happening, nor why I was there, just a strong knowing of my attempt to stop a group of people from doing something. Suddenly, there was considerable chaos, followed by a huge explosion—then white.

Listening to Rae share the details about the Atlantean Realm was beyond astonishing and filled in missing pieces for me. Being the High Priestess took me by surprise, yet when Rae looked into my eyes and addressed me as Arianya, it felt like a meeting of dear friends. There seemed to be such closeness as he spoke, which caused me to remember our connection. Rae's warm, heartfelt affection was completely different than my professional relationship with Gary. The conversation with Rae felt much more personal, with his fondness deeply apparent.

Since Gary and I had never discussed my experience with Atlantis, he had no knowledge of my personal memories. Therefore, he could not have described the details of what I remembered the way Rae did. This experience, coupled with my own memories, served to validate what Rae was saying. The knowledge of why I was in this crystal chamber at Rae's behest made perfect sense and offered closure to something that had long concerned me. Discovering that some Atlanteans were trying to create a portal through time confirmed my suspicions that something was not right. Rae affirmed that the Universe only allows travel through time on what is called the quantum level, using the power of the mind.

Rae's comment that Arianya was more than seven feet tall reminds me of archeological remains of humanoid skeletons that were exceedingly tall. Historical texts describe giants and ancient drawings depict races of larger-than-life beings. Were these truly references to Atlanteans? The information was captivating.

Rae tells us the mainland of the Atlantean Realm was in an area of Peru called the Altiplano and Atlantis comprised twelve islands located around the world with several in the Atlantic Ocean. It was a peaceful civilization ruled by a democracy of four governing bodies: the hereditary King and Queen; the Thirteen elected representatives; the First Prime of the military representing the army and navy; and the peace-keeping High Priestess representing their Patron God, Rae.

Since the crystal generators were interconnected, an overload to the generator in the capital city of Muir caused the generators on all of the islands to explode. The explosions were so huge they caused the complete destruction of the Atlantean Realm and opened a rift or tear in the ocean floor and energetic boundary layers in that area. While the Collective attempted to repair the rift, there are times when it can reopen, allowing some things to come through and others to be lost.

Several Atlantean islands were located in the region we now refer to as the Bermuda Triangle. There are numerous documented cases of unusual phenomena in the area, including mysterious disappearances of ships and aircraft. Some believe the ones who were lost in those areas may have been affected by electromagnetic wavelengths and were transported into another realm. They might still be active in other realms, just not able to return to their original human state.

In addition, explosions of this magnitude probably created tsunami-force tidal waves that spread across the Earth. If each of the islands exploded, that might explain some of the more circular land and sea formations noted in topography of the areas. Subsequent flooding might also explain the origin of relics of ancient civilizations mysteriously discovered under the seas. Prehistoric cities that were once buried in mud are currently being excavated.

Rae explained how early civilizations developed on Earth, beginning with nomadic Neanderthal tribes. Early civilizations formed in what is now known as Asia, Africa, and North America. Traveling tribes encountered others on their journeys, and either fought over the land or combined to create new tribes. When tribes stayed too long in one place, they outlived the land's ability to provide, which caused them to fight over food and resources. This may explain the origin of many competitive behaviors humans exhibit today.

Rae affirmed that our Earth is alive; Gaia, the spirit of our planet, is a good mother who welcomes new spirits who want to grow through experience. While she has only the best intentions for her children, she is suffering. "So many humans have lost the ability to hear her; they no longer strive to care for her." Rae says it is most important to encourage humanity to connect with the energy of our Mother Earth. We need to respect nature and do what we can to take better care of our planet and each other. There are countless people who have dedicated their lives to helping our planet. Many work to protect our land, care for our water, nurture our endangered animals, and restore our rainforests, along with so many other life-saving measures. We must encourage and support those who are making strides to heal our Earth.

Rae spoke of other worlds with corporeal life that evolved without conflict or competition into a different type of civilization. Although humanity is truly one civilization, one type of being, we continue to experience competitive tribalism. The Collective would like to see us outgrow this deeply engrained part of human nature.

Rae answered questions about aliens helping humans over the eons. He explained that it is extremely rare for most intelligent species to travel faster than the speed of light. I found it curious that he states it is not only difficult, but species who develop this type of technology tend to exterminate themselves. Is this because of conflict? Humans do experience alien visitation. However, what is perceived as physical visitation is truly spiritual visitation and is referred to as astral projection. Humans can develop the ability to project themselves across time and space using the power of their minds.

Our minds are amazing computers that we can engage if we train ourselves. Everyone has the potential to tap into extra senses that they are unaware of. Some people come by these gifts naturally, while others work to develop them. We refer to these individuals as being psychic or telepathic, or having a sixth sense. Have you ever thought about someone, and soon after, they contact you? That's an intuitive connection. Many people also have the ability to see or sense spirits of those who have passed over.

While in a light state of trance, most of my hypnosis clients are able to easily communicate with loved ones, angels, or Guides.[46] They also readily recall past memories. When reflecting on old memories, even past-life memories, although the visions seem real, they are truly illusions. These mental constructs are accessible to help us understand or relate to situations. The only true reality is this present moment of now. Similarly, we can use our mind to develop skills to communicate with others by projecting ourselves in a trance or dream state. We can develop extra-sensory communication abilities, yet Rae states: "Why you want to do a thing is always more important than what you are actually doing."

---

46. Metaphysically, a Guide is a wise spiritual energy that assists an incarnated human when called upon. This can be a wise master such as Jesus, a passed-over relative, a guardian angel, or even a helpful Earth energy.

Rae says some otherworld species have the ability to project solid structure by forming material together. Humans do not have this ability, yet. There are benevolent races from other worlds who would like to exchange information. They want to see other races evolve to their level and want to be visited in return. So, yes, there has been extraterrestrial communication, just not as we think of in the physical level. It is at the spiritual or quantum level.

Rae spoke of spirits being energetically matched with bodies at birth as a *magical thing.* Since the spiritual and physical bodies are matched for life, it is rare for another spirit to take over another's body. When the physical body dies, the bond is broken, and the spirit moves on. I have read of and experienced instances of what are called "walk-ins," where another spirit takes over the body of someone who wants to leave their physical body, while the body is still alive. Each situation is unique. In this case, Rae wanted to get a message to us, yet because his energy is too great to incorporate as a physical body without destroying the body, he chose to communicate through Gary's for a brief period of time.

In early human life, the Collective attempted to make people think there was reward and punishment to encourage good behavior. Rae says there is actually no reward or punishment. There is no *good* or *bad;* everything is relative. When your body dies, your spirit reviews all the memories you had when in physical form, and you see your life with great clarity. This is known as a *life review.* Based on how they lived their life, the person's spirit determines what they will do next. Some might reincarnate to start over, others might move on, some come back to learn and experience again. Those who have been hurtful to others may sink to such a low vibrational level that they cannot reincarnate. Part of the work my clearing consultants and I do is to help lost spirits find their place in the Light. Some are so badly damaged that we call on the Archangels to guide them where they need to go. Based on years of work with lost spirits, Rae's explanation made perfect sense to me.

I appreciated Rae's clarification on the importance of maintaining a balance of vibrational energies within a dimension. When the dimensional energy lowers, it is easier for lower-vibrational energies to get in, causing disturbances. It also makes it harder for higher-vibrational beings, such as angels, to assist because of the greater differences in vibrational energy.

Again, we hear that good and evil are subjective. Something is only good in comparison to something that isn't. We make decisions based on our own biases. That said, Rae confirms there are lower-vibrational energies that *do not* have the best interests of humans in mind. In order to tell the difference between these entities, we must not be drawn in by the words a spirit says but must note the intention in their heart.

Rae affirms that it is right to call on the higher-vibrational energy beings of the Collective for assistance. When we call on specific Guides as I regularly do with Archangel Michael or Jesus, the names represent any number of beings in the Collective who assist when called. This Collective of High-Level Spirits is what many of us refer to as God. The ones at Rae's level, whose energy is too high to incorporate, we refer to as Archangels and may have been ancient Gods. Rae mentions his Child Jesus; those at the Children's Children level are able to incorporate, and when not in physical form, they assist humanity as angels. When someone calls for Jesus, any one of his 32,768 siblings in the Collective can answer. When those at that level incorporate, they usually help quietly in the background, like Gary. Jesus received more attention than most because he came at a particularly difficult time.

Rae reminds us that two thousand years ago Jesus said: "I am not God. Do not follow me. You (humans) are the Gods. Follow each other. Learn to love each other. That will solve all your problems." Many people blame God for their problems. When Rae points to himself and says: "I am not God, don't follow me," he is letting us know that as a wise spiritual being he is here to assist us, yet does not control us. We have free will to choose for ourselves. When Rae says "You are the Gods," he means we are the creators of our own destiny. What we think, say, and do generates creative energy that is made manifest by our intentions. Our thoughts are self-fulfilling. If we focus on negative, fear-based or angry emotions, we create or magnetically draw more negative situations to us. If we choose to rise above negative situations by focusing on positive thoughts, we can shift our energy to manifest a positive outcome.

Consider for example, what people call God (Divine Source, Universal Energy, Great Spirit) as being the ocean, and each of us is one drop in the ocean. Individually, we are one, yet collectively, we are all part of the *Group of Divine* beings or *God*. It takes *all of us* and the uniqueness bestowed upon us to come together with *love* as the common thread that connects us. When Rae struggles with the word "love," understand there are many types of love, and some languages have different words for these different kinds of love. Everything good *is* love. Yet, the word "love" is often taken out of context and split into many definitions based on the person's individual understanding. Each person experiences love in their own way, many without realizing or recognizing it. The message is the same one that we aspire to communicate today: "We must learn to cooperate and harmonize with each other."

Rae tells us the Collective helps on all worlds and has lost some species where technology outstripped wisdom. They are concerned that no world is at such a tipping point right now as Earth with our future on an accelerating curve. Humanity's future hasn't reached the point that it cannot be corrected; however, *that point is very near.* The balance must be brought back before it's too late. We must address the greed in our world. The fear of scarcity must be shifted. As we come to know there is enough for everyone, those who have much must be willing to give and those who have little must be willing to accept. There should be an exchange of resources, insight, or energy.

We do have the technology to fix our problems; arid places could be watered, trees might be replanted, rainforests can still be brought back. We must do what we can to nurture our Earth. Once the environment is gone, we cannot bring it back. The information one generation receives about fixing the environment via technology is like a blueprint or overall picture for what needs to be done. The problem humans have with repairing, correcting, or restoring balance on the planet is that the information acquired by one generation is not always passed down effectively to subsequent generations. The destruction of the environment is something that evolves over long periods of time, possibly a lifetime for one generation. If the information is not passed down, the planet will continue to deteriorate at an accelerated pace.

Embracing a message of hope will ease the despair in the world today. However, there are people whose intent is questionable, offering what they call hope. Those in need of hope are at risk of believing the wrong message. The fact that Hitler was a charismatic leader who delivered the wrong message that people followed had a strong impact on me at an early age. As a young teen, I lived in Germany for many years and remember going to the Anne Frank House in Amsterdam along with one of the concentration camps in Germany. The horror of what people are capable of really made a lasting impression on me.

Since then, I have met many who have been severely impacted by the atrocities of war. Many clients come to me with devastating dreams or nightmares with tragic memories of being raped, tortured, or brutally killed in times of war across the eons. The stories of genocide come from ancient times, to Native Americans, to revolutions, to concentration camps. I listen with a heavy heart to the cruelty others have inflicted on fellow man, woman, child, and animal based on disturbed people or those who follow misguided leaders who seek power. Be they past-life recall, genetic memory, or stories from an earth-bound spirit, the vivid recounting of the atrocities is intensely real and causes great despair to my clients. As I help to lift the abused spirit and heal the memory, I have also learned to look for the perpetrator who is often nearby in the shadows, feeling guilty for crimes committed. Each of these cases leaves me with overwhelming sadness, a pit in my stomach, and a questioning mind. How will humans evolve to come from a place of acceptance and treat one another with value, respect, and integrity?

Team Hope and I are making every attempt to reach people with these healing and life-altering messages before they follow false leaders down a path of destruction. My driving force is allowing me to deliver their messages in books, training sessions, presentations, and other media to inspire hope for peaceful solutions. Many others are taking similar actions. Rae says to trust the people who put the greatest good for the greatest number ahead of themselves. There are a lot of good people on Earth whose positive activities go unnoticed. If we emphasize their positive actions, we will make this world a much better place. Think of what *you* can do to accentuate the positive in your life. Rae tells us: "If you teach two people, and they teach two people, it doesn't take very long to reach everyone." Very encouraging, don't you think?

Rae speaks of his parents, the Anquietas, as more vibrationally distant to humanity; they are similar to historians. However, we understand others of the Collective have vibrational energies that relate more closely to humanity. These beings have a high-level energy that is much greater than most human beings, giving them an expanded awareness and high levels of empathy. However, the Collective has a difficult time understanding humans because we tend to "switch off" our emotions with the use of substances or are too busy and distracted to hear the messages meant for humanity. These messages have been presented continuously through the ages, while people continue to miss them, misunderstand them, or dismiss them. This has been a difficult challenge to overcome and will continue to be until we learn to look within and open ourselves up to the messages these Wise Ones have presented for us as individuals, and as a spiritual, yet human, collective.

It's important we find time in our busy lives to put down the technical devices and connect with nature by going outside, breathing the fresh air, and enjoying the simple things life offers. Our children are becoming addicted to technology; we must teach them to explore all that nature offers. In doing this, we will find ways to discourage conflict, set aside our differences, promote harmony, and truly listen to each other with open hearts and minds. Consequently, we will finally appreciate and save the beauty of our beloved world before it is too late.

Sharing the messages of the Anquietas in Book 1, I have found others who are receiving similar messages from their spiritual Guides. Paying attention to this wisdom will bring hope, peace, and joy back to our world. I'm delighted Rae agrees that disseminating these messages is good, though he says the controversy will attract both positive and negative attention. With his encouragement, however, I feel confident in presenting the messages and sharing these important teachings.

I am so grateful that Rae came through on this day to spend this special time with us, and for delivering his sage advice for humanity. The last time Rae communicated with me was through the High Priestess Arianya over fourteen thousand years ago in Atlantis. I now realize why he came to speak with me again. We had worked together in the past, and both have a sense that we failed Atlantis. He wants to join efforts again and encourages me to push forward that we may affect a different outcome this time.

It would be a much easier transformation if Rae could physically appear and tell people what he told me, but life doesn't work that way. I know he is always here with us in spirit, along with others of the Collective to assist. Joined by our human collective, we can do this. We will do this. We shall do this. We, Team Hope, are doing our best to spread the message of hope to you to help turn this world around. Thank you, Rae. Thank you, Collective. Thank you, humanity, for doing your best.

> *"One moment can change a day,*
> *one day can change a life,*
> *and one life can change the world."*
> —Buddha

Session 2 ~
I Am the Spirit Known as Jesus
I Am Always in Your Heart

"Do unto others as you would have others do unto you."
—Jesus

Intention

Gary, Paul, and I continued our journey to receive information that is to be shared with humanity. We started by discussing how we would deliver these messages. Would the information be best published as a book? Should we distribute it through social media or podcasts? We decided to organize the transcribed sessions in such a way that we would have multiple options.

As we reflected on the last session, we were all surprised by the information that came from Rae and speculated on who would visit us this day. We discussed what questions we would ask. Should we ask how to prepare for the changes we anticipate are coming to Earth? How are we going to inspire hope for humanity? What is our part in helping the world? What are the most important messages we are to deliver?

Since Gary suffered from chronic physical issues, I wanted to ask questions to help him heal his body. While assisting Gary, it also presented an opportunity to learn ways to help others who struggle with similar health issues.

Session 2 participants were: Lois, the hypnotist guiding the session; Paul, the clearing consultant observing the session and protecting the energy; Gary, the client channeling the High-Level Spirit; and Jesus, the prophet and teacher being channeled through Gary.

Conversation

Gary is guided into a quiet trance. When he is in a hypnotic state, I begin the session.

Lois: On this journey today, we ask for whomever Gods or Wise Ones of the Collective to come through. We welcome you to receive your guidance, your instruction, your wisdom, and your insight. We are here.

Jesus: [Takes a deep breath.] Thank you for calling me.

Lois: Hello. Who is with us today?

Jesus: [Speaks in a gentle, kind voice.] I am the spirit that was known as Jesus, some two thousand years ago.

Lois: We are *very* honored to have you here.

Jesus: I am honored to have been called. I have not been back since last I was here.

Lois: Really?

Jesus: Not in physical form. I have a particular fondness for Earth. I'm never very far away.

Lois: We know. You help us a lot. You help so many.

Jesus: We are aware of the work that you do. [Smiles at Lois.] Your spirit was coalesced out of the Universal Energy, much as mine was . . . just longer ago. Other spirits actually come from Gaia. [Looks at Paul.] You literally are Earth's son. You're not restricted. You can go anywhere you like. The origin of the spirit does not restrict one, not once the spirit reaches a certain age, anyway. But some spirits are intimately tied to the spirit of the Earth.

   The work you both do is very important, especially now. *A turning point is coming to the Earth.* I might not have taken a physical form again for quite some time, but I wanted to be here because you asked. You certainly have earned an audience. [Smiles appreciatively at Lois.] Otherwise, my kin would not be here speaking with you if they did not believe you had the ability to carry out the task we hope you will carry out.

Lois: What is the task? What is it you want us to do? What is the message you want us to share?

Jesus: It is the same message I gave two thousand years ago. [Sighs deeply, sadly.] That message has been distorted through time . . . distorted through people. It sometimes pains me that . . . [Long consideration, then sighs.] I am close enough to humans, as I can incorporate, to feel emotion, as opposed to my kin that you've spoken to have not (been able to incorporate or feel emotion). Although my father (Rae) has a particular fondness for you. [Smiles knowingly at Lois.] That is uncommon for us. But my generation [Holds a hand to his chest.] . . . the spirit that lives in this body day-to-day identifies very closely with the corporeal world. We interact with it constantly and can become part of it . . . and it pains us greatly when people suffer needlessly.

That's an important word, *needlessly*. Suffering is necessary. You cannot enjoy pleasure unless you experience pain. Every coin has two sides. However, there are those who bring willful harm to others. That is a development which hurts us greatly. We have always sought to teach the message that people need to . . . I don't want to say: "Love each other." [Shakes his head.] That word is so abused. It's just a matter of simple *compassion*. Not all intelligent races have emotion. Some do have a limited amount. Compassion is not a strictly human quality to be sure, but . . . it is rare in the Universe. And it saddens us to see compassion wasted so often.

Not all worlds have their own spirit. Gaia is the spirit of this planet and cares for all of you. In some sense, *you are all her children*. You are all made of her bones. Gaia provides well for her children. There is no real scarcity on Earth. There is enough to go around. It hurts Gaia when her resources are wasted, but there is enough. It is not necessary that people take more than they need. [Sighs heavily.] There is too much greed in this world.

What ultimately brought down the Roman Empire[1] . . . arguably one of the strongest civilizations . . . physically strongest civilizations . . . they lacked quite a bit in morals toward the end. What ultimately brought the empire down was not attack from outside; it was decay from within to the point that they no longer even had the will to defend themselves. There are civilizations that have avoided that problem. The Anasazi[2] of the American Southwest . . . they literally evolved out of the need for corporeal existence. Some civilizations were simply destroyed from the outside, like the Incas. They had practices which modern man might have questioned, but they had their moral code, and they stuck with it.

It's not so much what you say, it's the belief in what you say (that matters). Pick your frame of reference and stay with it. If you can be true to your beliefs . . . if you do no harm . . . that essentially makes you a good person. There are . . . there are too many people who don't live that way. They do not . . . they do not even believe what they say. There is a reason why *honesty* has always been a most valued quality among humans. If you cannot be true to your own beliefs, how can you possibly be true to anything?

So, the message that we give is the message that we have given throughout time, not just in my previous incarnation. That one (incarnation) became more famous than we usually experience. It never ends happily for us. [Sighs sadly.] But, we've all been through it. Our incarnations

---

1. The Roman Empire (27 BC–286 AD) consisted of large territories around Europe, North Africa, West Asia, and the Mediterranean Sea. Principalities were ruled by emperors. Rome was the capital city.

2. The Anasazi (ah-nuh-sah-zee), also known as the Ancestral Puebloans, were an ancient Native American culture. Their territory included what is now the Southwest region of the United States.

as Buddha[3] and Muhammad[4] . . . many of the great prophets
. . . not all of them have been my kin. Most of the Gods who
have been worshipped have been my parents. [Pauses to
reflect.] It's interesting that there have been civilizations that
recognize the existence of . . . [Searches for wording.] . . . I
don't want to say . . . I'm trying . . . English is a very difficult
language sometimes. Words have definitions and then they
have connotations, and it is very difficult to speak literally
without being misinterpreted.

There have been civilizations that have recognized
there are . . . planes of existence beyond the physical . . .
that there are beings, such as myself, who live in these other
realms, without necessarily believing that they were Gods.
These beings had natural superior abilities, just as there are
different abilities among your own kind. It is . . . a bell curve
that exists everywhere, even among my kin.

There are those who believe that some level of
competition is necessary. [Smiles knowingly.] There are those
who, like me, believe that there is always a peaceful answer.
We are not the one true God that many human religions
believe. *There is not one, all-knowing, all-seeing, all-powerful
being.* As a group, my kin come close to that. Given all of
our years of existence, we have knowledge, but not down to
the microscopic level. There's no being watching everything
that everyone does, and certainly there's no one judging
everything you do. *The only judge you ever have to face is
yourself.* The only people you have to be better than are the
people you are today. I have kin who wouldn't give you that
particular message, and they are not wrong either.

If you do what you believe is right . . . [Shakes his head.]
Again . . . the word "right" is so wrong to use. [Shrugs, then

---

3. Buddha (Gautama) was a religious leader and is the primary figure in Buddhism.
   Gautama lived in ancient India between the sixth and fourth centuries BC and
   taught the Middle Way between indulgence and severe asceticism.

4. Muhammad (570–632 AD) was a religious, social, and political leader and
   founder of Islam. He is considered a prophet of monotheistic teachings, as were
   Adam, Abraham, Moses, Jesus, and others.

long pause.] Hippocrates[5] said it best: "First, do no harm." If you want to put a message out there, that would be on my top five list . . . First, do no harm. The message that I gave, "Do unto others as you would have others do unto you," seems so self-evident. Why would you ever need to tell people that? [Speaks with intense sadness.] Yet I see in the world the need to remind people of something that should be so obvious. [Long consideration.] Those two messages are probably the most important that I can leave you with [gestures widely with his arms], having left them with humanity once before.

Believe in yourself. You are the only ones who make reality exist. Your scientists today are only beginning to understand what that actually means. We, for example . . . when we are without physical form, and my parents and their parents, who never have physical form, are at once everywhere and nowhere. When we focus our conscience on a point, that's where we are . . . for the time that we choose to be there. It's very similar for corporeal life as well. It's only the time span that's a little different.

You were everywhere and nowhere until you chose the body into which you wanted to be. Now, you're here. This is your point of focus; this is where you will be, until it's time to move on again. You are limited by being in physical nature as to . . . the travels you can take. I can be anywhere, anytime, because I have no body that I need to worry about. If you depart your body entirely, then your body dies. That doesn't hurt your spirit, but you can't come back. When I depart this body, my brother's spirit returns, and the body continues. And, in fact, we are . . . close enough (in vibrational level) that he has not had to completely leave. He will remember what we say here . . . most of it.

Lois: Wonderful. He'll be happy to know that.

---

5. Hippocrates (460–370 BC) was an ancient Greek physician considered to be one of the most remarkable figures in the history of medicine. His teachings are the basis of Western medicine.

Jesus: It will be a little disorienting for him, but he's been through
   this before. We are sufficient kin that we can retain this
   relationship for a considerable period of time. But, if you
   were to look around us, you would see the merger of our
   spirits outside the body. You have been told that the spirit
   cannot wholly exist within the body. A physical form cannot
   contain that level of energy. What you call an aura[6] is the
   result of the spiritual part of the body that resides without.
   We both reside within and without right now. So, he will
   remember most of what we say.

   Do you have a specific question? Is there something I
   can tell you?

Lois: I have a question related to Gary's physical body. He seems to
   have many physical issues. You were an amazing healer. [Jesus
   smiles knowingly.] Is there anything that can be done to help
   Gary heal himself?

Jesus: That's an interesting question. You see . . . my brother's
   spirit that resides in this body is equally adept at healing. For
   every disease, there is a cure. For every individual, the cure is
   unique. There's a good message for you. Many healers have
   wondered: "How can I do so much for so many, and I myself
   have all these problems?" It's because, at some level, they
   put the greater good before themselves, and they would
   consider it a waste to use their abilities on themselves.

   The spirit, as it resides in a body, does not retain much
   in the way of memory of previous lives, or without training,
   much in the way of knowledge that there is anything other
   than what is. At some level, this is necessary. The physical
   brain can only handle just so much information, remarkable
   a development as it is. There are many forms of intelligent
   life. The human brain is . . . the pinnacle of corporeal
   development. It's not always used correctly, but it's there if
   you know how to use it. And . . . old spirits know more than

---

6. An aura is the energy field that surrounds all living things. It is the spiritual
   part of the body that doesn't fit completely into the physical body. The older the
   spirit, the larger the aura that extends beyond the body.

is good for their physical body to know. They realize that this is a very tiny piece of existence, especially for a very old spirit. When they pass away, it is only the physical body that dies. Older spirits are somehow, sometimes unwilling to help themselves.

Lois: We are concerned about our mission to help shift this planet to the positive, and we have all expressed concern about what's going to happen. There's a sense of wondering what *we* can do to keep humanity from annihilating itself again.

Jesus: Yes. [Takes a deep breath.] My older kin . . . tend not to make much in the way of recommendations. They will answer most any question. If you were to ask my father you know as Rae . . . how to build an Atlantean Crystal Generator, he would not tell you, because he saw what happened once before. My parent's parents will tell you even less. They will give you all the history of the Universe, but they won't make a recommendation. At some level, I can understand their reticence. There have been times when my kin have interfered. . . and the result was not what we intended. [Sighs regretfully.]

    We are not all-knowing. We cannot predict the future. We see trends and probabilities. But, we do not know with certainty what will happen. For that reason, we do not interfere with corporeal beings' development. We do not steer it one way or another because we do not know with absolute certainty which path ultimately will be best, at a macroscopic level, for the entire civilization and at an individual level. We make no recommendations. However, my generation, because we can take physical form . . . the very act of taking that form . . . represents change. Our simple existence, my being here right now, has incalculable changes in the probability timelines. My brother's existence . . . corporeal existence . . . makes changes in every life he touches, but that's true of all of you, even the newest soul. Every person you touch puts them in a particular direction, one that perhaps they would not have taken on their own.

Having knowledge of the future, even if it's just statistical knowledge, makes us unwilling to share that knowledge. Imagine, if you knew the precise date and time of your death, what would you do with that information? Would you try and avoid it? By avoiding it, you may cause it. By avoiding it, you may bring it nearer. Some knowledge is simply not useful. We try to share general messages. We try to steer civilizations based on our experience with other civilizations.

We've been around a long time. We've been on a lot of worlds. We know that certain things will *almost* always produce a certain result. It's the *almost* . . . that must make us hesitate, but we are happy to share . . . pearls of wisdom with you. The messages that we have given you . . . the messages I gave two thousand years ago are not so specific that we would be concerned about steering people in the wrong direction. There are a lot of things that I could say that I would not say, but the general messages are really all I can give you. So, forgive me if at some point you ask a question that I decline to answer. [Shakes his head apologetically.]

Lois: Thank you. In one of the earliest meetings with your parent's parents, the Anquietas implied that humanity was on a negative trajectory, and there is a choice that is coming. Humanity must make a choice on which path to take before it is too late.

Jesus: It is coming faster than we had predicted.

Lois: Yes. Is there any sense of how fast? I shouldn't ask that question, should I? [Smiles knowingly.]

Paul: Well, you can always ask. [Paul has been observing in awe.]

Lois: How fast are we talking? Twenty years . . . one hundred years?

Jesus: Time doesn't work for us the way it does for you. I knew that you wanted to speak with me in the moment between . . . the point at which my brother's conscious slipped aside. To me, it was a long period of time. I had to decide and think:

"Did I want to come? It's been two thousand years since I've taken physical form." That was true corporeal form, as opposed to the sharing that I do now (through Gary). Seeing what humanity has done with the messages that I left has made me hesitant to return.

You wanted me here and so I came. I hope this message is kept true. We trust you [gestures to Lois] or we would not be here. But there will be those who will try and take the words you write and use them for their own purposes. We hope you will defend the words, and it will not be easy. No one who has ever brought a world-changing message, on any world, has ever had it easy . . . and it usually doesn't end well. We want you to consider that. If you choose not to . . . [Looks directly at Lois.] If you choose not to proceed, we will understand. You do not have to do this.

Lois: I have been through enough in this life, and others, that I feel committed to helping humanity again.

Jesus: We thought you would feel that way.

Lois: With your guidance, I feel safe.

Jesus: We are always here with you.

Lois: I know that. Thank you.

Jesus: But, there is a limit as to what we can do for you. [Pauses to reflect.] When Rae reassembled your spirit, that's not entirely in keeping with the tradition of my kin. Not that we object. [Smiles kindly at Lois, then pauses.]

You have questioned the work you do. [Looks at Paul.]

Jesus seemed to know of Paul's dilemma. As one of my clearing consultants, Paul had previously expressed concern that we might be interfering with a person's destiny when we remove negative energies or spirits from someone.

Jesus: It comes down to the message that I gave you. *If you intend no harm, you cannot do the wrong thing.* You will make mistakes. I make mistakes. It's much more about the intent than anything else. Atlantis was destroyed because we made a mistake. [Hesitates as he chokes up with regret.] Many civilizations have fallen because we made mistakes. [Pauses to reflect with deep sadness.] *All anyone can ever do is the best that they can do.* Maybe the best . . . that some can do is better than others. It depends on what they are doing. We all have our strengths, we all have our weaknesses, we all have our blind spots. That's normal, even for us. [Motions to himself.]

Don't let fear of making a mistake stop you from doing what you believe to be right. We've given you that message before. We have to give you the choice, but we know you'll choose correctly, or we wouldn't be wasting our energy here. The important thing is to get people to listen. [Chooses his words carefully.] The message has to be delivered in a way, not just that they will understand, but in a way that they will hopefully accept.

The newer the spirit, the more limited its frames of reference. The fewer lives you've had . . . even though the memory of previous lives is blocked from you in an existence . . . the elasticity of thought stays with you. The more lives you've had, the more you've learned. Even if the specific memories are not immediately accessible to you, they all can be accessible. We don't typically encourage people to go hunting for them. But even if the specific memories are not accessible, the ability to realize that there is more comes from having experienced more, even if the experiences themselves are lost. Remember that.

One of the reasons that Earth is having so much trouble now is that there is such a high percentage of very new spirits. We prefer not to use the term "souls." Again, definition versus connotation. Essentially, it is the same thing . . . the non-physical part of your existence. There are so many new ones (spirits) on Earth that they do not have the elasticity to accept certain things.

The problem is . . . given a small box, once it's full, it's very difficult to . . . [Pauses to think.] If someone has picked up a bad habit, you can't . . . you can't give them a good habit. You have to get rid of the old one (habit) first. This is part of what you do. [Affirming nod to Lois, then speaks with strong emphasis.] This is what you have to do on a global level. People have got to . . . unlearn . . . before they can relearn. Many people will accept your message because they already know it. Some are simply afraid to be the first to step up and bring a message of being good to one another. I was tortured and put to death for it.

Lois: I am so sorry.

Jesus: It's all right. [Nods sadly.] We know that our lives move on. Physical existence is very fleeting, even if you keep coming back, even if you keep coming back to the same place. [Glances to Paul.] I can't tell you how to frame this. [Gestures emphatically to Lois.] I've given you some concepts, the same ones I've given before. The message got lost . . . somehow. [Shakes his head in frustration.]

The concept of reward and punishment after death was introduced as a way to control people. "If you're good now, it'll be good for you later." Karma.[7] The entire concept . . . which is not a wrong concept . . . the *payback* for what you do exists, it just does not come from the outside. There is no external judgment for what you do. There is no external reward and punishment. There is no vengeful God. There is no devil. I have kin that come close. [Nods knowingly.]

Reward and punishment do come from within. You may deceive yourself in your corporeal existence into thinking that you've had such a wonderful life. But, when that life ends and your spirit reflects, it will see with much greater clarity what happened in that life. If you have done more harm than good, you will punish yourself. There are spirits who have done such harm that they have . . . dissociated themselves. They have

---

7. Karma is the spiritual principle of cause and effect, where intent and actions of an individual (cause) influence the future of that individual (effect). Karma in the present life affects one's future in their present and future lives.

terminated their own spirits, released their energy back (to the Universe), never to return. Bits and pieces do return; they all get reused. Nothing is ever lost, but that consciousness, that individual consciousness, is gone. That doesn't happen too often, but it does happen, and not just here; it happens on all worlds.

The bell curve . . . given a level of intelligence, there will always be a few at each end. One hopes it is an even balance. On Earth, it may not seem this way to you, but the bell curve actually is skewed more to the positive. [Mutters in annoyance over the words.] Positive and negative . . . there are fewer people who do more harm than there are people who do more good. It . . . makes one wonder why things are so skewed to the negative. [Shakes his head.] It's a question that my kin have pondered. It seems that . . . the voices of the people who do more good than harm . . . don't seem to attract the attention of the people in the middle. And, the voices of the people who do more harm than good seem to be heard more clearly. This is a conundrum that, in billions of years, we have not resolved. We are not sure we could do anything with that knowledge if we did. It is not that we have rules, but we have traditions.

You need to make known the voice of the people who do *more good*. They *need* to be heard. It's easy to complain when something goes wrong and also very easy to say to yourself, "that was nice," and move on. Pointing out when somebody does wrong seems to be easier than congratulating somebody on having done right. That's a good message for you. *Speak the compliment aloud.* It's important to let people know when they've done well. A system based on . . . entirely on punishment without reward can never work. Whenever you must say something to somebody to correct an action, try if you can, to compliment them on a positive action at the same time. One, then the other: "You shouldn't have done that, and this is why. Then, thank you for doing this, that was a good thing." It takes the sting out without reducing the importance of the message. [Speaks more softly.] That message . . . I don't know how it got lost.

Lois: That's my curiosity. What do you think happened to your messages? How did they get changed? How can we take what you've learned and apply it differently this time?

Jesus: It was such a simple message: "Do unto others." [Speaks very sadly.] I don't understand where it all went wrong. [Shakes his head in regret.] I think it was timing. I think that . . . there was so much turmoil at the time . . . See, the bell curve exists, but it's not static; it moves each way. As each new life comes in, as each old life goes out, with every interaction the curve moves one way or the other. I came here when I did because the curve was moving in the wrong direction, and I think my timing was simply off. Perhaps I should have come sooner. Perhaps I should have waited until the pendulum had swung as far as it was going to. Then, maybe I could have . . . pushed it . . . given it more energy in the direction it needed to go. I came, and I pushed when the pendulum was still moving the wrong way . . . I wasn't able to apply enough force to make any difference, and the message was simply forgotten. I'm sorry . . . it wasn't really forgotten. People still know that message, don't they? [With tears in his eyes.]

Lois: Oh yes. They do.

As I interacted with Jesus, as channeled through Gary, I was struck by my own emotion of slight confusion. I am used to experiencing Jesus as a kind, yet strong, protective, and supportive Guide when he comes to clients during hypnosis sessions. I always feel a loving calmness when he comes to me in prayer or reflection. But in this interaction, he seemed different. He exhibited human emotions of intense sadness and concern. It touched my heart deeply to see him so sad. We have learned in these teachings that human emotions are unique in the Universe and can be very intense. Watching Jesus emote in human form solidified just how powerful our emotions can be.

Jesus: I know it became a tenet of some religions. (*Do unto others.*) But there's a case of: "We say these things because they are good things to say." But the actions do not follow. Not that they haven't done good things. Everybody does good things. But, *so many deaths* have been justified in the name of a God that doesn't *even* exist. Maybe that's a message.

Lois: That's what is happening now with some extreme religious groups.

Jesus: Still happening. [Shakes his head.]

Lois: Yes. Still happening. Death being justified in the name of a God.

Jesus: In . . . in . . . in my father's name, who isn't the father they think. [Speaks with great frustration, then a heavy sigh.]

Paul: You did such wonderful things when you were in physical form two thousand years ago. Such wonderful things, and you were treated with utmost cruelty and brutality.

Jesus: Sadly, that is the fate of many a prophet. [Sighs deeply.] I can't help but think of those who inspired followers with unhealthy messages, but their fate was never any better. The creation of change . . . even when it is change for the good . . . is painful. We understand that. Most corporeal beings understand that. I have kin who believe that change should be constant, and at some level, it always is. Nothing remains the same. You stagnate, and you perish. It's one of the basic laws written into the fabric of the Universe, but it's possible to change too much too quickly.

When you shake a person's beliefs, whatever they are, too much . . . the result is always going to be negative. [Pauses to consider.] Present these messages as reminders because it is not a new system. I'm not telling you anything you don't know. I think . . . humanity needs to be reminded . . . not told . . . not led . . . but reminded . . . that there is enough for everyone. Gaia is alive and cares for them. *If humans need to pray to something more powerful than themselves, let that be Gaia.* There have been many religions on Earth that were natural . . . that worshipped nature.

Lois: Nature-focused. Yes.

Jesus: Yes. There's nothing wrong with that. Gaia is more real than this imaginary God. Gaia is more powerful than this imaginary God. What happens when a volcano erupts? [He asks rhetorically.]

Honoring the sacred entity, the living spirit of Gaia, was significant in this session. It is remarkable how Jesus tells us to call on her, something that has been done by Earth-based cultures throughout the millennia.

Lois: I would like to make an observation. At your death, there was what we refer to as a solar eclipse. And, it is said that three days later you appeared to your followers. [Jesus nods knowingly.] Today, this day is three days after a solar eclipse that just traveled across North America, and you are appearing to us. Isn't that an interesting coincidence?

Jesus: The Universe is full of coincidences. [Smiles gently.]

Lois: Amazing coincidences.

Jesus: Total eclipses are not that uncommon; they occur about once every eighteen months. [Nods knowingly.] It just hasn't happened in this particular country in a while.

Lois: Correct.

Jesus: When my physical body died two thousand years ago . . . it died. [Deep breath, then sighs.] I breathed my last breath in the arms of the woman I loved after they took me down off the cross.

Based on historical and biblical references, some people believe that Jesus was married to Mary Magdalene.

Lois: It is said that after three days, your body disappeared from the tomb. What happened to your body?

Jesus: I do not know. I did not care about my body. It was so badly damaged. I suffered such pain. I know my followers were in anguish to see my body so damaged. *My . . . resurrection was one of spirit.* I had followers with whom I was very close. Having been corporeal only days before, part of my spirit was still within them, and I was able to appear in their mind's eye. I told them to keep the message alive.

In the same way that you and my father Rae were very close, he could communicate with you in your mind. [Looks at Lois.] Had he not been a part of you, he would not have been able to reconstruct you, and your spirit would have been gone. Many Atlanteans were destroyed. I don't believe he made any attempt to restore others because they were responsible for the accident. [Long pause.]

I realized then that my timing had been off, that my message was going to be lost. [Looks down as he shakes his head in despair.] I relied on my followers . . . if not to do the job I had tried to do . . . to keep the message alive . . . and try to bring peace to the world. [Sighs heavily.]

Lois: Is it true that Mary Magdalene traveled to France to teach your words?

Jesus: All of my followers taught my words. Mary was very special. [Smiles softly.]

Sadly, the message was changed. Instead of . . . following the simple message, leaders tried to force people to obey the message, and it was never meant as a command. [Pauses to consider.] The Ten Commandments were written by good men who wanted people to be good to each other. The message was simple. But, trying to enforce it on people . . . as I said, you cannot force people to change. Even if you give them something that they know is right . . . even if you give them something that they know is better to do . . . if you force them to do it, they're going to resent it. And that is where it all went wrong.

When the Christian religion was created, based on the messages that I gave, leaders tried to force people to follow their rules . . . [speaks with great remorse] and then worse, executed people who did not . . . in my name. [Long pause, then speaks with deep regret.] These are those moments that . . . these are the moments that hurt us. These are the moments . . . that at some level, we regret having gotten involved. That's why we try not to get involved. Even . . . *we* . . . . as well-meaning as we can be . . . [shakes his head with heavy sorrow] . . . think of the number of deaths that went down in my name. It was not what I had intended.

Lois: Yet there are many who did get your message.

Jesus: I know. [Continues to speak with intense sadness.] The message hasn't died.

Lois: It's the negative that always seems to be amplified. There are many more good people; much good came out of your message. Truly. And we are here to help perpetuate the good as best we can.

Jesus: What saddens me most is not the death itself, because I know that these spirits continue on and are reborn. [Takes a deep breath and buries his face in his hands.] What saddens me most is the harm to the people who are doing the killing. So many don't recover. [Speaks with frustration as he shakes his head.] I don't understand how anyone can profess a belief in any God, and then knowingly do something that they must realize is contrary to anything that any God has ever said! What do they *think* will happen? How can you believe in any kind of reward and punishment and do the kinds of things that people on Earth . . . not just Earth . . . it's more prevalent here. How can they believe in reward and punishment and do what they do?

Lois: Do you think that there's any sort of external, negative influence? In the work that Paul and I do, we find negative entities that manipulate humans. They seem to be malicious and tend to enjoy causing disturbances.

Jesus: Such do exist. But it doesn't begin to explain what happens. It (conflict) is part of human existence. It's part of civilization on this world. There are worlds in which, for one reason or another, no conflict ever developed . . . ones with sufficient resources, sufficient willingness to spread out enough to not crowd each other. Frequently, on some worlds, life begins in a single place and spreads, and remains essentially as one civilization.

Much of the conflict that occurs is not over a physical thing, although there is plenty of that, but is over beliefs and ideals. Some people grew up being taught one thing, and other people grew up being taught another, and that's fine. Difference and divergence are necessary for health and strength. *It's the desire to enforce what you believe on someone else that generates the conflict*. It is a concept with which we have a great deal of difficulty. Perhaps it's because we . . . again the language fails me but . . .

Lois: You don't interfere with free will . . .

Jesus: Hmm . . . no . . . I was heading for . . . *My kin are of one kind, we don't have that conflict,* which is not to say we don't have differences of opinion, but the fundamental conflict is not there. *Humanity is a single species*. [Pauses to consider.] That's an important thing to remember. You're not . . . it's not the case of *Homo sapiens* versus Cro-Magnon; you're all the same. That *should* be important to you.

You're not fighting aliens. You're all one people. It doesn't matter where you are born. It doesn't matter what you were taught when you grew up. [Reflects hesitantly.] I think some of my kin have thought that a belief in a single God might unify people. But, even the major religions that believe in a single God have gone astray . . . and don't realize that it is one God (they all believe in). They seem to think that *their* God is somehow different than the next person's.

The polytheistic religions[8] don't seem to have these conflicts between each other. There are many religions that live in many regions adjacent to each other, and they have their set of Gods [indicates a space with his left hand], and they have their set of Gods [indicates a space with his right hand], and nobody has ever fought over that. For some reason, when it's my God versus your God . . . Gods that don't even exist . . . somehow, they can't accept the fact that somebody might believe something different than what they believe. And within Christianity [speaks emotionally] it's even sillier, because the differences between God in the different sects are so minuscule. How could you fight over this?

At least in the polytheistic religions, there *are* multiple Gods . . . if I call my parents that. [Explains more calmly.] Like I said, there are civilizations who understand the existence of non-physical beings and beings greater than themselves without having to resort to calling them Gods . . . without attributing totally natural things to them . . . like the Greeks or the Romans did, or the Norse. Thunder came from Thor. Thor was one of my fathers, and he's thrown a few thunderbolts in his day. [Breathes in hopefully.] But . . . perhaps we could get humans to believe in what is *real* in the Universe, and not what they would *like* to be real.

Ultimately, these are going to be your decisions: what you choose to pass on, and how you choose to pass it on. Clearly, I have made mistakes. I won't tell you to do what I did because I know that's not the right thing. [Smiles tenderly.] We all do the best we can do. [Pauses to reflect.] *Get people to understand they aren't alone in the Universe . . .* get them to believe there is something greater than themselves, even if they don't attribute it to the one "God." They (the Collective) have experienced enough and seen enough to know that people who believe in ghosts are not wrong. You know that. [Gestures to Lois.]

---

8. Polytheistic religion is the worship of or belief in multiple Gods and Goddesses as Guides for a civilization.

If we can get them to understand that these God-like beings exist . . . awful term. [Huffs annoyingly.] Maybe they won't fight about it. Then, you're likely to just cause a fight between the people that will believe you and the people who won't. I don't see how to not create two sides. *There will always be people who believe and people who don't . . . and people who don't care* [shrugs his shoulders]. And they're the safe ones. Maybe a certain degree of apathy is needed. It's always the people who *care* that cause the trouble. Most people are perfectly happy to just say: "Life isn't too bad. I have what I need. I'm good." The vast majority of the population on this planet is exactly that. It's only the few who rattle the cage. Have I helped you at all, or are you hopelessly confused?

Lois: No, this is wonderful. Thank you so much. I do have another question.

Jesus: Of course.

Lois: Would you be willing to return if we ever needed you, as a spokesperson through Gary?

Jesus: I . . . am not sure how comfortable I'd be with an audience. [Shakes his head regretfully.]

Lois: That is my question.

Jesus: I will always be here when you need me. [Nods in affirmation.]

Lois: Thank you so much. Are there any of your brothers or fathers or sisters or mothers who we should speak with?

Jesus: We are not so different. [Smiles knowingly.] You can . . . speak to any of us on anything you like. My parent's parents tend to be a little long-winded . . . but whose parents aren't? [Chuckles light-heartedly.]

Lois: So, is there one last message? Is there a question that we haven't asked that we should?

Jesus: I don't think I could tell you if there was. [Laughs heartily, then sighs heavily.] I can think of several questions you should ask and none of them have answers that I can give you. We have great faith in your ability to do the right thing, especially with this information. [Nods expectantly to Lois.] We recognize that a lot of it . . . is going to stir things up. We do not envy you for your task, but we appreciate that you are willing to take this on. It will not be easy for you. I had my time in the spotlight.

Remember, I am never far away. I am always in your heart.

Lois: I know. Thank you. We've had your presence long enough. I appreciate all that you do. Thank you so very much for honoring us this day.

Paul: Thank you.

Gary's head drops back momentarily. I give him a few minutes to rest, then slowly bring Gary back by filling his body with light energy and invite his spirit to come back fully into his body. I encourage him to take a moment to align his physical body for health as he returns to full awareness.

Since Gary was able to remember most of what transpired, as Jesus said he would, the three of us discussed this session. Gary described moments of discontinuity at the beginning and end, yet he said he seemed to be present for most of this session. He expressed having trouble processing it all. As he was going into trance, Gary connected with Jesus outside of the physical body. In the brief moment before Jesus entered, Gary described having what seemed to be a long, private conversation between them. He stated the time "in between" is much different than physical time. As spiritual brothers, their energy was more closely matched, allowing this session to be the longest yet at an hour and thirteen minutes.

Gary experienced much more emotion than in prior sessions. He commented that he didn't feel much emotion from the Anquietas, and he felt some of Rae's feelings. However, Jesus' spirit had a great deal of emotion that he could feel strongly in his heart. We discussed the concept that there may be a relationship around the heart being the seat of emotion. We felt a need to touch people's hearts with Jesus' many messages.

We spoke of the caution from Jesus about choosing to accept this mission. In many of our past lives, we were beheaded, were burned at the stake, or died in other tragic ways for bringing positive messages. This time, we hope to make an exception, and know we are here for this reason, to deliver the messages of the Collective. We also discussed that Jesus is always here when we call on him. We are never alone.

Reflection

In this powerful session, we speak with the spirit of Jesus, prophet, messenger, teacher, brother, and friend. I was overjoyed to have an actual conversation with this dear Guide whom I call on daily. Jesus comes to many of my clients while they are in trance. As the observer to their sessions, I have the privilege of hearing Jesus' messages on a regular basis. He always speaks of love, kindness, compassion, and forgiveness. He encourages people to lighten up, often saying we are too hard on ourselves, that we need to enjoy our lives and each other. Jesus brings a warm, glowing kindness that is truly profound. Clients always express a sense of calmness when he visits them. I encourage people to call on him regularly, especially when stressed or worried. I've learned that Jesus will take away our fears, and when we remember to call on him, he will be there. Always.

In this conversation, Jesus was even more animated than Rae. He sat upright in the chair, holding his hands lightly in front of him, gesturing regularly. He opened his arms wide with his hands gently welcoming, as he is often portrayed in pictures. At times, he rubbed his chin, moved his head from side to side, even buried his face in his hands in exasperation. His energy was intensely palpable; I could feel his warmth, tenderness, and sincerity deep in my heart. Jesus was quite personable, exhibited a sense of humor, and expressed a variety of emotions. He had tears in his eyes when he spoke of the sadness over his messages being lost, and I could feel the depth of his suffering.

Conversing with this dear teacher and Guide triggered a host of my own feelings. Imagine how emotionally charged this session was, from the excitement of having a very real conversation with Jesus and the sadness he felt over his message being lost, to the concern he shared on how I would spread these messages. I came away with even more drive to follow through on my commitment to re-share the lost messages Jesus taught so eloquently two thousand years ago.

When reflecting on how messages are lost or distorted over time, one theory is that as people gain power, they begin to feel superior.

Their traditions, thought processes, and actions shift toward being more self-serving. As they become more ego-based and less communal, these power-centric people change the initial messages to suit their own purposes. This causes confusion among the people and the collective energy spirals out of control.

There was great turmoil in Jesus' time with controlling rulers who subsequently adopted and distorted his messages. While others have historically changed messages to suit their agendas, this trend has continued with perhaps more frequency. With today's ability to communicate globally, I am encouraged that we have the opportunity to present these messages as they were delivered to us. Our hope is we that may come together as a human collective in a way that wasn't possible in Jesus' era.

As others do, I have my own heartfelt connection with Jesus. I have learned to call on him regularly to assist myself and my clients with everyday issues. In my powerful connection with Jesus, I am able to feel his guidance and actually hear him speaking to me in my mind. This is in contrast to Gary, who was non-religious and had no interest in a relationship with Jesus. So, this session came as quite a shock to him.

Some of my Jewish clients have been surprised to discover that Jesus came when they called for assistance while in trance. Because of their Jewish background, they expressed confusion as to why Jesus would come to assist. I remind them gently that Jesus, the human being, was indeed Jewish, and the eternal spirit of Jesus helps everyone. This made sense to them and would often continue a meaningful relationship with Jesus as a spiritual teacher and Guide. It is society who began to associate Jesus with specific religions after his death. The eternal spirit of Jesus does not have a religious affiliation.

Both Rae and Jesus referenced past lives. Reincarnation is mentioned throughout the Bible and other holy books, yet some deny or downplay this concept. There is a belief that our spirits choose to come to Earth for the experience: to learn, to teach, or to grow. Some people wonder why anyone would choose a life that is challenging. We choose our parents, our family structure, our social and environmental situations for reasons related to our intended purpose. I have learned that experience is the best teacher. I often take clients to a place known as life-between-lives so they can learn for themselves why they chose to be born into their specific life situation, or why they were asked to incarnate.

Memories of previous reincarnations are typically blocked from us when we are born, though some do have spontaneous prior-life recall. We can choose to access these memories through guidance, such as hypnosis, when we are ready to understand, process, and learn from them. Numerous people have past-life recall of being alive at the time when Jesus was on Earth. Many of my clients knew him, or of him in their past lives, where he had a meaningful impact on them. Some were soldiers who carried such guilt for not stopping the cruelty against Jesus. One client was a peasant farmer whom Jesus taught to irrigate crops. Others were disciples, both men and women. These were simple people. Jesus never discriminated against anyone and welcomed everyone into his flock: men, women, children, rich, poor, healthy, and infirm. No matter what race or denomination, his consistent message was: "We are all one."

I have my own past life memories of being with Jesus, where I listened to him teach to crowds, both large and small. As a young teen in that life, I traveled in his circles and experienced the simple peace of community without strife. Unsure of my exact relationship with Jesus, other than that my parents were among his followers, I remember being in a large household with a wonderful open court-yard. It was a gathering place where people told stories, recited poetry, listened to musicians, and children enjoyed games. The excitement was evident when Jesus would return from his travels. He was so kind and engaging, and we always enjoyed his inviting presence. There was gentle laughter and much introspective discussion as he shared his insightful stories.

I also have vivid recall of being extremely shaken by what the soldiers did to Jesus and how they destroyed our home. Because I have visceral recall of him being crucified, to this day I am deeply disturbed by the portrayal of Jesus on the cross. It seems strange to me to focus on the cruelty of his death when he was such an amaz-ingly charismatic teacher with a message of peace and love. It is diffi-cult to imagine why one would prominently display a photograph of a loved one on their deathbed. Shouldn't we prefer to remember their happier, healthier times? Why does our civilization focus on cruelty and venerate suffering? What if we were to focus on good, uplifting teachings instead of sadness, sorrow, and pain? When I was a child in my current life, I much preferred to sit at Mother Mary's altar with her statue lovingly holding baby Jesus in her arms. To this day, Christmas is always a special time for me.

I feel honored to have received this special audience with Jesus. I believe he came because of my own deep connection with him. Jesus guides me in my day-to-day interactions both personally and professionally. I pray for his assistance for others, call for his help with clients, ask for the words to say to guide them, and connect clients while in trance to his kindly energy. I also teach clients how to ask for his assistance and live in the light of his peace. Jesus wants to remind people that the guiding spirits we call the Collective, of which he is one, are always there to assist when asked.

Jesus clarified that he died after the crucifixion in the arms of the woman he loved. He declined to verbally acknowledge Mary Magdalene as his wife, simply stating she was very special. I felt he knew what I was asking and chose to not answer that question directly as he considered the details of his human life and death to be less significant than his messages. He assured us that his resurrection was of spirit, communicating with his followers spiritually and telepathi-cally. The Gnostics,[9] of which his followers were considered to have been, had the ability to directly commune with "God" in their prayers. I believe Jesus was able to connect with his followers in a prayerful, spiritual, channeled way, similar to how the spiritually-aware commu-nicate with him to this day.

Jesus shared how the Collective thought a belief in one God

---

9. Gnosticism is a system of religious concepts among early Christian and Jewish groups that emphasized personal spiritual knowledge. Many texts focused on enlightenment and direct communication with the divine.

might unify people. However, the opposite was the result. He was distressed with the absurdity of people fighting and killing over beliefs that are so similar among religions that are almost identical. The worst dissension is between sects of the same religion. Killing in the name of God hurts him and the Collective tremendously. From Christians in the crusades, to protestant reformers, to those who conquered nature-focused tribes, isn't it time to stop the bloodshed in the name of God? When will we learn to accept other religions as if they are simply different languages? One is not right or wrong. Each belief is unique to the individual, just as each spirit is unique to the person.

Clearly, much conflict is generated over similar religions enforcing their way of living as the only path. Those who force beliefs on others or argue about others' beliefs miss Jesus' foundational message of mutual respect. *Chronicles of Hope* invites us to tap into our own knowledge, wisdom, and belief systems. As we digest these messages with openness, we enhance and renew our own understanding. Those who base their life on the honest teachings of the Bible, and pray to God, may wish to consider this series a companion text.

Medical professionals are aware of the Hippocratic Oath: "First, do no harm." This was one of Jesus' favorite messages. Who are we to judge another's thoughts, beliefs, or life choices, unless they are causing harm? Jesus also referred to the Golden Rule: "Do unto others as you would have them do unto you." He emphasized the simplicity of this message and wondered when people will learn to be at peace with themselves and each other. This book encourages every individual to truly listen, live, and share the messages Jesus gave us many years ago.

Jesus affirmed that there is not one, all-knowing, all-seeing, all-powerful God, just as Rae and the Anquietas reminded us. People often wonder how God could allow terrible things to happen. The Collective neither controls nor causes. Their energy serves as a group of guiding spirits, assisting in times of crisis. They are all one, yet have individual personas, much as humanity is all one species, yet different individuals. Think about your hand with individual fingers that operate independently yet are all connected together as one hand.

Jesus reminds us that we can use the words "soul" and "spirit" interchangeably. Soul tends to have a religious overtone, while spirit is more universal.

Jesus said to avoid belief systems that don't value spiritual growth, encouraging humanity to believe in something that is real, that has value. He reminds us it is good for people to pray to one God, if that is where their heart is. If people are open to call on the Collective of spirits to assist us every day, then humanity will see positive shifts. We are invited to capture people's hearts to allow them to create a more personal relationship with their own spirituality. We could use the words "God" and "the Collective" interchangeably. You could think of "God" as a "Group of Divine" beings (GOD).

We are on this Earth to learn, to experience, and to grow our spiritual selves. When the human body dies, the spiritual part of our being continues since our spirits are eternal. As our spirits mature, we learn the value of asking for guidance and being grateful for answers. The members of the Collective God cannot interfere with our free will. When we request assistance, guidance comes in a variety of ways from many sources, people, and spiritual beings, including living friends, as well as passed-over loved ones.

Years ago, I remember feeling frustrated when my stubborn young son refused to ask for help with his schoolwork. While the teachers were willing to help, he had to learn to ask. They could readily alleviate his distress. Similarly, the more confident we are with our spirituality, we realize we are not in this alone. The more we practice humility to invite help and the more we increase our awareness, the more we receive answers that come in a myriad of ways. It could be through the lyrics to a song, an impromptu meeting with a friend, or a series of sequential numbers. The true spiritual power is in the asking, believing, and receiving.

It is remarkable and surprising how Jesus tells us to call on Gaia, the spirit of the Earth. This has been practiced by Earth-based and native cultures throughout the millennia. We know nature is pure, authentic, and good, yet has her own harsh side as part of the circle of life. At their inception, nature-focused practices such as witchcraft,

Wicca, and paganism were pure in their initial intent. Some of these ancient beliefs have been distorted in practice with shifts in perception over many thousands of years. Nature-based practices honor and respect nature. Native cultures ask Mother Nature in their own way for sun, rain, bountiful harvest, good hunting, and healing. Their practices are interconnected in ways that can show us how to survive.

Connecting with nature has never been attributed to Jesus' teachings in the past, yet it makes sense. His relationship with celestial energy has always been strong. There was a bright star in the heavens at his birth, which was the convergence of several stars shining as one. Then, there was a total solar eclipse the moment Jesus died. It is said that he rose from the tomb and appeared to his disciples three days later. It was interesting that this channeled visit from Jesus was exactly three days after a total solar eclipse crossed North America. Although eclipses happen regularly, the last time one had crossed this part of the country was ninety-nine years ago. I found that to be an amazing "coincidence."

Honoring the sacred entity, the living spirit of Gaia, our Earth, is one of the cornerstones of the Collective's teachings and was memorable in this session with Jesus. Gaia provides us with what we need to heal disease, sustain life, and thrive. If humanity is to be saved, getting to know Gaia, appreciating her gifts, and showing her respect is essential.

Jesus referred to Earth-bound spirits as ghosts. In the work that I do, it is gratifying to connect clients with spirits of loved ones who have lived a good life and have passed into the Light. Other spirits are simply lost because of confusion at the time of their death and seek assistance. I work with the beings of the Collective to help these lost spirits find their way to the Light. In my session work with clients, I often find lost spirits who died as victims and help them safely into the Light. I also look for perpetrators who may be hiding in the shadows around their victims. Jesus was very concerned about what happens to spirits of people who do harm, who have committed murder, or worse, killing in the name of a God. These kinds of actions damage the eternal spirit, and these damaged spirits can cause trouble to the living they are drawn to. In addition to draining the energy of their host, they influence the living with their negative emotions.

It does not surprise me that Jesus is concerned about damage to the lost souls. In Biblical stories, Jesus was always looking for the lost lamb. In the work I do, it feels deeply rewarding to assist lost spirits into the Light for healing. And it feels especially fulfilling to rescue the damaged ones who are stuck in the shadows. It is not up to me to redeem their spirits; that is part of the karmic work the spirit does in their own life review. Although, I have noticed that the spirits of the perpetrators are taken by Jesus or Archangel Michael to different places than where other lost spirits are taken.

There seems to be a code of honesty in the spiritual realm. Spirits do not lie. When asked if they hurt someone, the spirit will say yes if they did, often with remorse. Many Earth-bound spirits do not feel worthy of going into the Light because of the harm they have done to others. They express feelings of guilt and may be concerned what will happen in their life review. When I encourage them to go to a place of healing and forgiveness, where they may have a chance to start over, they eagerly go into the Light with proper guidance from the Collective. Their release helps my client's energy to shift to a lighter, quieter, more positive place.

It is imperative that we clear the Earth and living humans from these damaged souls, or they will continue to wreak havoc on the living. While we encourage positive energy practices, it is equally important to support the lost spirits who are willing to make the transition. Relate this to the parable in the Bible of the prodigal son who was lost, and when he returned, the father celebrated.

It seems many are struggling with increasing health issues today. Our physical body is essential to human life on Earth. It is important we take care of this vessel to sustain health, and in the process, gain experience. Jesus tells us there is a cure for every disease, and the cure is unique to each individual. There are many who have healed themselves from debilitating illnesses with natural remedies and mental shifts. Integrating medicine with holistic practices assists the healing journey. Many use wholesome lifestyle changes, body movements,

Reiki, special magnets, toxic substance elimination, mindfulness practices including hypnosis, and other techniques to heal themselves.

I can understand how often healing professionals put the greater good of others before themselves. Many are driven to help others and unfortunately ignore themselves in the process and hesitate to take time for self-care. Their mission is selfless, and their passion is to serve, first and foremost. As a result, some get bogged down from the negative energy attracted to them from being around others who need help. Much like catching germs from patients, they pick up negative energies that drain their energy. They become fatigued, overloaded, overwhelmed, and retreat in physical or emotional sickness.

Other healing professionals go so far into their discovery journey they tap into painful past life memories where helping others ended tragically. One of my greatest joys is helping to awaken healers to their mission and purpose as they heal the trauma of their past. As they clear their emotional energies and understand their past, they can clearly envision their calling. Humanity needs each sleeping healer to awaken to their mission so we can individually and collectively shift the energy around humanity to save this beautiful planet.

The Collective cannot predict the future because our future is subject to actions humans will take. Unfortunately, we are an unstable society, and at best, an ever-changing civilization. The Collective is obviously concerned for our future or would not be holding these intense conversations with us to raise awareness of the consequences of our actions. There are humans with psychic abilities who can foresee potential outcomes. They offer insight as to what might happen in the future, which is always based on actions people *choose* to take in the present.

Many carry painful memories from this life or past lives that hold us back from growing and cause us to be stuck in negative thoughts. In past lives, many have experienced death for saying or doing good things, so they may be reluctant to speak out based on fear from the memory of persecution. Based on my own past lives, I have suffered from that same fear. To unlearn or shift emotions tied to old memories, we must strive to understand, forgive, and release the pain of the past. Only then can we empower ourselves to make better choices based on experience and maturity.

I love how Jesus spoke about giving positive feedback: "Speak the compliment aloud." This was one of the most memorable messages for me. Some of my parents' generation was of the opinion that a child would get a "big head" if you complimented them. Therefore, many children raised in that time frame grew up lacking self-worth. Subsequent generations were overly praised, which can tend to create self-centeredness. Jesus spoke of the balance and wants us to give appropriate compliments regularly and offer thoughtful critique so it will be accepted constructively.

Give praise when someone does well, offer information with kindness about what can be improved, and encourage positive change. Amplify the good in people to overcome the negative. There is much good in this world. Yet, we most often hear from those who are unhappy about something, while those who are more content are silent. The negative is generally louder and sensationalized by those in the spotlight, including journalists, celebrities, and politicians.

Unfortunately, some people seem to be drawn to horror and cruelty. There have been good news programs in the past, yet they were not very popular. It takes more effort to focus on the positive, though it is worth it. This is why my team launched a "good news" radio show,[10] to shine the light on inspiring people who are all around us and amplify their positive voices.

While writing this chapter, I continuously asked for guidance from Jesus to make sure I was keeping true to his words. I am grateful to hear him guiding my thoughts on a regular basis. Yet, I wondered why some phrases in the conversation sounded different than how many of us hear Jesus in our hearts and minds. Then, in a personal hypnosis regression session with a respected Team Hope member, Jesus spontaneously and surprisingly channeled through to offer me several confirming insights, one being: "Remember, Gary is my

10. *Inspiring Hope with Lois Hermann* is a good news radio show featuring everyday people who are doing inspiring things to help each other and our world.

brother . . . he is not me. Listen in your heart for my words. You will know." Gary often expressed heavy sadness and seemed to feel the weight of humanity's suffering. I realized that while in his expansive spirit form, Jesus is strong, majestic, loving, and protective. However, while lowering his vibrational energy to be in corporeal form, Jesus experienced the vast range of human emotions much more intensely and expressed them fully in our conversation. He was deeply saddened by what had happened to his teachings, and also seemed to feel the collective suffering of humanity, which touched my heart.

I was curious about the memory of my relationship with Jesus at the time he was on Earth, and why they asked me to deliver these messages. In this channeled session, I asked Jesus how he knew me back then and he explained: "You always had flowers in your hair. You danced and sang. You were a happy little girl. I was in a marketplace talking with people who were coming up to ask me questions, and you were with the youth who stood back from the adults to watch. I loved being with the children. They gave me such joy, especially when I was feeling such sadness."

This explains why I continue to think of Jesus with such joy in my heart. His reminder gives me the knowing that I am to hold onto the innocence of youth in this project, without personal agenda or bias. Jesus said it is your faith that will help you, heal you, save you. I *know* this deep in my heart and have seen results so many times. One of his greatest messages is that when you ask for help, it will be given. We must remember to ask, then listen in our hearts for the answer.

Jesus clarified he never intended to create a revolution when he was in corporeal form two thousand years ago. He shared a concern that coming back as human in this day and time might create a situation of worship and dependency, which he does not want, as it could cause more distraction, disturbance, and division. He affirmed that he is ever here for us in spirit to call on and advise us whenever we ask.

While Jesus' messages were kept alive by his followers, they were distorted and changed over time. How extraordinary that he is giving us the messages again in this collection to help people remember his true intentions. My team and I hope you will embrace Jesus' heartfelt teachings in your own way and take what resonates into your heart. Encourage each other and lift each other up. We have faith many will make changes in ways that will cause ripples of hope for a positive, healthy, and happy future for our world. Jesus' parting message to me was: "I know you will share my words with truth. Trust yourself. *I am always in your heart.*" Thank you, Jesus, for your continued guidance, assistance, and love.

"And I say unto to you,
Ask, and it shall be given to you;
Seek, and ye shall find;
Knock, and it shall be opened unto you."

—Jesus

Session 3 ~
You May Call Me Aurora
I Am a Sister Spirit of the Collective

"The path that humanity is currently on, if it makes no changes,
will invariably lead to its own end.
Humanity has a simple choice,
either they learn to live together or face extinction."

—Aurora

Intention

Gary, Paul, and I gathered to do another discovery session. We ruminated over what had transpired in the last session with Jesus and were still in awe of the messages he brought to us. He gave us insight that we applied to the work we do to guide lost spirits into the Light. We feel and appreciate Jesus' guidance every day.

We wondered who we would speak with in this session. Our goal for these messages is to reach a diverse audience, beyond religious beliefs and spiritual practices. Today, we thought about asking one of Jesus' brothers, Muhammad, to come through. At the time, there were issues and situations with religious extremists who were killing in the name of God. Would it be prudent to ask his opinion on what could be done?

We also discussed what questions to ask. Those in the Collective who have come through Gary have spoken of humanity's two probable outcomes. They have not given specifics on what those outcomes might be. We wanted to get more details. We were ready to learn more from these amazing ones.

Session 3 participants were: Lois, the hypnotist guiding the session; Paul, the clearing consultant observing the session and protecting the energy; Gary, the client channeling the High-Level Spirit; and Aurora, a sisterly spirit of the Collective being channeled through Gary.

Conversation

After guiding Gary into a deep trance state, I begin the session.

Lois: As you allow yourself to relax deeply, peacefully, I would like to invite the Anquietas to send whomever they would like for us to connect with on this day and this time. We are curious as to whom you would like to send to teach us lessons for humanity.

Gary: [As he lifts his head from a reclined sleep-like pose, he slightly gasps. His eyes slowly blink as he stretches his mouth open and closed.]

Lois: Hello?

Gary: [At the sound of Lois' voice, Gary turns his focus on her, and stutters softly in a light voice.] Um . . . um . . . forgive me . . . this is . . . my first time . . . in a human body. [His eyes continue to slowly open as he shifts his shoulders in the chair and murmurs something about being uncomfortable. He sits up, leans forward in the chair, clears his throat, folds his hands politely in his lap, looks directly at Lois, and smiles.]

Lois: To whom are we speaking?

Aurora: Friend, Lois. [Smiles at Lois with a slight nod.] Friend, Paul. [Nods to Paul.] We have never met. I have never been on Earth before. You may call me . . . Aurora.[1] [Tilts her head slightly from side to side as if to get comfortable in the body.]

Lois: Aurora?

Aurora: Yes. I . . . am a sister to the spirit that motivates this body. (Aurora is one of the Children's Children.) I understand who you were seeking to speak . . . but I have . . . intruded. [She says with a soft voice and gentle smile.]

---

1. Aurora was the Roman Goddess of the dawn, who announced the coming of the sun by painting the night sky with beautiful colors. Ancient Greek poets used the name Aurora to reference dawn's play of colors across the dark sky.

Lois: Well . . . welcome. [Returning a gentle smile.] I'm sure you are here to bring us amazing insight.

Aurora: There are things that I will share with you. [Looks at Lois and Paul, then pauses to exercise the jaw with another tilt of the head.] Part of why I have come is . . . to give you a perspective from a spirit who hasn't been on Earth. I think you might find that useful. You have specific questions . . . that you would like to ask?

Lois: There are questions we would like to ask based on the messages from your kin. One is, we have been told by some that humanity has two distinct futures if we do not change. We were curious as to whether you would be able to share what those two outcomes are. And another question is: what would you recommend that humanity do to change the future?

Aurora: There are only probabilities for the future . . . it is not cast in stone. The two most likely outcomes . . . [Drops her head with a deep sigh.] It is very dangerous for someone to know too much of their own personal future. It can be even more dangerous for a civilization.

Lois: [Speaks quietly.] I understand.

Aurora: The path that humanity is currently on . . . if it makes no changes . . . will invariably lead to its own end. [Makes intent eye contact with Lois, then Paul.] Civilization will fall first. Civilization is very fragile, especially on Earth. Humanity as a species most likely will survive but . . . it is hard to see the future. [Long pause, searches for words.] *All I can tell you for certain is that the world as you know it is heading for an end.*

Some will survive to start again. The ultimate future of the species depends largely on . . . who the survivors are. The people who cause the most trouble, the people who are leading civilization down the path of destruction . . . are the people who will make the strongest effort to protect themselves. However, they won't necessarily succeed.

Two thousand years ago, my brother (Jesus) said: "The meek shall inherit the Earth." That is *still* the probable future. That is still the most likely outcome for civilization . . . a new civilization . . . based on equality. There is too much inequality in the world today. Gaia provides people with all they need. There is no scarcity . . . yet civilization on this planet seems to be based on the premise that there isn't enough to go around. This leads to greed . . . and it is unnecessary. There is *more than enough* of everything. It is important to get that message across. It seems self-evident and obvious, but there are people who have no food, no clothing, no shelter . . . people whom civilization has simply discarded. [Shakes head sadly.] These people have no voice . . . and so they receive no help . . . and it isn't necessary. There is more than enough for everyone. Everyone should contribute what they are able.

The only other alternate path that civilization can take . . . would be to make changes that support those who are now forgotten. It is necessary to distribute the resources so that everyone is included. [Tilts head slightly.] Sadly . . . the people who need to make those decisions . . . are the people who have decided to send humanity down this path in the first place. We have no recommendation as to what to do other than to speak out. There is no force that we can bring to bear . . . to help. We would not . . . even if we could. It is not our place. We can only advise. That is what my siblings have done for countless millennia.

It is sad that our messages are so often twisted or forgotten or buried. [Looks down sadly.] My brother has not returned to Earth in the last two thousand years for fear of producing another revolution that . . . might be even more harmful. It was never his intention to create friction between groups of people. He preached . . . that people should be as one. [Takes deep breath.] In a sense, you are all one. *You are all children of the Earth. You are all one species.*

We know of many species on many worlds that do not have the internal conflict that seems so pervasive here. Even reviewing the history, we have trouble determining from whence this comes . . . It is not unique, but it is a very peculiar trait of humans. They thrive on conflict. For a new species, that is necessary. It strengthens the species. It weeds out those who are too weak to survive. But beyond a certain point . . . [Sighs heavily as she shakes her head.] Beyond a certain point, it becomes excessive and leads to what you would call the class disparities that seem to exist now. We would hope that simply reminding people that you are *all one people* would be enough. We doubt this will help, but it is the only recommendation that we know how to make.

In Book 1, the Anquietas told us much about the evolution of our planet, of civilization, and the many other worlds that exist with life that are more evolved and more peaceful than Earth's humanity.

We have sent many messengers; many of my siblings have been on Earth before. They have all said the same thing . . . *and the message has been lost every time.* [Looks down.] One of my siblings has recently returned to us. There are now only two spirits like us (the Children's Children) on Earth. In a very short time, another will return to spirit. The spirit that motivates this body (Gary) will be the last of our kind to remain. [Sighs deeply.]

In the early sessions captured in Book 1, the Anquietas told us that Gary was one of three Children's Children who were in physical form on Earth at that time. Gary's spiritual sibling, Aurora, tells us that one of those three has since died and another is about to leave their physical existence on Earth as well.

So, humanity has a choice . . . and it's a very simple choice. *Either they learn to live together or face extinction.* [Long pause.] Gaia loves all the children she creates, but sometimes one species . . . one species must be lost to allow another to develop. [Pauses with a sigh.] This has happened five times in Earth's past. Several of the events were beyond Gaia's control, but some of them were her own doing. She still weeps for the species that are lost. She weeps for every life that is lost, but . . . sometimes it comes down to the greatest good for the greatest number. *Earth is at that tipping point right now.* [Clears throat.] It is several hundred years sooner than we had predicted.

We have discouraged new spirits from being born as humans . . . in an effort to allow the older spirits more of a chance to bring the Earth back into balance. We do not stop it. We cannot stop it. A spirit will be born where it wants to be born. We try to make suggestions to send the new spirits elsewhere.

Lois: I understand.

Aurora: You specifically mentioned that you wanted to talk to the spirit who was Muhammad. He is in visible (corporeal) form on another world right now. It is interesting that he's with a species not dissimilar from your own, perhaps . . . twenty thousand years your junior . . . on a world, in a galaxy for which you have no name. [Smiles knowingly.] However, there are other prophets, other spirits who are around you in spirit form . . . but all they can do is repeat the same message if you ask them to come. And it is the same message that my brother (Jesus) gave you a short time ago.

It is difficult for humans to have their faith shaken. Most of the information that you have been given . . . from my kin . . . is potentially very destabilizing. [Looks directly at Lois.] The message is important, and you do have to get it out there, and *you have to get it out there quickly.* Humanity doesn't realize how little time it has left . . . and no, I can't tell you exactly when. [Shakes head.] I wouldn't if I could. [Smiles sadly.]

The message has to be delivered in a way that people are going to be willing to accept. For two thousand years, most of humanity has believed in the *one true God* . . . Perhaps it would be best not to try to dispel them of this idea. The concept of one true God was created by men in order to motivate people to behave in a way that they believed was . . . the word they would probably use is *righteous,* but *right* is sufficient. They believed that without the promise of reward or the threat of punishment that the strong, the physically strong, would simply dominate everyone.

If you examine civilization today, you'll see that is exactly what has come to pass; only the definition of what *strong* means has changed. It's no longer the biggest and the physically strongest. Those who have managed to gather more than they need is your modern civilization's definition of strong. But, considering that most of the resources of the world are controlled now by only a very small handful of people, that is *not* a stable civilization.

Gaia . . . doesn't like the way that people treat each other . . . but likes even less the way they treat her. You know this. [Looks at Paul.]

Paul: [Speaks quietly.] Yes.

Paul has been told his energy coalesced from Gaia's energy, therefore he is truly a child of the Earth and feels greatly for Gaia. Others, like Gary and myself, come from the energy of the Universe.

Aurora: Her reactions to civilization will become much worse in a *very short* period of time. Sadly, she . . . she cannot target the people whom she realizes are responsible. She can only paint with a very broad brush . . . and she weeps for the innocent who suffer because of her actions. But she takes the only actions that she can. She . . . is with us in our desire to find a less violent way to evoke the change that is *so* necessary.

It is very unusual for us to speak directly to a physical species . . . partly because it is so difficult . . . mostly because our efforts backfire. [Long pause to reflect.] We almost wish there *was* an omnipotence in the Universe incapable of error, but there is none such. [Shakes head.] We . . . make mistakes. We have before. We will again. The reason that we talk to you . . . is because *you are human*. You will recognize flaws that we cannot see.

When my brother spoke two thousand years ago, the words were simple enough . . . but somehow, they were not accepted. We hope that coming from . . . [Long pause to consider.] . . . native humans, the words might be better accepted. Not that people understand from whence the message comes. The knowledge of what Jesus truly is . . . is in your hands right now. That he was more than simply human is understood. But he wasn't the son of God . . . I suppose you could say he was the son of Gods. But . . . *we have no desire to be worshiped.* We would be happy to have humans simply take our advice. [Long, heavy, reflecting pause.]

Have you another question?

Lois: Yes, the reason we thought to invoke Muhammad is because there are those who cause harm in the name of God . . . some, not all, are Muhammad's followers. How can we touch their hearts to help them change?

That's one question. The other one is more personal. I'd like to know more about you. Can you tell us about yourself?

Aurora: [Takes deep breath.] To answer your first question . . . it is probably best not to specifically target any particular religious group or belief. Humans do not react well to having their beliefs challenged. Your history is written in blood. All I can suggest is to reiterate those messages in a very generic way. My brother's first message: "Love thy neighbor. Do unto others as you would have others do unto you," is a very simple message. It can be delivered without the draping of religion . . . as it originally was.

Humans have evolved beyond the need to believe in Gods. They have science now. They don't need to think that it thunders because a God is angry. If they want to attribute something beyond themselves to what they see around them . . . they should be more respectful of Gaia. *By any human definition, Gaia is a God . . . a Goddess.* [Shrugs gently.] The Native Americans, the Druids,[2] there are many cultures that

---

2. Druids were members of a professional class in ancient Celtic cultures and best known as religious leaders. They were legal authorities, lorists, and medical practitioners who possessed great respect for and connection to the natural world.

respect nature . . . not worship . . . respect. [Looks intently to both Lois and Paul.]

Humanity is also worthy of respect. It is not a majority of people who are causing the majority of problems. Present the message of peace, of restoring balance . . . pause to reflect before taking an action. It is very simple to give in to a reflex. It takes maturity to stop and consider your response. Any struggle can be stopped by only one side . . . if they simply choose not to fight. It really is as simple as that. If my brother's message: "Turn the other cheek," was one of the basic tenets by which people lived, most of the problems would go away.

People need to be reminded in a *secular way* of the basic messages that all religions have. It is only the religious trappings that cause difficulty. We find it hard to understand how some religions, which on the surface seem *so similar* . . . could *hate each other* so much. And yet, there are religions vastly different . . . that do not possess that level of hatred. As well as we know the history of the world, we do not know where that comes from. We do not know how that hatred became so ingrained in humanity. We understand that love and hate cannot exist independently, any more than dark and light cannot exist independently. But *it is not necessary* to give into hatred so easily. It only takes a simple effort of will.

People need to be reminded that they're better than they think they are. Somehow that message has been lost. There are ancient civilizations on Earth . . . that were not only peaceful within . . . but were able to interact with others and still remain peaceful. Humanity is probably unique in having evolved to the point of having civilization . . . but then . . . devolved back into conflict. We have never seen that on another world. [Shakes head sadly.] We have seen conflict in younger species, but once they grow out of it, they leave it behind. Humanity has not only carried it with them . . . they wear it like a badge of honor. It's very self-destructive . . . and . . . that destruction is coming. *Humanity will destroy itself* if it does not learn to live with itself. Those are the only two outcomes. [Shakes head strongly.]

I chose the name Aurora because it was simply on the top of Gary's mind when I came in. [Looks at Lois with a smile.] We have no names that we could speak among ourselves. We do not even communicate in a way that you would understand because we have no bodies. As much as we are all one, we are also individuals. We are individual in a very different sense than a physical being (human) would understand, but we each have our predilections and avocations. Mine . . . I watch out for my siblings. Some of them can be very passionate about their particular avocations, and . . . with great passion can come great stubbornness. There are times when they do not know when to let go of their passion, and . . . they can hurt their own spirits. [Long pause.]

You are aware that a human has four parts. A physical part, which is the receptacle in which the etheric parts reside. Humans have a mental part, which is the intellect. They have an emotional part and a spiritual part. When a human is conceived, the physical body begins to develop. At some point during that development, the intellectual and the emotional bodies are created . . . not necessarily at the same time, and the time that they are created differs for each individual. At some point before birth, the spiritual body is . . . [Searches for words.] synchronized . . . and joins, and now you have a whole person. Again, all the points at which this happens vary depending upon the individual. The physical body will develop with life, throughout its entire life.

The spiritual body is fully formed and developed when it enters. Even if it is a brand new spirit having never been in a body before, in and of itself, it is complete. It will learn as the human body develops. Most of the changes that happen to a spiritual body occur at the end of the physical life, when the vessel is broken. The spiritual being can review the mental and emotional parts and keep parts they choose. [Brings hands to chest.] That is how all spirits develop. Newer spirits develop more quickly, because they have less to build on. It is like momentum, they have very little when they begin.

The reason that I chose to come here today is in the hope that you can do something that might relieve some of the human struggle. If . . . if there is any hope left for humanity at all, it's in the work that you are doing. My other siblings on Earth . . . one has given up, and one is about to. Gary will be all that's left. None of my siblings will return to Earth . . . until it survives. *These messages will be all you have left.* We . . . we wish you the best. We hope you succeed. [Long, heavy pause.]

I think I need to leave.

Lois: Thank you so much. We will do our best.

Aurora: We know you will.

Lois: Thank you for coming.

Aurora: Thank you for allowing me to come.

She takes a deep breath and departs as Gary slouches back into the chair. Moments later, Gary starts to shake violently with deep, heavy, sobbing cries.

Lois: Are you okay?

Gary: Pain. There is so much pain. [Crying and gasping for breath.]

Lois: Where does it hurt?

Gary: My heart. My heart is in such pain. [Cries out loudly, sobbing heavily.]

Lois: Let me do some Reiki for you. [As Paul holds Gary's hand to comfort him, I place my hands on Gary's head to share Reiki, which starts to ease him. Using soothing words, I help him slowly integrate his spirit fully back into his body. It takes a few minutes for him to become calm. He takes a deep breath, shifts to a more relaxed posture, and opens his eyes.]

Gary: What happened? Why am I watery? [Wiping his tears.]

Paul: You're back. Welcome home.

Afterwards, we debriefed the session and expressed amazement at the information that came from such a sweet, wise, feminine perspective. Gary said the pain he felt in his heart was extremely intense. He wasn't sure if the pain was from returning to the physical body after having been in such a euphoric spiritual state or if he was feeling the intense pain and despair of humanity deep in his heart.

We were intent on getting these messages to others as quickly as we could.

Remarkably, it was dusk as we walked to our cars after this session. Suddenly, we were awestruck by the brilliantly painted sky overhead. We stood in amazement to take in the beauty of our own *Aurora* and thanked her for sharing such a spectacular display of colors: deep purples, bright blues, soft pinks, golden yellows, bright oranges, and dazzling reds. I have never seen our New Hampshire sky look so exquisite before or since. We were grateful for the wonderfully affirming gift with which she blessed us that evening.

Reflection

This was a very different session from the previous two. We met Aurora, a gentle sisterly spirit who looks after her brothers and sisters of the Collective. Gary had told us about a recent trip to Alaska, where he was disappointed at not seeing the aurora borealis.[3] Initially, we felt his spiritual sister chose to be called Aurora because this thought was present in his mind. Upon researching, I discovered that Aurora was the name of the Roman Goddess of the dawn, who painted the night sky with brilliant colors.

One of the Anquietas' Children's Children, Aurora has long helped humanity and her siblings in a spiritual way, though she had never taken physical form before. She seemed uncomfortable in Gary's body, repositioning herself frequently, with a lot of head and neck motions as she shifted in the chair. She spoke softly, sweetly, yet intently, with her hands folded properly in her lap.

In discussions before this session, we thought it might be helpful to speak with the prophet Muhammad to get another perspective on what could be done to stop bloodshed and bring peace to humanity. It was a delightful surprise that Aurora stepped in, telling us Muhammad was helping another civilization grow in a distant galaxy. She thought it might be useful for us to gain perspective from one who had never been in a corporeal body.

Aurora explains that the individuals of the Collective have no names we would understand because they have no bodies; it is humans who give them names. They are one Collective of spiritual beings, yet are individuals with specific dispositions and avocations. For example, Archangels have distinguishing areas of focus and assistance: Michael

---

3. Referred to as northern lights, auroras are natural displays of multicolored lights in the Earth's sky. They are seen in the extreme northern (borealis) or southern (australis) magnetic poles of the Earth.

is a protector, Raphael[4] assists with healing, Jophiel[5] brings illumination, and Gabriel[6] is a messenger.

Many call on individual saints like Mother Mary[7] or Mother Theresa[8] for help or comfort. I call on a variety of Guides to assist with situations and encourage clients to seek the wisdom and direction of the spiritual Guides who resonate with them. We are reminded that calling on any combination of the Collective of these spiritual guides is not a new concept. It has been practiced by numerous cultures throughout millennia.

There are many Gods and Goddesses across diverse belief systems, such as Isis,[9] Shiva,[10] Lakshmi,[11] and White Buffalo Calf Woman.[12] Each has their own personas, passions, and areas of influence.

---

4. Raphael is the Archangel of consecration, dedication, and healing. Raphael is associated with the angel who stirs the water at the healing pool at Bethesda in Jerusalem and is also referred to as Israfel in the Koran.

5. Jophiel is the Archangel of illumination who brings light and truth. There is a belief that the Statue of Liberty was modeled after this Archangel.

6. Gabriel is the Archangel of visitation and resurrection, whose name means "God is my strength." Interpreter, revealer, and communicator, he is believed to be the one who communicated with Muhammad.

7. Mother Mary was the beloved mother of Jesus and is known for her compassion and gentle love. She is exalted in many Abrahamic religions as one who helps mothers and children.

8. Mother Teresa (Mary Teresa Bojaxhiu) was the venerated modern-day Saint Teresa of Calcutta. She was granted a Nobel Peace Prize in 1979 for her tireless charitable work helping the poor, sick, and infirm in India.

9. Isis is an Egyptian Goddess who represents feminine strength and power. She assists with balance in family and career. She is said to help spirits transition into the afterlife and restore spirits of the departed.

10. Shiva (shee-vuh) is the Supreme God in the Hindu religion. He is one of the Hindu Trinity, along with Brahma and Vishnu. Shiva is the Supreme Destroyer of evil, and the God of arts, meditation, and yoga.

11. Lakshmi is the Goddess of abundance, good fortune, and beauty among both Hindu and Buddhist followers. As the mother Goddess and wife to Vishnu, she transforms money worries into prosperity and financial flow.

12. White Buffalo Calf Woman is a sacred Lakota prophetess who brought rites to honor the Earth with a sacred pipe that connects prayers from Earth to heaven. She helps with peace in relationships and our world.

The Children's Children also have their areas of assistance: Jesus is a healer and teacher, Buddha brings inner awareness, Quan Yin[13] inspires compassion, Lao Tzu[14] teaches the way of life, Ganesh[15] removes obstacles, and Aurora watches over her siblings while they are in corporeal form. She frequently reminds her family of their chosen mission when they get sidetracked by human emotions.

Several months before this hypnosis session with Aurora, the Anquietas told us about three Children's Children who were on Earth to help humanity. Aurora disclosed to us that one of those has since died, and now there are only two of them left on Earth. She expects another will leave soon, and Gary's spirit will be the last of his kind (Children's Children) to remain in physical form. Further confirming the urgency, Aurora discloses that her kin will not return to corporeal form until humanity makes its choice. The time is now. Civilization must learn to live together without conflict.

Of the spirits we have met, Aurora is the most adamant of the Collective about the world's potential demise. Specifically, she told us if we do not change our ways of hatred, conflict, and greed, humanity is headed for extinction. Although she cannot tell us when this probable extinction will happen, Aurora expressed concern that the original timeline is gone. What the Collective calls "the tipping point" is coming much faster than predicted. It was alarming to hear her say that the world as we know it is heading for an end, and that we don't realize how little time is left. Aurora and the Collective urgently implore us to get these messages to humanity before that tipping point is reached.

According to Aurora, civilization is very fragile on Earth and will

---

13. Quan Yin (Guanyin) is the beloved Buddhist Goddess of compassion and mercy. Guanyin hears all prayers and assists those who ask for her help. She represents forgiveness, compassion, peace, gentleness, and love.

14. Lao Tzu (Laozi) was the ancient Chinese sage who created the *Tao Te Ching*, translated as The Book of the Way and of Virtue. Believed to date to the late fourth century BC, this text is the basis for Taoism, Confucianism, and more.

15. Ganesh (gah-nes) is the elephant-headed Hindu God of new beginnings, the remover of obstacles, and the God of wisdom and intelligence.

fall first. Humanity as a species will most likely survive; some will endure to start again. Yet, the future depends largely on who the survivors are. It would seem that in the event of an apocalypse, those with power would survive. Aurora says that will not happen. She reminds us what Jesus said about the meek inheriting the Earth. In the event of an apocalypse, some humans will live on and create a new civilization based on peace and respect for one another.

Aurora emphasizes that challenge is necessary for a species to become stronger and eliminate those who cannot withstand hardship. Yet I wonder about the extensive level of conflict at this stage of our civilization. Species are supposed to mature, and as they confront challenge, they are intended to overcome disagreement, be more accepting, and together, form a healthy civilization. This has not been our course.

Humanity has regressed into immature patterns of hatred, conflict, and greed that are damaging to individuals and our civilization. Are these immature patterns really a direct result of our primitive conditioning? Is there a lack of knowing what to do because there are few positive role models, elders, or teachers who can provide guidance to help us work through these challenges?

Ancient civilizations on Earth were able to interact with each other from a place of respect. Humanity evolved to the point of civilization, then devolved back into contention and aggression. Aurora tells us conflict is normal in younger species, who then outgrow it and leave it behind. Unfortunately, humanity has continued to live in conflict, often wearing it like a badge of honor. This self-destructive behavior will be our civilization's undoing. Aurora advises that humanity will be destroyed if we do not learn to live together in harmony.

For thousands of years, many have believed in one God. Aurora reiterates what Rae and Jesus said: the concept of one God was created to get people to behave better toward one another. Without the promise of reward or threat of punishment, the physically strong would dominate. Our civilization still experiences this today, except the strong are those who have more than they need. Many of our resources are controlled by very few people. Aurora says we do not have a stable civilization. Some inherit wealth; many are driven to achieve; others have no incentive to participate or contribute; and some simply have no hope. There is great imbalance.

Aurora tells us there is a small number of people who cause most of Earth's problems. When people come from a place of greed or fear, they lose respect for others and seek to forcibly exert control. They speak, write, or act based on negative emotions such as anger, hate, and blame, which causes a cycle of retaliation. This lowers vibrational energy for everyone involved. She encourages us to present this message of peace to restore balance. We must learn how to pause and reflect before taking an action and giving in to a primitive reflex.

Most humans react instinctively from a place of self-preservation. To stop conflict, Aurora says it should only take a simple effort of will. However, it does not feel simple at all. Humans tend to ruminate over wrongs others have done to them, allowing destructive thoughts to control their minds and actions. Unfortunately, many have difficulty releasing those negative thoughts without reactions that incite anger or retribution. Others retreat from tension with self-destructive thoughts, habits, and behaviors.

Negative mindset causes so much stress, anxiety, depression, and sickness in humans today. This also lowers vibrational levels. How can we create conscious awareness to shift internal distress, change external reactions, and respond from a place of peace, honesty, integrity, and respect? More than a simple act of will, it takes pause, reflection, conscious awareness, self-control, and choosing our actions more mindfully. By thinking, acting, and responding more positively, we are able to forgive, accept, and move on.

Aurora teaches it takes maturity to stop and consider your response to any struggle. We must simply choose not to fight. Most of our problems would go away if we learned to live by Jesus' simple message: "Turn the other cheek."[16] I truly wish it were that simple. When people push our emotional buttons, we seem to be hardwired

---

16. "Turn the other cheek" is a passage from Jesus' Sermon on the Mount that refers to responding to injury without revenge. This passage has many interpretations.

to react with responses that are less than honorable. We must *stop* to reflect, *ask* for assistance, and *remember* to come from a place of honesty, integrity, and respect.

There is even division over the meaning of the passage "Turn the other cheek." Some victims allow their offender to continue to mistreat them, believing that being submissive as Jesus was to his persecutors will make a difference. Having been involved in abusive relationships, I did just that. I thought my passivity would help the situation; I was wrong. My current interpretation of this passage is to turn the other cheek and *walk away* from toxic people, places, and situations.

You must protect your energy without aggression or retaliation. Do not allow others to drain your energy, which leaves you in a weakened, confused, and hopeless state. Ask the Collective for the strength to walk away. Request that they help the troubled ones so you can redirect your focus to heal yourself. To recover from any challenging person or situation, seek help to regain your power and increase your energy on all levels: physical, mental, emotional, and spiritual. Surround yourself with positive people, places, experiences, and uplifting energy to create a life of inner and outer peace.

From a global perspective, leaders can apply the principle of turning the other cheek in many ways: stop posturing or fighting, agree to disagree, set clear boundaries, remove support, avoid meddling, show respect, embrace ethics and morality, and focus on the good. If we incorporate these values in our policies, national and international relationships would change dramatically. People need to remember they're better than they think they are.

Aurora explains the description of the four human parts. The physical body is where the three etheric ones reside: the mental-intellectual, the emotional, and the spiritual. The physical body begins to develop at conception. During gestation, the intellectual and emotional parts are created. The spirit synchronizes with the other parts before birth to create the whole person. The point when they join varies based on the individual.

Although the physical body develops throughout its life, the spiritual body is fully developed when it enters the fetus. Brand-new spirits who have never been in physical form before are complete when they enter the body and learn as the body develops. Most spiritual changes occur at the end of life when the physical body dies. As the spirit reviews its life, it keeps the mental and emotional parts it chooses. This is how the spiritual body develops and grows.

Newer spirits develop awareness quickly because they have fewer experiences and less momentum to build on. This is also why old souls or spirits have greater awareness. They have more experiences to draw on from the many lives they've lived. Upon death, they review their actions, learn from them, and usually return to assist or teach. It was noteworthy that the Collective is discouraging new spirits from being born right now to allow older spirits to bring Earth back into balance. While they encourage new spirits to go elsewhere, spirits will be born where they choose.

After death, human spirits who have gone into the healing Light are able to see the actions they took in life more clearly from this high-level perspective. However, while in physical form, we typically forget who our spirit truly is, lose sight of truth, and can get caught in low-level human emotions. We often react to situations from instinctual fears, without reflection, forethought, or concern for consequences.

The Collective is relying on us to come from this human perspective to help people learn to be more positive. We must develop ways to regularly shift our energy to be more positive: to first pause, then respond, rather than react, to situations. When we come from a place of inner peace and self-awareness, we bring positive influence to every situation.

While in hypnotic trance, many of my clients can recall being a fetus in their mother's womb. There, they experience sensory feelings and emotions. They also respond to external stimuli, such as a tender voice, a loving touch, or angry words. In my past ultrasound career, I observed many fetuses react to their surroundings. For instance, moving their hands over their ears when the ultrasound transducer lingered too long over their head.

In hypnosis, while remembering being a fetus, clients often experience emotions such as joy and excitement, or sadness, fear, and worry. While some of these feelings may be their own, at times they are truly sensing their mother's emotions. Assuming the feeling as their own, they carry this unexplained emotion throughout life. Additionally, many carry guilt for believing they caused their mother distress. This emotional carry-over can influence clients throughout their lifetime. When clients come to understand the origin of the emotion, the old feelings can be released and replaced with a sense of peace and empowerment. Recognizing that emotions can be passed generationally, this carry-over may explain what causes the instinctive negative responses that many humans demonstrate. There are hypnotic techniques to heal soul wounds that can be very effective across generations. This may be one of the answers to heal the persistent anger and hate in our world.

Our actions and reactions are perplexing to those of the Collective, and Aurora is no different. They observe all of creation from their high-level spiritual perspective and are confused by the more singular viewpoint of individuals. Their expansive awareness identifies less with the emotional impact that comes from being in mortal form. For instance, since they do not experience extreme negative emotions in the spiritual world, they do not understand why humans have so much hate. The Collective believes it should be simple to release those negative feelings. However, when humans are stuck in those low-level emotions, their vibratory rate is lowered, and it does not feel that simple. It takes determination and dedication to shift the heavier emotions to be more hopeful, more positive, and uplifted.

The Collective is also relying on humans to recognize emotionally charged issues and situations they cannot fully comprehend. They want humanity to succeed, yet their hands are tied. These Wise Ones are often constrained, ignored, and even dismissed by humans who lack awareness in anything other than themselves. As part of our evolution, we must make our own decisions, which includes trusting our wise mind to call on Guides and Wise Ones to assist us in a partnership of purpose. We are never alone on this planet—we all have Guides, angels, and loved ones in the spiritual realm who are ever willing to help. When we learn to trust our inner guidance system—our intuition—we will truly sense and feel responses to our prayers. Over time, with practice, we come to fully communicate with these Wise Beings in a very real way.

As we evolve to higher levels of consciousness, we come to live as one, with acceptance, respect, and care. We truly know that we are all children of the Earth, we are all one species, one people. Throughout the ages, prophets and teachers have delivered messages of hope. Aurora reminds us that many of these messengers came to Earth to communicate similar messages. Yet most of their teachings have been lost.

The messages we have received from the Collective are foundational to many belief systems. Aurora recommends using a more secular approach to communicate with people. They do not understand why people who practice similar religions have so much hate. How has hatred become so ingrained in humanity, and why is it necessary to feed into conflict? Since conflict comes from enforced beliefs, it is our intention to present the information without targeting, blaming, or challenging any belief system. Aurora reminds us of Jesus' simple message: "Love thy neighbor. Do unto others as you would have others do unto you." It was originally delivered with positive intent in a secular way. While challenging traditional thoughts, much of the information we have received in these sessions has the potential to be destabilizing. Our intention is to invite acceptance with a fresh perspective and renewed awareness.

Coming from their vantage point of peace, unity consciousness, and true acceptance of each other, the Collective is wary of making mistakes by forcing actions that could cause unforeseen consequences for humanity. The Wise Ones never interfere with our free will, yet provide guidance when asked. When we pray for assistance, we open our hearts to guidance. With the recent wave of anti-religiosity, many have moved away from the concept of prayer, of communicating with God or higher levels of consciousness. Some have been raised devoid of awareness for anything greater than themselves. Once we gain the realization that there *are* infinitely wise spiritual beings wanting to assist and learn to trust our intuitive guidance systems, we'll feel more comfortable asking the Wise Ones for their assistance. When we *ask* from our hearts and *believe* in our minds, we will *receive* answers in a myriad of unexpected ways.

In Book 1 and now Book 2 in this series, the belief in one omnipotent God has been challenged by those of the Collective. Aurora suggests humans have evolved beyond the need to believe in a controlling God. We now have science to explain natural occurring events. "If we want to attribute something beyond ourselves to what we see around us, we should be more respectful of Gaia." Doesn't this make perfect sense? Mother Earth gives us food, water, shelter, and so much life. Native Americans, Druids, and other Earth-based cultures understand this and have long shown respect for nature. They honor the Earth and all life that thrives on her in a symbiotic relationship. If we destroy the trees, we will have no oxygen to breathe, animals will have no shelter, and soil will erode. The now barren Easter Island[17] is an example of the disastrous results from excessive tree harvesting.

I was especially moved by Aurora's discussion about Gaia. In session 1, Rae tells us, "Gaia is a good mother." Then, Jesus goes on to tell us how Gaia cares for all of us, and we are all her children. Aurora provides greater detail, telling us that Gaia loves all the children she creates, but sometimes one species must be lost to allow another to develop. Gaia doesn't like the way people treat each other, but likes even less the way they treat her. She appreciates that there are many who do good things to help. However, some only care about themselves, without regard for her, others, plants, or animals.

Wasteful behavior has long been at epidemic levels in our society. Food waste occurs in all steps of the supply chain from production to consumption. Some food is thrown away because it is misshapen, instead of giving it to those who are hungry. With the COVID-19[18] situation, farmers are destroying products instead of finding ways to deliver them to others who would benefit. Although recycling exists,

---

17. Easter Island is an island in the southeastern Pacific Ocean famous for nearly a thousand enormous statues called *Moai*. It was settled around 1200 AD by Polynesian travelers, who created a thriving culture.

18. COVID-19 was the pandemic of coronavirus disease beginning in 2019 that swept the world in 2020.

a large percentage of plastic bottles, bags, and wrapping end up in landfills and our water. Businesses worldwide produce large amounts of paper waste. These products consume many valuable resources and represent just a few examples of overconsumption. We must be more respectful of what we have been given and find ways to be more resourceful.

Since many have stopped caring about the Earth, Gaia is reacting. She cannot specifically target those who are responsible; she paints with a broad brush. Unfortunately, Gaia cannot protect the innocent. We experience her anguish in the form of hurricanes, tornadoes, floods, wildfires, and drought. The result is increased animal, plant, and human disease. Gaia cares for her children and is sad for those who suffer or will be lost because of her actions. She mourns for every life and every species that is lost. Gaia recognizes sometimes choices are based on the greatest good for the greatest number. Is humanity about to be one of her lost species very soon?

In Book 1, the Anquietas gave us details about the five mass extinctions.[19] Aurora also emphasizes this. She mentions several of those events were beyond Gaia's control, but some of them were by choice. Aurora feels Gaia and the Collective are hoping to find less violent ways to inspire humans to make necessary changes. Is the coronavirus pandemic one of those less violent yet strongly impactful wake-up calls for humanity?

What can we do to be more mindful to help alleviate Gaia's suffering and decrease these natural disasters? Interestingly, many resources are seemly being conserved during social distancing and quarantine due to COVID-19. We are using less fuel with decreased travel by car, boat, and plane. We are learning to conserve food and other household resources that are in shorter supply. We have taken small steps in learning to be more efficient. It is interesting to realize how living simply with a smaller footprint is not only possible, it can be healthier and enjoyable.

---

19. Mass extinction is an event during which the preponderance of life (all life—not just human) dies off. There have been five recorded mass extinction events on Earth.

We are encouraged and grateful that Gaia, our Earth Mother, provides all we need. Those of the Collective have consistently told us there is more than enough for everyone, that greed is unnecessary. The desire for more drives many humans, along with the subsequent pressure, fear, and stress that destroys lives. Inequality in our society today is largely due to the few who control resources, leaving many with nothing, with no voice and no hope. Truly, there are many who work hard to make a living, others do what they can, and some simply expect a handout. That disparity must be minimized. We need to support those who are forgotten, give a hand up to teach people how to survive, and balance the inequality in our society.

We must also increase the care we have for our Earth, and all who live on her, including ourselves. When we treat Gaia with well-deserved respect and are good stewards of this world we are blessed with, we will be rewarded with health and happiness over the long term.

The concept of *worshipping* God has also been questioned. Aurora reiterates the Collective *has no desire to be worshipped.* Instead, they want us to request assistance, listen for answers, and follow their advice. I have found this to be true in my personal life, which has resulted in miracles. While working with clients, I regularly request assistance and am often surprised by the insight that comes through. Usually, it is exactly what the client needs to hear. I allow my superconscious mind, the one connected with Wise Guides, to embrace their guidance. With continuous practice, I have learned to ask, listen, trust, respond, and be grateful.

Although Jesus' words were simple enough at the time he walked our Earth, they have not been fully understood. Even in his lifetime, his communities were hesitant and conflicted over accepting the simplicity of his messages, challenging core beliefs of the time. Aurora hopes the messages might be better accepted coming from what she calls "native humans" this time. Although some may not understand or doubt where the messages come from, she tells us: "The knowledge of what Jesus truly is, is in your hands right now. That he was more than simply human is understood, but he wasn't the son of God. He was the son of Gods."

As one of the Children's Children, Jesus is the son of the Children of the Anquietas, therefore he is considered to be the son of many Gods. The Anquietas told us their Children are known as Gods throughout mythologic and polytheistic history. We invite you to look to this Collective of spiritual beings, who act together as one "Group of Divine" as a source for guidance.

One of Aurora's recommendations is to share these messages far and wide. The Collective is giving us solutions to increase our positive energy through the messages in *Chronicles of Hope*. While Aurora wishes the Collective could help more directly, it is not their place to interfere; they can only advise. They *have* sent Gary to be the channel for their insightful wisdom in this day. She mentions her brother Jesus often in this session and reminds us of the important messages he taught: "We are all one. We are children of the Earth. We are all one species."

If we heed the advice of the Collective and take action to change ourselves, we hope to be able to make a difference. As we release our individual patterns of negativity and conflict, we will raise the spiritual collective consciousness of humanity. While Aurora expresses deep concern for our world, she is hopeful. If we do change to come from a place of acceptance and equality, there is hope for a bright future.

Interestingly, Aurora is also the name of the Disney princess in *Sleeping Beauty*. This story is based on a fourteenth-century folk tale in which Briar Rose was placed under an evil spell and slept for one hundred years. She could only be awakened by true love's kiss. This is a compelling metaphor for where humanity is today. We may only have less than a hundred years before our own spiritual awakening. We hope to turn our world into a place of peace with the kiss of true love for each other and our Mother Earth.

I am so grateful Aurora chose to speak with us. The reason she came was in the hope that we can relieve some of the human struggle. She says: "If there is any hope left for humanity at all, it's in the work that you are doing . . . We wish you the best. We hope you succeed." Aurora's visit left us with hopeful hearts and an enhanced dedication to deliver these messages to humanity. We hope you receive them into your hearts, make changes in your own life, and do what you can to make a difference. Collectively, we *do* have the ability to bring positive change to humanity and our precious planet. One person at a time. Thank you, Aurora.

"When you want to hate, be love.
When you want to judge, be love.
When you want to fight, be love.
When you want to be right, be love."

—Quan Yin

Session 4 ~
One of My Names Is Samael
Bringer of Light

"Do not let the fact that you have technology delude you
into thinking that you are evolved.
I want humanity to survive,
but I want it to survive with strength."
—Archangel Samael

Intention

Gary, Paul, and I were excited to gather for another session. The last session with Aurora was particularly insightful. I had been working to incorporate her teachings in both my personal life and in work with clients. Paul was especially transfixed by her messages. We shared concerns over delivering all of these messages promptly as there are so many people who are looking for direction.

Gary expressed feeling the sadness of many people on Earth who are in distress. We really wanted to understand how best to encourage them to embrace positive thought and hopeful behavior. Many seem to simply go through the motions in their daily spiritual practices, without much thought or intention. Aurora commented that humans do not do well when their core beliefs are challenged. Paul, with his own Christian upbringing, had been quite intrigued by this series of sessions, and was concerned about how these messages would be received by humanity.

I knew we needed to avoid giving into fear and to trust the Wise Ones of the Collective to guide us. We are simply the messengers presenting to humanity this information that was entrusted to us. Our role is to remind people of the teachings and messages that have been presented for thousands of years, with a deep knowing the Collective is always here to help. Reflecting on the task of delivering these messages, we needed to avoid becoming overwhelmed and take this one step at a time. Feeling inadequate to save the world, we thought if we could simply help one individual at a time, the positive shift would spread "one person at a time." This seemed more achievable.

Seeing many clients turn their lives around quickly as a result of the clearing techniques we use, I had the privilege of experiencing how powerful this change-work can be on an individual basis. To reach more people, I was excited to have launched a new energy-clearing training program that was based on many years of experience in this field, coupled with the teachings and urgings of these Wise Ones. Their wisdom brought much insight, encouragement, and clarity to this work.

Paul and I were experiencing more clients with negative energies. We questioned if we were doing everything possible to assist our clients to shift their energies. We sought to gain more insight and were curious who we might ask to come through. I mentioned since Jesus said there is no devil, it might be good to get clarity on that statement.

The night before this session, I watched a documentary on the Nag Hammadi library,[1] a collection of documents that included a description of Lucifer.[2] One of the seven Archangels, he brought knowledge and Light to humanity. Ancient Sumerian[3] hieroglyphics

---

1. Nag Hammadi library (from the second century AD) is a collection of early Christian and Gnostic texts discovered in 1945 that had been buried in a jar near the town of Nag Hammadi, Egypt.

2. Lucifer is the Archangel considered the Bringer of Light, who has mistakenly been associated with the devil based on historic lore.

3. Sumeria (2000 BC) was the first literate civilization of ancient Mesopotamia, which scribed writings on stone tablets and regarded deities as responsible for all matters pertaining to the natural and social order.

also depicted a serpent God bringing knowledge to humans. I wondered if Lucifer had been trying to assist humanity, but instead had been demonized. The Anquietas told us we cannot have light without darkness. Since we had been enlightened about our misperception of God, were we also misinformed about Lucifer? To gain his point of view, we were curious to speak with him.

Paul was nervous about invoking this potentially negative energy. He was concerned about calling Lucifer because of how Gary reacted after the session with Aurora and was worried the energy might be too overwhelming for Gary. While Paul and I encounter negative energies often, Gary had not. We considered him an innocent and wanted to keep him safe. Gary was open to call on Lucifer and was willing to participate for a short time. He had confidence in us to protect him. I had faith in Archangel Michael for protection. Gary commented that technically we would be asking his spiritual father to come through and was assured his father would not harm him. We voted on whether to call on Lucifer and agreed to do so.

We understood that we had been called to do this work and thus trusted our Wise Ones to guide us in this session. Paul and I took a moment to set our intentions and invited the Archangels to be with us. We started with a prayer to clear our energy and asked that we be guided, guarded, and protected in our work this day. Archangel Michael and his Legions of Light were asked to lift any negative influence that may affect us. Paul intuitively sensed the energies lifting around us. As the room was shielded, illuminated, and protected, we were ready to begin this journey.

Session 4 participants were: Lois, the hypnotist guiding the session; Paul, the clearing consultant observing the session and protecting the energy; Gary, the client channeling the High-Level Spirit; and Archangel Samael being channeled through Gary.

Conversation

After our decision to call on Lucifer, we offer prayers of protection, and I guide Gary into a trance state to begin the session.

Lois: It is my understanding that . . . the Angel of Light, the one called Lucifer, has been trying to help humanity. We have questions we would like to ask you. We're here as curious humans wanting to make a difference.

Samael: [Slowly lifts his head. Speaks in a deep, strong, resonating voice.] Well, this is an interesting experience.

Lois: How so?

Samael: Despite what the lore may teach, I have never taken human form before. I do not possess people. [Looks intently at Lois.]

Lois: May we ask to whom we are speaking?

Samael: By what name would you like to call me? [Still looking at Lois with a slight smile.]

Lois: Whatever name you would like to share with us.

Samael: I think Lucifer is the name you're most familiar with.

Although Lucifer is the name he first mentioned, we came to refer to him as the lesser-known Archangel Samael from the Old Testament.

Lois: Welcome. You've never taken human form before?

Samael: [Barely moving his body, he slowly shakes his head no.]

Lois: We are curious. Can you tell us your story?

Samael: I understand what you want. It was foremost in my son's mind when I arrived. You were very brave to seek me out. Usually, there are only two kinds of people who call on me: children playing with fire and souls so badly damaged that they wouldn't understand my response. [Sits motionless for a while, then takes a breath.]

It's a very old story you're asking for. [Long deep breath.] At the dawn of humanity, I took on a role of . . . the God of the underworld. You might know me as Osiris[4] (Egyptian), Nergal[5] (Mesopotamian), or Hades[6] (Greek). I gather from the conversation you had before you summoned me, you want to know how the persona by which I am currently viewed came about. [Pauses, takes a breath.] It wasn't until the birth of Christianity that I was painted in such a negative light. Oddly enough, one of my names is Samael[7] (Hebrew), the bringer of Light. You might think of me as Prometheus[8] (Greek), although I wasn't *actually* Prometheus. [Long pause to reflect.]

The creation of me as a dark force was . . . viewed by the creators of Christianity as a necessary counterpoint to the creation of an all-powerful, all-positive force. And, at the same time as they were trying to convince people of a reward in the afterlife, so they had to convince them of punishment in the afterlife. [Pause.] That sort of control over individuals . . . can be understood. What I have trouble forgiving . . . is the need that the Church had, and still has, to force their belief on others. [Long pause, looks down at his hands.]

---

4. Osiris is the Egyptian God of fertility, agriculture, the afterlife, and the dead, and is the brother to Isis. Osiris was judge of the underworld, and the kings of Egypt were associated with him.

5. Nergal is the Mesopotamian God of war and pestilence and became known as God of the underworld. He represents the destruction brought by the summer solstice and is also called "the king of sunset."

6. Hades is the Greek God of the underworld, who was often portrayed as stern, yet passive rather than evil. His role was to maintain relative balance and held his subjects accountable to his laws.

7. Samael is the Archangel who brings Light, as well as discord and challenge. One of the seven Archangels in the Old Testament, he is considered the angel of death. He is associated with bringing the tree of knowledge to man.

8. Prometheus was a Greek Titan who defied the Gods by stealing fire and giving it to humanity. He is known for intelligence and considered a champion of humankind.

I can feel that I'm burning up this body. My brother Rae had a lot more experience in blending with humans. [Looks knowingly at Lois.]

Lois: We do not wish to harm Gary. Please let us know when we have exhausted the time.

Samael: We have time. [Long pause.] This body has been strengthened by these sessions that you have had. And my son . . . my son is very strong of spirit. [Laughs quietly.] He will hold the body together. What would you have me tell you? [Looks at Lois.]

Lois: In some historical writings, you are described as being the one who brought knowledge to humans.

Samael: The Promethean story.

Lois: Yes.

Samael: Remember that all my kindred . . . even as we are individual . . . so we are also one. Any of us can respond. [Long pause with a heavy sigh.] We are all here to offer information. The information is the same regardless of who of us (in the Collective) it comes from. I did . . . bring much knowledge to humanity . . . and to evolving intelligent life on many worlds. We all do. We . . . are judicious in what we teach. There is knowledge that humanity is not ready for. [Sighs deeply.] Were I in a generous mood, I would say that humanity is still in its infancy. As of the moment I am *not* in such a generous mood; I would say that *humanity is being infantile.*

In all of the races that we have known throughout time and throughout the Universe, evolution is along a single path. [Pause.] It can end in failure. Civilizations can simply die, obliterate themselves, or succumb to some external force. Or they can end in . . . enlightenment. [Sighs.]

The Anasazi . . . one of your previous incarnations. . . evolved beyond the need for a physical form. [Nods at Paul.]

So, too, did the Lemurians.[9] The Atlanteans were destroyed. The Incas[10] were destroyed. [Long pause.] But . . . these cultures represented peaks of evolution on this planet. Somehow, the current state of civilization is considerably less than what those civilizations enjoyed. [Speaks strongly.] Do not let the fact that you have technology *delude you* into thinking that you are evolved.

Yes, I bring knowledge, but . . . I bring *discord* as well. I am one of my kindred who believes that conflict is essential to the survival of any civilization, even as that conflict can bring about the end of the civilization. If it cannot survive the challenge, it does not deserve to live. That is not a popular message, even among my own kindred. My parents would not tell you that. [Long pause with a sigh.] Despite that belief, it disturbs me greatly to be remembered as I am being remembered. At some level, humanity is still my children. [Pause.] It is my desire to see humanity survive, but only if it can be a *strong* civilization. I have no desire to promote survival of the weak, because that is *not survival* . . . that is existence.

Lois: How would you choose to be remembered?

Samael: The Mesopotamians had me described quite well as Nergal. (I noticed he pronounced it *Ne-gral*.) The Norse had me described quite well as Loki.[11] Even the Egyptian Osiris was a reasonable form for me to take. [Pause.] You know that all of my kin are beyond such mortal conceptions as good and evil. I do not desire to be remembered as evil. Even if I

---

9. The Lemurians (le-moo-ree-uhns) were highly spiritual beings who evolved beyond the need for physical form, belonging to the ancient lost civilization of Lemuria. This civilization pre-dated and possibly spawned the Atlantean civilization.

10. The Incans were originally a pastoral tribe in the twelfth century and became the largest pre-Colombian empire in South America. Their empire existed from the fifteenth to the sixteenth century.

11. Loki is the Norse God of mischief, who sometimes assists the Gods and sometimes behaves in a malicious manner toward them. A shapeshifter, he appears in many different guises and is associated with knots, loops, and webs.

were capable of such . . . that was never my intent. [Looks up.] *I want humanity to survive, but I want it to survive with strength.*

Lois: How can we help to make that happen?

Samael: The knowledge that has been passed on to you over these last few months . . . needs to be disseminated across the world. [Takes a breath.] Here is an area where modern technology will help you. [Long pause with a sigh.] When there was less technology on Earth . . . there was less struggle. Civilization has become too technocratic. It has forgotten its roots in nature. It has forgotten . . . it has forgotten that all humans are humans. You are *one* species. The fact that you grew up in a different place . . . the fact that your ancestors came from a different continent does not make you any less related. Every living human . . . every living *creature* on this planet . . . can be traced back to an original common ancestor, primitive as that ancestor may be. [Long pause.] Remember that you are *all* brothers and sisters to each other.

Remember that your spirits . . . the young ones and the old ones . . . are immortal spirits. You need have no fear of death. Taking on the role of God of the underworld in so many ancient civilizations has never been a pleasant task. No one looks forward to meeting what I represent. [Long pause, then looks at Lois, then Paul.] I believe you are the first two humans ever to address me directly.

Lois: We are honored to hear from you and to be advised by you. We encounter what we know as spirits who interfere with humans in a negative way, and have been told historically that they were sent by you. We don't always know what to do with them. Please advise us. Who are they, and how do you recommend we deal with these entities?

Samael: Most of these entities are not *sent* at all. [Speaks strongly.] Certainly not by me. As I said, I have no desire to bring harm. [Softens his voice.] It's difficult to strengthen a herd without

culling the weak individuals. Still . . . we would prefer that
selection to be natural. No, I have never sent . . . entities. Had
I wanted to hurt somebody, I am more than capable of doing
that on my own. Most of the entities that you deal with are
of two categories. The first are simple non-physical beings
. . . creatures of energy of a lower order. They seek merely to
feed. Every living thing must feed. The fact that they have no
body makes them no less living. I gather that they never give
you any trouble when you ask them to go.

Lois: No, they don't.

Samael: The other form you see are spirits that have had physical
incorporation (human beings who have died) but are
damaged souls. [Long pause, takes breath.] They, in some
cases, are simply clinging to a life . . . even if it wasn't their
own. In others . . . they seek to regain the energy they need
to resume incorporating. I take it these are the spirits you
have the most trouble getting rid of . . . because there is
conscious will behind them?

Lois: Yes, that is true.

Samael: [Long pause with a sigh.] The number of humans on
Earth right now with souls so badly damaged that they will
not reincorporate, or some so extremely damaged that they
will dissolve, is considerable. When the body dies, the spirit
lives on, but if the spirit realizes that it has led a life that has
been *so* harmful and hurtful and hateful to others that it can
no longer tolerate its own existence . . . that spirit simply
dissociates . . . evaporates. The energy is not lost. It will be
used to create a new soul . . . but that (the original) soul is
gone. It is sad that the number of people on Earth right now
in that condition has never been higher. [Looks down sadly.]

Lois: What causes the intense hate in these people?

Samael: That is not a uniquely human condition, but it does occur
on this planet a great much . . . with much more regularity
than it does on most others. [Sighs deeply.] It is . . . difficult

for non-physical beings, such as myself, to understand how
that can be brought about. [Pauses.] Having never taken
corporeal form before, that is not a question I can answer
with certainty, I surmise by observation. [Stretches his neck.]

You are aware that humans, the individuals, are of
four parts: physical, which is physical body; and the etheric,
which includes the mental, the emotional, and the spirit
which motivates the body. Be that spirit new, in its first
incarnation, or be it as old as one of my Children, the mental
and emotional etheric parts of an individual are new for each
incorporation. They develop as the physical body develops . . .
as the individual develops . . . independently of the spiritual
body. It is possible that the conditions that an individual
developed under in a particular incarnation . . . will result in
mental or emotional bodies that are damaged . . . poisoned.
[Looks up.] For individuals with well-developed spirits . . . this
presents an almost inescapable conflict between the nature
of their spiritual self and the nature of the individual self.
Many humans that you think of as insane suffer from this very
problem. [Long pause.]

From my observation, I believe that this condition has
never occurred in so many people as it has *right now* on this
planet. The environment under which new individuals . . .
not new souls, new individuals . . . develop is producing this
discord between essential parts of their own individuality.
This results in . . . undirected anger. They do not know why
they hate . . . any convenient target is suitable. There have
been many dictators in the history of Earth who have used
that very principle. They build power for themselves by
channeling the unfocused hatred of people who become their
followers. Normally, the focus of that hatred is undeserving of
it.

Lois: Someone like Hitler?

Samael: Yes, as Hitler did with the Jews. *Remember* that the
citizens of Germany were the first to fall to the power of the
Nazi regime. [Deep breath.] This is why I seek to strengthen

humanity . . . to prevent people from being able to gather a large enough number of people. If the people had more self-determination, and if the individuals did not have this unfocused hatred and anger, it would not be so simple for a dictator to gather them up into an army.

The work that you are doing . . . you seek a way to bring hope back to humanity . . . these are the people who you target. If you can *be the voice that rallies them*, rather than somebody who would use them for ill, you will have accomplished your goal. It is very easy to make that statement. It will not be easy for you to do it. [Long pause.]

Do not fall into the trap that my son Jesus fell into two thousand years ago. Do not become the objects of adoration.

Lois: We don't wish to be. We're actually feeling very inferior for this challenge. [Speaks nervously.] We wonder why we've been asked to do this.

Samael: No! No, far from inferior. [Shakes his head.] There are only a handful of people on the world right now who can do what you are trying to do. There is only one other like Gary on this world right now, and she will not be here much longer. [Long pause.] When Gary passes, and my son's spirit is freed, he will be the last you hear from us (directly) . . . until the world decides one way or another what its fate is going to be. [Long pause.]

There are others who, in their own way, are trying to bring about positive change for the planet. If this work does not succeed . . . it is *not the end of all hope* for Earth, but *it is Earth's best hope right now*. [Pause.] No one else is in possession of the knowledge that *we* have given you. [Pause.] If we did not think that you were perfect for this task, you would *never* have heard from us [shakes his head].

Lois: Thank you for your belief in us. We *are* nervous as to whether we're up for the challenge.

Samael: [Looks kindly at Lois.] Do not be sad. Do not be frightened.

Paul: Thank you for sharing your knowledge with us.

Lois: Is there anything you would encourage us to do? Anything specific that we should be aware? Anything more we should be asking?

Samael: Everything you need to know is already within you.

Lois: [Softly.] Okay.

Samael: We aren't going anywhere. You can always come back to us to ask.

Lois: Thank you. Is our plan of action correct? Would you say our plan to write a book is a good plan?

Samael: It is as good a plan as can be.

Paul: Would you have any suggestions on how to improve it?

Samael: The material we have given you speaks for itself. We would have said that two thousand years ago, too. Humanity is in worse shape now than it was two thousand years ago. You have an upward struggle. However, you will find groups with similar goals who have not had the benefit of communication with us . . . Vet them carefully when they seek to join you.

Lois: How do we know who to trust? How do we vet?

Samael: That is a question I cannot answer. [Shakes his head.] That is something that must remain between humans. We trust you will make the right choices. [Long pause with heavy sigh.]
There have been many who have said, "My way is the only way." Nothing could ever be further from the truth. [Long pause.] Humanity is . . . too complex to believe that there is ever *one* course of action. As I said, there are other groups doing similar work, and of necessity, they are on different paths. We try to make *your* path as smooth and straight as possible.

Lois: Thank you. We will do our best.

Paul: Thank you for telling us your story.

Samael: It will be nice . . . to *not* be so vilified.

Lois: Many people got so much wrong. It speaks to power and politics, and people wanting to control others. We still have that. Is there anything we can do with the political insanity that's going on now?

Samael: When individuals become empowered . . . when the dissociation resolves between spirits that are essentially positive and other parts of their etheric selves that have developed negatively . . . when these people see a clearer path . . . when they believe in their own internal power and do not seek to place it in the hands of another, we hope then most of those issues will resolve themselves. [Sighs deeply.] Many of the people in power today have their power only because it was given to them. Remember, Hitler was elected chancellor before he became dictator. We see that in several individuals on Earth right now.

Lois: Is there anything we can do without interfering with the karma and destiny of those individuals? Is there anything that we could do help shift them, so they are on a more positive path?

Samael: There is nothing that forbids you from that. If you had the power and the will to reach out . . . to clear the people . . . that has nothing to do with either destiny or karma. Paul, because you've had so many incarnations on this world, you are particularly good at removing external negative sources from people. Yes?

Paul: I guess so. [Nods hesitantly.]

Lois: Yes. He is.

Samael: It will be much more difficult for you to remove *internal* negative influences [looks at Lois] . . . partly because it is a literal part of that individual . . . partly because those forces will have been there for so long and become more entrenched. To a large extent, this is something that people must do for themselves. You need . . . you need to teach people a lesson that everyone needs to learn. How to . . . [deep breath with a sigh] . . . it is not possible to completely remove the dissonance between a spirit that is naturally positive from emotional and intellectual bodies that are essentially negative . . . but the effects of that dissonance can be mollified. The problem is that most people, if not all, don't realize *why* they have the anger and the hatred. They don't understand the true nature of their own selves, and therefore cannot see the dissonance between pieces of themselves that they are unaware they even have.

I understand that this work you do is to bring hope to the world . . . which is a laudable goal. [Nods his head.] It *must* contain some instruction. The individuals must *heal themselves* before you can heal the world. If the people do not understand their own natures, let alone the nature of the Universe, then nothing else you present will make any sense to them. Even if they don't dismiss it . . . even if they want to believe . . . even if they want to follow . . . they won't be able. [Long pause.] They need to *understand* their own true natures.

Lois: I understand. Thank you. Can you speak to us of the role Gaia has in this? We have a sense that she's not very happy with her humans either.

Samael: You have *no idea.* [Slowly shakes head in frustration.]

Lois: Is there anything we can do to help her?

Samael: First, do not mistake Gaia's frustration and anger for a lack of love for her children. But . . . children require discipline. Discipline is something else lacking in modern civilization. [Shakes his head again.] And, Gaia is, by right, frustrated right now. I believe that in the very near future you will begin to see a drop-off in population growth. That will be in part Gaia's work. It isn't that she cannot support more people . . . but only if the people become more thoughtful. And it comes down to the same issue . . . if people do not understand their own true nature, you cannot expect them to understand a living planet.

Not all planets have a spirit like Gaia . . . not all planets have a spirit . . . even the ones with life. I believe all planets with intelligent life do have a spirit . . . it is probably a necessary factor. Yes, Gaia requires healing as well. When there are a sufficient number of people who understand, there will be a sufficient number of people to help. Right now, all of the energy that the people who do understand could muster would not be enough to even mollify her, let alone heal her. She hears your words. What she decides to do with them is up to her. [Looks to Paul.]

Paul: As I would expect.

Samael: What else?

Lois: I'm honored that you would come and visit with us. Thank you.

Paul: Likewise, very much so.

Samael: It is the first invitation I have ever accepted on this world.

Lois: We are honored. We will do our best to share the truth.

Paul: I'm sorry for what humanity has done to you.

Samael: I suppose if I were not there to absorb it, they would have simply spread it out among all my kindred. [Heavy sigh.]

Paul: Thank you for being so strong.

Samael: I would say the same to both of you. [Deep breath.] . . . I think it's time.

Lois: Thank you.

Gary: [Exhaling.] . . .

Gently allowing Gary's spirit to reintegrate into his body, fully, slowly, and completely, we allowed a few extra minutes of quiet before Gary took a deep breath and returned to present awareness peacefully. He shifted in his body, stretched his arms, rubbed his hands, and shook them as he awakened. Gary stated that he felt a bit sore, even stiffer than when the Anquietas came through. He only remembered the first and last few seconds of the session, the period of overlap; however, he *definitively* knew who had come through.

Reflection

This was truly an incredible session with intense, palpable energy. We experienced the majestic power of Samael's presence as we conquered our inner fear of conversing with him. We were surprised and honored to have the unique opportunity for an audience with this ancient God of the underworld. His persona was considerably different than the others we had met from the Collective. From his deep, vibrating, baritone voice, to his penetrating gaze as he slowly, deliberately shifted his head, we were captivated. Other than a few subtle motions of his hands, Samael barely moved in Gary's body. He conversed eloquently, while sitting motionless and regal.

Samael exuded massive power, even commenting that he felt like he was burning up Gary's body. Compared with the gentleness of Jesus, the light and inviting presence of Rae, and the kindly energy of Aurora, Samael's commanding strength drew us in. This forty-five-minute session was one of the most profound we had experienced from the Collective. He willingly gave us solid instructions and educational information on what we needed to do to help humanity. Instead of being afraid, I was unusually comfortable in his presence. I felt a real sense of respect for him and was compelled to converse with him. We were grateful for his visit and felt this information would add considerable value to the clearing work we do for clients. It would also help clarify some important questions for humanity.

I am a medical professional and don't consider myself a literary scholar or mythological expert. However, my research on the different names Samael had been called over the millennia revealed his presence consistently represented the shadow side and the underworld of death and rebirth. Also known as the bringer of Light, he represents fertility and growth, strength, knowledge, and enlightenment.

In the Greek mythos, Hades was one of the Olympian Gods, the grandson of Gaia, or Mother Earth, and Uranus, or Father Sky. His brothers were Zeus, who ruled the air, and Poseidon, the sea. Hades was given watch over the underworld, the land of the dead. Being more connected with the Earth than his brothers, I can readily understand Hades' relationship with Gaia, his intense respect for her, and his great concern over the harm humans are inflicting. He seemed equally disappointed that much of humanity has lost their connection with our Mother Earth. I think it is probable that, as one who brings light and fire, he might be involved in some way with the earthquakes, volcanoes, and fires that persist across our beloved planet.

In early biblical texts, Lucifer is associated with the morning star, the planet Venus, and is considered the son of Aurora, Goddess of the dawn, whom we spoke with in an earlier session. There is no biblical reference to this Archangel being the devil. The transposition of Lucifer being associated with the fallen angel came about through lore in later centuries.

There are disturbed people who call on, invoke, or worship shadow figures of darkness. They are worshiping whom they think to be Lucifer, based on the false portrayal of this Archangel through history. Indeed, there are shadow spirits, mean ones who delight in creating chaos. These disturbed spirits relish being revered as powerful, enjoy inflicting pain on humans, and can be called to perform malicious deeds. However, these dark ones have falsely associated themselves with this Archangel, and people have bought into that deception. This is truly a case of mistaken identity.

Once, I had a young client who wanted to speak with Lucifer. Instead, I invited him to converse with Archangel Michael, who is considered Lucifer's brother. Archangel Michael told this young man that Lucifer is not who people think he is, and that he is doing good work in his own way.

In this session, instead of using the name Lucifer, which people often associate with the devil, we chose to refer to him as the lesser-known Hebrew Archangel Samael, a persona that was deeply respected by the Hebrew culture.

This Bringer of Light has brought so much to humans in his various roles over the ages, including the seeds of thought, knowledge, intelligence, and even technology. Sadly, he has been vilified by most modern religions and portrayed as evil, which, as we learned from this session, he is not. In early mythologies and Earth-based cultures, his persona may have been feared, yet he was deeply respected and highly regarded for his valuable position.

Archangel Samael admits his task has always been to strengthen humans through discord or challenge, which is not an easy role to fill. He has introduced temptation to test humans and strengthen their resolve to make the right choices. And he will be present when their spirit experiences their life review. Many people will continue to throw accusatory stones at him even as they read this session. It is said coal doesn't become diamonds if it is run through feathers. We need to recognize that hardship stimulates growth and is an ever-vigilant teacher that introduces the challenges we each face. A seed doesn't grow unless it pushes through the hard exterior shell to the light. How we react or respond to any situation is what makes all the difference in our spiritual growth toward enlightenment.

While developing this session for Book 2, I had been extremely busy helping clients, developing trainings, and teaching classes. I knew that I needed to take some time to reflect on the serious information delivered by Samael. In a clearing session with one of my consultants, quite spontaneously, Samael came through strongly, offering specific clarification on some questions. In parting, he left me with instructions to sleep deeply and take care of myself. The next morning, I awoke with a strange virus that kept me nearly comatose in bed for almost a week. As my body was racked with fever, chills, and pain, I had to completely surrender to allow the healing process to unfold. While my body was shut down, my mind alternated between deep sleep and sorting through memory sequences from all aspects of my life, beginning with early childhood. It was as if my brain was rewiring itself. Through it all, I felt a sense of spiritual peace and serenity. Knowing I was being prepared to delve into the unknown, I came through to the other side with clarity and purpose.

As I laid there immobilized, I asked for assistance with my healing from my beloved Guides, Jesus, and the Archangels. I felt amazing energies surrounding my spiritual, mental, and emotional bodies, and was completely at peace as my being filled with rejuvenation. I could feel the loving energy sent by dear friends from both the

Earth plane and the etheric. It took another week to slowly recover. This precious time allowed me to reflect on Samael's messages, delve into the deeper meaning of what he wanted to convey, and pace myself to make sure the information was articulated and communicated accurately.

In this same time period, my elderly mother, who had suffered from years of back pain, had been placed in a rehabilitation center for a spinal injury. A pessimist by nature, she was being combative with the staff who were trying to help her. As I was bedridden in such pain, I prayed for her and reached out to help her spiritually. This is a woman who traveled the world, never had to work outside of the home, and was blessed with a lovingly supportive family. Yet she was deeply mired in chronic negative emotions of anger, fear, blame, and resentment. She could only express these intensely damaging emotions.

The contrast between our viewpoints was remarkable. In answer to my prayerful meditation, Jesus told me that she must reach out for assistance. I could visualize members of the Collective waiting to lift her suffering, but they would not interfere with her free will. All she needed to do was come from a place of gratitude for what she had received in life, relax into acceptance with her reality, and ask for graceful relief. Days later, I was finally able to talk with her and encouraged her to pray for help. Once she changed her mindset, her misery lifted, and she shifted into a place of gentle peace.

We all know those who look at the world through rose-colored glasses, as well as others who are stuck in such anguish and despair that they can't see their way out of their self-imposed prison. This is what Samael means when he says he brings challenge. Daily, we are faced with choices on how to respond in any given situation. How we respond is based on our mindset and will determine our ultimate outcome.

Contrast this with a woman whom I call my spiritual mother, a dear mentor and friend named Agnes. A Holocaust survivor, she was a single mother of seven with very low income and was challenged with many health issues. Yet Agnes always shared a cheerful smile, a welcoming heart, and a loving message of kindness. Years ago, as a single mother of two with a solid career, when I found myself mired in my own self-pity, I would look to Agnes to lift my spirit. Even though she has now passed, to this day she is ever with me in my heart, where she planted seeds of glowing inspiration.

I now wonder if that strange virus I had in February 2020 may have been COVID-19. Considering I would be in the high-risk medical category, I recognize that my sickness took place prior to the public awareness of this disease. Since I did not have the extreme fear associated with this sickness, I simply prayed, embraced healing, and got well. Instead of fighting in anguish, I embraced it as another of the many challenges life has presented to me for growth, understanding, and clarity.

If we come from the low-level negative energies of anger, fear, blame, and resentment, we spiral into the abyss of darkness until we knowingly reach for help. When we ask for assistance, we are given opportunities to shift our perspective and are able to look at situations from a higher vantage point. With fresh eyes, we can review what we are learning, like examining the corrected answers after a test, and can finally choose to integrate the lesson into our spiritual selves. When we stay stuck in the muck of negative emotions, we are not learning, we are not growing, we are moving backward. Instead, let us use positive thought to raise our vibrational energy and grow on the path toward enlightenment.

Encouraging people to do more inner reflecting, review their actions, and integrate what they are learning allows their spirit to grow. Samael says humans are acting infantile. Many act like spoiled children full of spite, throwing temper tantrums when they don't get their way. We should strive for a high-level, intellectual place of wisdom balanced with honesty and integrity. The current state of our civilization is considerably less evolved than many prior civilizations. This is evidenced in much of our religions, government, media, business, and entertainment arenas.

Samuel tells us: "Do not let the fact that you have technology delude you into thinking that you are evolved." Humanity has become so dependent on technology that we have forgotten what is most important. Technology is linear with processes, tasks, and impersonal structure. It is a valuable tool, yet it has come to define and control our way of living, our way of being. All life, including humanity, is truly circular by nature, co-existing in a world that is rich with rhythm and flow. Day follows night and spring follows winter.

We need to remember our roots in nature and discover ways to tap into the natural flow of the cycles of our days, our seasons, and our lives. As we find ways to escape from our rigid technocratic schedules, we allow our spirits to experience the seen and unseen world that stimulates growth. We must connect with others in an open, interpersonal way to see another's perspective, and come from a place of curiosity without the immature need to force opinions on another. It is vitally important to find the balance between connecting with technology and communing with nature and other human beings.

At the time of this writing, we are immersed in the coronavirus pandemic with a worldwide practice of social distancing. The use of technology has been valuable to keep people connected in work and play. People are learning new skills, using video to communicate, playing online games together, staying connected, and keeping each other uplifted. Without technology, life would be lonely for many. By the same measure, instead of going to restaurants, people are spending time outside, playing in yards, walking on paths, singing in the streets, and sharing music from balconies and windows. In our separateness, there is a sense of oneness, of coming together as people, as one human collective.

As much as Archangel Samael was a huge powerful energy, my heart went out to him. I could sense his deep sadness over being vilified and labeled as evil. He brings discord, which is similar to the concept of tough love. As a fatherly figure, Samael feels for his children and wants us to succeed, with strength. It is not that he enjoys the type of tension that incites war, nor is he inferring we must remove the infirm.

The struggle that is essential for personal growth is based on internal conflict that must be mastered. If children are given everything without challenge, they don't tend to grow into responsible adults. Those who are given much without having to earn it have a tendency to be dependent and never learn to support themselves. Give a person a fish and they will eat for a day; teach them to fish and they will eat for a lifetime. As we learn to rise above our internal and external struggles, we evolve into a place of strength, peace, and empowerment.

The concept of rising above challenge is true for civilizations as well. As we collectively elevate our consciousness, we avoid contention. Knowing that conflict stimulates growth should cause us to rise above conflict, seek a higher perspective, and understand another's point of view. We learn to respond with loving hearts, rather than react from anger or disagreement. When we remember we are all one species as humans, we realize no one is better than the other. We are unique individuals with varietal differences. Just as each flower is different, all are flowers with an array of sizes, shapes, colors, fragrances, and vibrations. When we learn to celebrate the wonder of our differences, we will embrace our similarities as true brothers and sisters of one tribe called humanity.

Whether old or new, our spirits are immortal, and we need not fear death. We live on to learn and grow again. We were a bit surprised and honored to have Archangel Samael tell Paul and I that we were the first humans he ever addressed directly. Maybe we were less fearful because of the many years spent dealing with the unseen shadow side. Our purposes are similar: we help lost spirits into the Light. I've often encountered the type of damaged spirits that Samael describes as they attach themselves to and interfere with my clients' lives. I have held conversations with spirits who claim to be the devil. However, when confronted with the light of love and compassion, they acquiesce into a place of acceptance and submission, and are often ashamed of their actions.

Particularly onerous spirits readily surrender when we call on Archangel Michael. He transports these lost ones to a place that is somewhat different than the Light, assuring us he is taking them where they need to go. I now understand that Archangel Michael might be taking these dark spirits to the realm of Archangel Samael, where they are held accountable as they perform their own life review. During one client session, Paul felt like punching a nasty spirit for their unbelievably cruel treatment to a child. Archangel Michael intervened, explaining it is not for us to judge. We are reminded that even the dark ones are spiritual beings who should be treated with compassion and without personal judgment or bias. They will judge themselves in the light of truth. We must refrain from retaliation or hate of any kind.

We are ever learning in this journey of life. I had believed that some of these extremely negative energies were commanded or sent by Samael to interfere with humans. Samael assured us that he never sends entities to bring harm to humans; he has no need to do this, since he intends only growth. He reminds us some of these energies we encounter are the low-level entities of which the Anquietas spoke, who are only searching for vibrational energy as food. These are easily dispelled. Some we encounter from other dimensions willingly allow Archangel Michael to return them from where they came.

The more stubborn are actually spirits of humans who believe they are demons because of the life they have lived. These damaged spirits cling to mortal humans to draw energy to sustain themselves. They are more resistant to leaving, because they have their own beliefs that were formed at the time of their mortal existence. Some of these lost spirits who claim to be demons state they were sent by Lucifer. If these spirits believed they were evil in life and were doomed to hell at the time of their death, that belief remains, even centuries after their physical death.

Some disturbed people invoke dark spirits through spells, curses, and incantations, directing misguided spirits who respond to these requests. Situations like these are very real, though are caused by damaged spirits of the living and the dead. The nasty spirits are sent by vengeful humans, not by Archangels, to attach to the human target of the spell. These dark spirits have no real energy of their own, so in effect they drain the living host of their life-force energy. When encountering such dark entities, I strive to convince them to go with the Archangels into the Light, where, with forgiveness, they have an opportunity to start again. Perhaps they are given another chance at life. It is their choice. My intention is to help each spirit find their place while freeing my client of the spirit's draining energy. As the spirits release their hold, my clients feel tremendously lighter and are freed of the heavy burden of negative energy that interfered with their thoughts, actions, and lives.

I have communicated with and released thousands of Earth-bound spirits over the years and knew there were many more in need of help. Yet I did not comprehend the gravity of the situation. Before this conversation with Samael, I had not realized that many of the damaged spirits will never recover. My intention was to send them into the Light. He explained the number of extremely damaged spirits on Earth right now has never been higher, and that many of them will not reincorporate. When spirits do their life review, if they were full of hate and misery, they may choose to destroy their eternal spirit. Once that spirit is gone, it evaporates, and that energy is used to create a new spirit. The insight that there are so many damaged spirits on Earth right now explains the origin of the large numbers of new spirits. Archangel Samael helps transform the residual negative energy from the damaged spirits into positive energy for new life, new growth, and new beginnings. He is basically a master of spirit recycling.

Attempting to explain the root cause of hate in our society, Samael described what happens with the four parts of our beings, which was similar to what we have heard before from others in the Collective. Yet he added that regardless of the age of the spirit, the mental and emotional parts of an individual are new for each incorporation or reincarnation. These two etheric parts develop along with the physical body to create what we know as the individual. This individual person develops independently of and alongside the timeless spiritual self.

At times, adverse conditions in human life damage the mental-emotional parts of the body, creating a poisoned effect that incites conflict between the spiritual self and the individual self. This inner dissonance can cause damage to the individual, resulting in self-loathing and hate. Many humans become insane from this inner struggle, which is prevalent in society today. Additionally, our techno-logical environment causes individuals to develop under too much pressure, which can produce inner discord, also resulting in misdirected anger. People do not know why they are angry, and so they direct their hatred at unrelated targets, including humans, animals, or our planet.

Dictators use the principle of inner dissonance to build power for themselves by rallying the unfocused hatred of the masses to develop a following. Some leaders on Earth today have risen to power seeking to control others for their own gain. Humanity is at risk. We need to strengthen ourselves by developing individual self-determination, which will prevent those in power from gathering forces based on hatred and control.

Similar to two thousand years ago, when Jesus walked the Earth, humanity is experiencing extreme turmoil and unrest. Those who feel compelled to force beliefs on others are the ones who cause the most distress. There is no one-size-fits-all answer to any course of action or belief. People should be encouraged to think for themselves, embrace inner reflection, and practice self-discipline and spiritual discernment. Many paths lead to enlightenment; each person must choose the path that resonates with their true selves.

Based on the teachings from the Collective, I started holding regular clearing sessions with my clearing consultants to remove negative energy from around people, places, and things. These consultants have become exceedingly adept at removing external negative influences. However, a person's internal negative influencers are more challenging to release by others. Since these are personal, each individual must learn ways to release their inner pain, grow from a place of forgiveness, and embrace healing for themselves.

Many sessions, classes, and trainings are available to help people understand the nature of their problem and learn ways to clear their negativity. Each person is unique, each cure is unique to the individual, and each person is able to cure themselves of their inner dissonance to establish peace. Most important, when individuals heal themselves through discipline, dedication, and resolve, we can collectively raise our vibrational energy to heal our world as a whole.

This world offers many ways to assist people to connect with their wise mind, their higher power. Be it ascension through nature, meditation, prayer, dancing, drumming, or chanting, the methods are plentiful and uniquely suited to each individual. They are all intended to assist humanity to raise the collective consciousness, by relating to the interconnectedness of all that is. As we align with the divine energy of unconditional love, we become self-empowered with balance in all parts of ourselves: physical, mental, emotional, and spiritual. Working with inner harmony, a clear path will be revealed. We will be less easily influenced by others who seek to control us. When we come from a place of positive energy, inner power, grace, and unity, we will help our planet survive. We welcome the gathering of those who support this healing journey.

As I listened to Samael and compared his message to others who have spoken, I felt the fundamental issue with humanity is one of misunderstanding our true eternal spiritual self. The real healing for humanity will take place when people understand they are spiritual beings having a temporary human existence and are interconnected with every living thing on this planet. Our lives are driven by mental and emotional beliefs that are usually based on our upbringing and can be incorrect, incomplete, or misguided. We hope to shift this perspective by inviting people to connect with their true selves. The question is, how do we help open minds to new awareness? When humans learn to respect our Mother Earth, are grateful for all they are given, and learn to ask for assistance, we will begin to raise our vibrational energy and shift civilization to the positive.

How remarkably accurate Samael seems when he mentions Gaia's frustration, and believes that in the near future we will see a drop-off in population growth. This certainly seems to be happening with COVID-19. As people experience the vast numbers of deaths worldwide, some are becoming more aware of how interconnected and similar we are as a civilization. Samael wants us to be more under-standing of ourselves, each other, and our connection with Gaia. This virus is stimulating a new awareness among many. People are being forced to stop their robotic lives and return to nature, a practice Native

American and other cultures have long embraced. The connection with our Earth Mother is deeply engrained in their history.

Gaia and the others in the Collective can help humans develop their spiritual self. People need to experience nature, to truly listen for and receive the message of inner peace and atonement. Once people affirm their true identity, old patterns will slowly dissipate, culminating in the fundamental knowing that *I am enough.* I encourage people to be open to the traditions of indigenous cultures that have long been misunderstood, much as Samael was misunderstood.

Humanity needs unity and inspiration. We all have flaws and our lives are far from perfect. Yet if we each do our own personal work to gain understanding, achieve clarity, and connect with what is true in our hearts, we can shift anger and hate toward peace and acceptance. In this work to bring hope to humanity, we aspire to be the voice that rallies those who are hurting, to bring comfort and harmony. Samael cautioned about becoming objects of adoration. We are only sharing these powerful messages, feeling at peace with the request, and willing to accept the task without the desire to be famous.

Team Hope and I are mostly grateful for those who share the journey with us. Our wish is to help humanity bring peace to itself and our precious planet. Armed with this knowledge and these messages from the Collective, we feel empowered to share this roadmap of hope with humanity, along with these guidelines for living. Many people are doing beneficial things to bring about positive change in their own way. We must each contribute to do what we can to make a difference in the lives of others and our planet. Let us join with each other to grow into a united sense of purpose with gratitude.

Samael has a heavy responsibility to spur humanity's growth through challenge, and we need to accept and embrace our own personal trials. Transforming ourselves with positive energy as we face adversity allows our spirit continuous growth toward enlightenment. The intention of this book series is to invite introspection, offer tools to empower a personal healing journey, and help people gain an understanding of our true spiritual natures. From there, others will begin to recognize and respect the heart of our living planet.

When a sufficient number of people become enlightened, that collective energy will help Gaia heal our world. Samael tells us Gaia is doing what she can to maintain equilibrium. She knows we want to alleviate the stress she is experiencing, and we want to help nourish her growth. She is grateful for any care we can give.

I am grateful for Archangel Samael's wisdom. What advice can you take from this Wise One to help make a difference in your own way? Thank you, Archangel Samael, for your powerful insight and encouragement.

"The strongest among you is the one who controls his anger."
—Muhammad

Session 5 ~
I Am the Spirit of the Universe
All Living Things Are Part of Me

"Terrans never truly realize how each of their lives affects each other because they do not feel what each other feels."
—Spirit of the Universe

Intention

The day that Gary, Paul, and I met to do another informational session was also the day of a global prayer for universal peace. The prayer had been started by Tibetan Monks and was to circumnavigate the globe with people joining at specific times in different regions around the world. The intention was to surround our planet with continuous prayer for twenty-four hours. Coincidentally, our team was meeting at the exact moment our time zone was scheduled to join in this universal prayer.

We agreed it was important to participate in this collective prayer. It was in alignment with our own intention to help this precious planet and all that live in and on her. Since we needed to join at our designated time, we did not have the opportunity to discuss much of the prior Samael session. At this point, I knew meeting Samael was very meaningful, yet it wasn't until I digested the messages more thoroughly later on that I truly understood their full interpretation. Looking back, it was as if we were not intended to have this discussion until we were able to better discern the messages.

We had no expectations or preconceived thoughts as to who might be channeled through Gary today and decided to allow the Collective to send whomever they felt best to speak with us. We were ready to begin the session while uniting in prayer with others around the world.

Session 5 participants were: Lois, the hypnotist guiding the session; Paul, the clearing consultant observing the session and protecting the energy; Gary, the client channeling the High-Level Spirit; and the Spirit of the Universe being channeled through Gary.

Conversation

I begin the session with an invitation for Gary, Paul, and myself to join in a universal prayer for world peace.

Lois: Our intention is to inspire all people to come together to care for each other and to care for our beautiful, living planet. As we join in this prayer for world peace, we would like to allow Gary to relax into this moment. We are grateful that the spirit who inhabits Gary's body has elected to come to Earth to assist in saving humanity. We would like to join in the prayer for universal energy with a desire to heal our planet Earth. Let us take a moment to join with others of like mind that we may contribute our own heartfelt energy.

Allowing Gary to relax into this moment, we join together in the universal prayer for world peace. After a few moments of silence, I start the session by speaking to Gary.

Lois: Who is coming through today?

Universe: [Long pause as the energy slowly adapts to Gary's body. Then, he begins to speak very slowly with only subtle movements, much like the Anquietas.]

I am the Spirit of the Universe made manifest. You spoke my name, and I am here. [Long pause.] Why have you called me?

Lois: [Surprised.] Thank you for coming. We have joined in prayer with others around the world to invite and envision peace. We are concerned about the future of our world and have been beseeched by the Wise Ones of the Collective to share their messages with all humans on this planet. Our mission is to help save humanity from imminent destruction, and to inspire hope, peace, and love. Is there anything you can advise us? Is there anything you can share that will help with this mission?

Universe: All life in the Universe is tied together. [Long pause.] All life in the Universe is brother and sister to each other. When conflict arises, it is . . . as though family were fighting within itself. I am aware of some of the issues associated with Terra.[1] They are common issues throughout my very fabric. I would tell you that *you are all the same*. Not only do you share a common physical ancestor, all life on any planet shares common physical ancestry. Terrans[2] have not yet realized that life exists throughout my whole fabric.

    Terrans need to understand that they are not alone. They need to know they are part of a greater family. You need to use that information to help bring them together. *Terrans are very isolated as individuals.* The immortal parts of themselves do not coalesce with other individuals, as happens on worlds without conflict. Terrans view themselves as being isolated and alone. This is not the case. They need to learn to share themselves with others. Terrans never truly realize how each of their lives affects each other, because *they do not feel* what each other feels. They believe that their actions occur in isolation. That is not the case. They need to learn that every action they take, and every *thought they make*, affects all those around them. When individuals learn to feel what their neighbors feel, when they experience the pain that they cause others, the natural desire will be to avoid inflicting that pain. *That is the true path to peace.*

Lois: There are many people on this planet who have so much hate inside of them. How do we help change that hate and inspire people to be at peace?

Universe: It is one that comes from isolation, the thought that they are alone. *Terrans need to learn to share,* not only the physical world around them, but their feelings and emotions . . . even their thoughts. The non-corporeal part

---

1. Terra is Latin for Earth. It is also the common name for the primordial Roman Goddess, Terra Mater, Mother Earth. In this book, Terra refers to the physical Earth itself, while Gaia refers to the living spirit of Earth.

2. Terrans are inhabitants of the planet Terra, also called Earth.

(the spirit) of each human strives to communicate directly with the non-corporeal parts of all the people around them. But the environment in which most Terrans are brought up discourages this from birth. The result is that Terrans as individuals are, in fact, more isolated than individuals need to be. By not being able to experience what others around them experience . . . by believing that others somehow have more . . . this promotes feelings of jealousy and greed that can ultimately lead to hatred.

There are many belief systems on Terra, and they are oddly mutually exclusive. Yet the Terrans never seem to notice that all of their descriptions of what they think the Universe truly is cannot possibly be right. When, in fact, most of them are quite far from the true reality. It would not be possible for me to describe myself (Universe). No corporeal mind can truly conceive of the infinite.

But by breaking down the barriers between individuals, by allowing Terran minds to share information directly, by striving toward the common consciousness, it would help each individual see that the people around them are not so very different. Much hatred is based on the belief of difference . . . that another individual is deserving of hatred because they believe differently. With true communication comes the realization the differences are not so great . . . so that the hatred dissipates. It is difficult to hate someone who you view as being similar. Closer individuals believe themselves to be brothers. Not only does that reduce the cause of hatred, but makes it more difficult for the individual to hate. Many conflicts on Terra are based on a group of individuals having been painted as different, providing a focus for hatred. By removing the belief in that dissimilarity, you remove the focus of the hatred. [Long pause.]

Lois: Thank you for that explanation. If I understand correctly, the first beings, the Anquietas, are your Children. Is that correct?

Universe: In a sense, they came of my own energy . . . My consciousness came about at the same time. [Long pause.] In a sense, they are more my brethren than my children. They came from my energy but, prior to their creation, *I was only energy*; there was no conscious thought. My own conscience . . . my own consciousness is . . . a representation of all conscious living things. You might say that I am the sum of all the consciousness that exists within me. So, I am the sum of the first 8 (the Anquietas). And I am the sum of that 8 and the next 512 (the Children). My consciousness grew again with the next 32,768 (the Children's Children). Once planets began to form with spirits of their own that were similar in that they were the sum of the consciousness of the creations on those worlds . . . my consciousness expanded again. Still today . . . parts of my energy go in to produce new spirits . . . that, over time, gain consciousness and again become part of my own. That is *why* all living things are kin to each other. Because *all living things are part of me, as I am part of all living things.* I do not exist independently. I am the sum of my parts.

Lois: We are the sum of our parts as individual humans, and the sum of the parts of humanity and the collective as a whole. Is that correct?

Universe: Yes. You exist as individuals. You exist as parts of collectives. You exist as part of the consciousness of your own world. Terra's conscious spirit is Gaia, the name by which you know her. Her consciousness is then part of mine, sister to *many worlds* that have their own conscious spirits. Not all worlds do.

Lois: There are so many questions I'd like to ask. Speaking for humanity, what has gone wrong with our civilization? Is hate the main issue?

Universe: Hate is a symptom . . . a cause. It, in turn, becomes a cause for the actions that occur. It is the isolation that Terrans feel that causes the hatred. Breaking down the barriers between individuals, allowing them to experience each other's thoughts and feelings . . . that is the cure.

Lois: I understand. We are concerned with presenting this material to the world. We have been told by some of the Collective that we need to "vet" carefully in order to place this information in the right hands. Can you advise us on that?

Universe: It is the same solution. Remove your own feeling of isolation. When you see into the spirit of the people with you . . . around you, then you will know without any shadow of a doubt . . . without any conscious thought . . . with whom you may share whatever you wish. [Long pause.] Someone has to be the first . . . to be willing . . . to drop the barriers isolating them from another. [Long pause.]

When you are well matched, and you trust and love one another enough, you don't need barriers between you. Yet, none of you actually realizes . . . none of you understands the methods by which you can allow non-corporeal parts of your existence to truly become one.

The . . . spirits that you refer to as the Anquietas' Children's Children . . . they have the knowledge, because they existed in both corporeal and non-corporeal form. They know how to drop their barriers when they leave the body and exist more closely to my own consciousnesses. Any of the Children's Children can teach you how to do that while remaining in corporeal form.

The Universe is speaking of having the Children's Children who have been in human form teach us how to blend our spirits together collectively while we are in physical form.

It is a process not without risk. It is a process not without discomfort. You will be opening yourselves up primarily to each other . . . but also to any free spirit near you. You will need to protect yourselves against unwanted intrusion. When you open yourselves up, your light will shine more brightly and will be visible across dimensions. This has happened only rarely on Terra before . . . and never by design. Your . . . your light will show brightly to those around you who desire the same change that you seek . . . who will respond to a feeling of openness. If you are open to them, they will . . . without conscious thought . . . become open to you.

You will be the first ripple in a very large pond. But any ripple, no matter how small, will eventually reach all the way to the borders of that pond. As more and more people around you become open, *it will spread*. You have the opportunity . . . and the ability . . . to make the moral change on Gaia. It's up to you to decide whether you want to do it.

Lois: You are talking about us coming together, to shine our light collectively, to lead the way?

Universe: Yes.

Lois: Thank you, we understand. I have a question about clearing the path of negativity. Would it be prudent for us to clear negative energies from specific people who are causing more hate on this planet? Or, would it be more prudent for us to shine the positive light? We could do either.

Universe: You will become a beacon. Those around you who want to experience the positive energy, will. However, you will attract . . . non-physical beings that seek out any source of energy. You have the skills to protect yourselves. But you must be vigilant with exercising these skills or you will become . . . burdened.

In Book 1, the Anquietas gave us explanations about non-physical beings, such as low-level entities that are from other dimensions and are attracted to both positive and negative energies as food sources. The Anquietas also gave us information on the Protective Bubble[3] to use for protection. It is detailed at the end of each book.

It would help make your process easier . . . if other Terrans had some conscious desire to want to experience

---

3. The Protective Bubble is a spiritual technique designed to protect one's energy from external interference. Outlined in each book, people can use this spiritual hygiene to keep their energy strong and protected.

what you are going to show them. It is possible to make your path clearer . . . by, as you say, removing some of the hatred. There are lessons that you can teach to help people, to be more thoughtful of their own thoughts and actions . . . to *not be so reactive and defensive.* Clearing your path in the physical dimension will help clear your path in the non-physical dimension. You *can* simplify your task in that way.

Lois: Thank you for that clarification.

Universe: I am . . . pleased to be of service.

Lois: Is there anything else which we should ask? Is there anything specific we need to know?

Universe: What I see within you is that you have all that you need. You have been granted audiences with the oldest spirits within me. Listen to those words and pass them on. Take them into your own heart and try to get others to do the same. Most importantly, your instincts are good. You need to trust them. You have no need to doubt yourself in any way. [Long pause.]
   I . . . I cannot stay any longer.

Lois: Thank you so much.

Paul: Thank you for coming.

Lois: We will do our best.

Universe: You . . . *can only* do your best.

Lois: We certainly will.

I bring the session to a close by encouraging the spirit of Gary to come back gently into his physical body, pleasantly, softy, quietly, and peacefully on this day and in this time.

As Gary started to return to awareness, he expressed feeling like someone was screaming inside of his mind, as if his head was spinning. I instructed Gary to breathe gently into the noise and offered to share some Reiki with him. As he was struggling to return to alertness, he moaned in pain, asserting it was an odd experience, like none he had felt before. He felt as if his hair was burning, while his mind was chattering with a loud energetic hum.

He sensed it wasn't one roaring tone; it was thousands of intense voices, like a chorus. They were all saying the same thing at the same time. He said it was similar to hearing people in a football stadium chanting together, just a bit out of sync. We wondered if he had been hearing the chants of people around the world who had joined in the prayer. For several minutes, Gary continued to hear the echoes of many voices like a murmur coming together, yet he could not pick out a single voice. He seemed to have tapped into the collective of universal consciousness, his mind opened to hear all the people who were praying. Even though the words sounded different, their intent was the same. Their hearts were joined in a collective effort for world peace.

Once we realized this, I invited Gary to relax into the chatter, and his pain slowly subsided. While still in somewhat of a trance state, Gary expressed that he felt expanded, like he was much larger than himself. As I continued to encourage him to calm his mind, he then saw numerous faces looking at him. They were repeating words, though their lips didn't match. They were chanting something he couldn't process, continuing to echo in his head.

I asked our Guides to help quiet his thoughts and fully integrate him back into his physical body on Earth. Suddenly, the voices changed. Gary commented they were speaking in a language that humans couldn't understand and were now smiling at him in a comforting way.

Finally, Gary relaxed into his body. Then, he suddenly cried out loudly, expressing an intense feeling of pain, of being all alone, and that this might be the collective pain of humanity. I instructed him to remove the feeling from his body, that it was not his to bear. As he removed it, he described the color as black. I asked Gary to wrap the black in a bubble of light, and called on Archangel Michael to assist with his healing, to take away the feeling of isolation and bring the feeling of connectedness to each other and all that is. As Gary eased into a state of peace, we sensed several Archangels, including Samael, surround all of us with healing light.

As the Archangels lifted the feeling of isolation, I continued sending Reiki through Gary to help ground him. I could feel the soft warm glow of gentle light surround us and move through us. Gary returned to full awareness as I talked him gently into this present day and time. Although he had no memory of what had transpired in the session, he conveyed that he felt a huge expansiveness while I was doing Reiki on him.

The feeling of loss from isolation hurt his heart tremendously. He was shivering, stating that he felt excessively cold with his hands freezing. He warmed himself with a hot cup of tea and enjoyed some dark chocolate. As he relaxed and began releasing the intense emotions of the session, he asserted: "You don't realize how truly lonely you are until you are not."

Reflection

In this fascinating session, we experienced the incredible magnitude and power of collective thought and prayer. As the three of us joined in a global prayer for world peace, we were shocked that the Spirit of the Universe spontaneously came through Gary to speak with us. Of course, it made complete sense. We had gone into the session with an openness to share our collective energy for world peace and had tapped into the actual energy of the Spirit of the Universe. This energy was so expansive that it interfered with our recording devices. From our usual video camera to recording apps on two cell phones, nothing worked. Thankfully, an audio software program I had running on my computer as a backup recorded it all.

Communicating with this powerful spiritual energy through Gary was similar to conversing with the Anquietas in Book 1. At times, the Universe momentarily glanced at me, but otherwise showed little facial expression or physical movement. The voice was soft and slow, with frequent pauses, as if to purposefully choose the correct translation for our "Terran" language. This was the first time I had heard our planet referred to by the name Terra, and Terrans as her inhabitants.

Also, similar to the Anquietas, the Spirit of the Universe was only able to spend around twenty minutes with us. Others of the Collective that were more closely matched to Gary's energy spent a greater amount of time. However, in this short dialogue with the Spirit of the Universe, we gained grand insight.

We learned the Anquietas actually came from the energy of the Universe. Initially, the Universe was only energy, so their (the Anquietas') collective consciousness coalesced about the same time. The Universe represents all conscious living things; it is the sum of all consciousness. So, all beings of the Collective, all of humanity, and all living beings on all planets make up the consciousness of the Universe. New spirits are being created who are also part of the Universe. We are all one, and the Universe itself is the sum of all.

The Universe reinforced that all life on our planet is interconnected, that we are brothers and sisters to each other. We exist as individuals, yet are part of the consciousness of Gaia, the conscious spirit of our planet. As we realize that we are all part of each other, we should be compelled to treat each other without bias and know that one person is not better than another. We are also part of a larger family of life across the Universe; we are truly not alone on Earth. We are one collective whole, one civilization of humanity.

When the Universe speaks of isolation, we may consider it as separation. Many people think of themselves as a being separate from everything else: from each other, from the animals, from the trees, from our Earth Mother, and from whatever God they might call on. This way of thinking is fundamentally misguided. How many people think of themselves as different, less than, not enough, or inferior? That feeling of separateness is what causes prejudice, judgment, bias, and wars, and ultimately may be the death of the human race.

How many people have given up on prayer, refuse to connect with something outside of themselves, or fail to express gratitude for what they have? What about those who do pray to a mysterious God who is far away, up in the sky, separate from and greater than them? In fact, when you pray, you are really communicating with your wise mind, your higher self, the part of you that is connected with the infinite or Divine.

Prayer can be as simple as appreciating a gesture, sunset, a rainbow, or the song of a bird. Life and everything in existence, seen and unseen, are part of an intricate web of the Universe. We are not separate from, but rather *part* of the infinite. I am not separate from you. You are not separate from me. My energy and your energy . . . my spirit and your spirit are together. We are one.

Primitive civilizations knew this. Native cultures knew this. When the Universe speaks of isolation, the word "separate" seems more applicable. When we are separate from each other, from communication with Divine sources, and from connection with nature, we become isolated and alone. Our hope in human survival is that we come together to be included with and part of one another and all that is.

Our modern way of life has caused us to be particularly isolated and alone, which creates division. Our dependence on technology has intensified our isolation. While we seemingly connect with others on social media, the absence of physical contact is problematic. When we allow ourselves to share with others, we realize how interconnected we really are. Each life affects another.

When you smile at someone, that simple action creates a ripple effect that may positively shift their entire outcome based on that one moment in time. Every interaction with another creates momentum in one direction or another, whether positive or negative. Unfortunately, at the end of the day, we usually remember the negative things that people have said or done. In actuality, we should focus on the good things we experienced throughout the day.

The Universe's message seems perfectly timed for our here and now. The coronavirus pandemic is sweeping the world, exacerbating the effects of isolation among many who are in quarantine with little or no touch or physical contact. Many are feeling alone and isolated, filled with despair, anger, blame, and anguish. Others are seizing this as an opportunity to simplify, slow down, spend quality time in nature, with family, or with self.

When you look at today's crisis of isolation from a broader perspective, the takeaway for all of us, be it positive or negative, will influence whether we shift and awaken, or drop into anger and refuse to change. Those who hold onto the anger are the ones Samael refers to as the lost spirits who, in the end, will wish they had made different choices when they had the chance. Now is our chance.

The positive side of technology is that it connects people. Though virtually, technology allows us greater access to each other, accentuating our similarities and creating common consciousness. During the shelter-in-place period, many benefited tremendously from the use of technology. We stayed connected with friends while at home, continued to work and learn via computer programs, had online doctor's and other appointments, and even tapped into positive practices such as meditation and yoga.

With the world at our fingertips, technology opens virtual doors, allowing us to visit people of countries and cultures many of us could never visit in person. Connecting with others virtually, we have the opportunity to see how closely we are related, share our similarities, and appreciate our differences.

Having traveled extensively throughout my lifetime, I recognize the uniqueness of each country and culture: the distinctly different sights, smells, and sounds of the land, and attitudes of the people. Our similarities are profound, as are our differences. Yet, being there in person, I could unquestionably experience and relate to situational divergences and the historic imprint of each culture more fully.

However, technology is a double-edged sword. We are at the mercy of whoever is sharing information from a potentially biased point of view. While we have the capacity for expanded knowledge and connection, we are also exposed to the potential for confusion and fear. A major challenge of technology is that it can readily be used to create instantaneous demonstration of global pain via our media outlets. Although negativity, anger, and rage do exist, they are often misrepresented, sensationalized, or amplified. While absorbing the increased fear, hysteria, and panic, observers succumb to desperation, division, and increased isolation.

Based on human perception, some see what appears to be lack in our world, because it's vastly different than their norm. They feel angry at groups, or sorry for those who appear to have "less." When, in fact, people in cultures who live simpler lives may actually be happier because they don't have all the external pressure or distractions. By the same token, some who live in impoverished countries assess those who live in what they consider to be "rich" countries with jealousy and contempt. They consider wealth to be so desirable, without under-standing the added burden of required performance that accompanies attaining even middle-class standards in many countries. Each sees the other from their personal viewpoint, their lens of life. Communal feelings are exacerbated by the intention of the person providing the information via technology.

Ultimately, we must come from a place of truth. As we remove our tinted glasses and attempt to experience what others may be feeling, we can more clearly see their viewpoint. It's all about perception. A person's perception becomes their reality. What someone needs to understand is *their* reality, not necessarily shared by others.

How can we allow ourselves to tap into another's reality with open-mindedness and come from a place of mutual respect? As we remove our deep residual anger and refuse to be swayed by others' opinions, can we be willing to listen to another without bias? Only then will we have the opportunity to truly come together as one.

One of the main teachings of this session is how the anger and hate many humans express can be caused by a feeling of isolation. Hate may be a symptom of isolation, which could cause division. The sense of being different fosters notions of jealousy that might lead to hatred and fear. We exist in a fear-based culture where even our children learn to be wary of everyone and everything. With electronic devices being the main instrument of touch today, have humans lost physical and emotional touch with each other?

In schools, our children are exposed to a variety of negative emotions and power struggles among peers. I see many of these diffi-cult challenges in working with young clients. Based on traumas and tragedy in schools, many of our children leave the safety of home with an intense fear of the unknown. Our schools have become like prisons, locked down, with children feeling unsafe. From this, they learn to exist in isolation and fear the person sitting next to them. As a result, they escape into electronic devices for fun and distraction, or to connect with friends. This exacerbates the feeling of isolation and adds other complications such as bullying, which causes even more withdrawal and fear.

Our range of emotions can be compared to the full range of keys on a keyboard, with one end expressing peace, happiness, and joy, while the other expresses sadness, fear, or anger. It is healthy to fully experience and express the entire spectrum of emotions. When some-thing sad happens, like the death of a loved one or pet, it is appro-priate to feel sadness. When something good happens and we want to celebrate, we should feel free to do so with joy. For optimum wellness, it is important to play the entire range of the keyboard of emotions.

Many live their lives with such fear they become numb to their emotions, and they develop strong coping skills to exist in a world that is bombarded with chronic negativity. Making ourselves emotionally numb can lead to destructive behaviors as we try to avoid underlying feelings of sadness, depression, anxiety, anger, and hate. Some reach for substances to ameliorate their pain, which causes additional health issues on all levels: mental, emotional, physical, and spiritual.

When we become open to understanding, embracing, healing, and sharing our emotions, we develop compassion for ourselves and others. Ultimately, as the healing unfolds, we may come to willingly share our feelings from a place of mutual trust and respect. As we allow ourselves to feel what another feels, to appreciate and accept the differences between us, we can relate more openly to one another and have the opportunity to avoid creating conflict or inflicting pain.

Once we develop ways to accept each other and communicate from a place of honesty and acceptance, hatred dissipates. Only then can the anger, rage, and violence that is pervasive in our world stop. Humanity can then shift to a place of true peace.

Those on a path of spiritual development may choose to explore coming together in groups. We experience the oneness of community through prayer, group meditation, and spiritual connection via many different avenues. A beautiful example of this kindred spirit sharing is the Native American people's custom of healing circles or talking circles, which have been around the First Nations' culture for eons.

In the circle, everyone is present as individuals and as a collective whole. A ceremonial clearing or smudging takes place with sage or cedar as each individual enters the circle. The ceremony continues usually with an elder sharing a meaningful story. Others are invited to participate by the passing of a "talking stick." Whoever has the stick can share what is on their mind in the way of gratitude. They can make specific requests for health, growth, or positivity, or share insight based on what is going on in their life at that moment.

Others in the ceremonial circle are fully present to listen and send healing thoughts or energy to the one speaking. The talking stick is passed to each member of the circle who wishes to speak, while the others listen without interruption or interjection. Wonderful people of like minds and intentions come together while truly being present for one another and the community as a whole.

Since there is so much negativity in our society, many become overwhelmed and unfortunately develop a mistrust of others. Many extraordinary, sensitive people have the ability to truly feel what others feel. An empath,[4] also referred to as empathic, senses the feelings of another in a visceral way, often resulting in deep emotional or physical sensations of their own. Empaths often protect themselves by avoiding interactions with others because of the extreme discomfort they sense from another's negative emotions.

I have empathic clients who have real struggles in today's climate of extreme negativity. To protect themselves from this adverse influence, many empathic people shut down, distancing themselves into isolation, which exacerbates their feeling of being alone and different. An empath does need to retreat momentarily for personal rejuvenation. Yet pulling completely away from others is ultimately detrimental to their mission and humanity. They are here as "way showers," literally to show us the way. If you have an empath in your life, respect their abilities and heed their keen sense of awareness. Much like the canary in the coal mine, they sense emotional distress before others feel it.

The Collective have told us to "vet carefully" those whom we should trust. When we trust our own intuitive knowing, our spiritual self, to truly sense the spiritual nature of others, then we know with certainty whom to trust and share. Empaths teach others how to relate and how to connect heart to heart on a spiritual level. Their abilities can bring us together and teach us how to relate to one another. If we pay attention to their sensitivities, intuition, and guidance, we can better develop understanding and compassion for others. Then, we can tune into the collective energy of our world and aid the shift to positivity.

Further, when we heal our own emotional issues by releasing the inner pain of hate in our hearts, we come to understand where the pain originated. As we empower ourselves to release the pain of

---

4. An empath is a person who is very sensitive to all types of energy. They are capable of sensing and feeling the emotions of others. Empaths must learn ways to handle the energy they detect and protect themselves.

the past, we come to a place of acceptance. Once at peace, we can be open to share our thoughts and feelings that break down the barriers of isolation. As we discover ways to more directly communicate with spiritual awareness, we empower the ultimate cure for hate and will be able to transform this world into a place of peace. When we allow ourselves to experience one another through our shared spiritual connection, we create one common consciousness with the ability to collectively manifest a healthy society.

It is difficult to comprehend the expansive power of the Universe available to us. When we tap into this power together, the potential exists for magnitudes of change. This can happen if we are willing to drop the barriers of isolation, then trust and love each other enough to allow our spiritual beings to truly unite as one. The spirits of the Collective can be called on to help in this process, as they understand existence in both physical and spiritual form.

The Collective knows how to drop the barriers we put up as physical beings in order to connect at higher levels of spiritual consciousnesses. The Universe specifically recommends we call on one of the Children's Children to teach us how to do this. Depending on your belief, you may look to Jesus, Lao Tzu, Buddha, Quan Yin, Krishna, Muhammad, Moses, or others. Any of these amazing teachers can give you instructions on how to connect to the higher spiritual realm.

This consciousness sharing should be taken seriously, since it does come with the potential for risk, even pain, as it did for Gary in this session. He experienced real feelings of pain, isolation, and loneliness, and it took my knowledge of the situation and use of Reiki to bring him relief. As we open ourselves to one another, we become vulnerable to other spirits around us that can create this type of real havoc. Book 1 describes in detail the types of energies and entities that surround humans on a regular basis. Energies we call emotional energy feeders[5] seek mostly to feed on negative emotions. Low-level

---

5. Emotional energy feeders (EEFs) are simple energy-draining Earth energies that feed off the negative energy given off by human emotion. EEFs neutralize negative energy, allowing opportunity for positive change.

entities from other dimensions seek all levels of energy as food sources and can cause harm to living beings.

When someone practices energy healing techniques to help others, the ensuing light created by their sharing shines exponentially brighter, which attracts attention. Some energy feeders are attracted to both negative emotions as well as the bright light of positive energy, like moths to a flame, especially across dimensions. Once attached, they can stay with you and drain your energy, bringing discomfort.

I encourage clients to practice daily spiritual hygiene. Like brushing your teeth every morning, my clients find that doing a spiritual clearing and zipping into their Protective Bubble before starting their day is helpful. You can use many ways to clear and protect your energy. Both books include a step-by-step description of the Protective Bubble, which is used regularly by my clearing consultants for spiritual protection. Before every group or clearing session, we surround ourselves with deflector shields to protect against unwanted intrusion. We have developed protective protocols for ourselves, as well as the space surrounding us.

As you become comfortable calling on members of the Collective to assist, you will discover their powerful energy is always there for protection, guidance, and empowerment. We never do this work alone; we consider ourselves to be the human component in partnership with the amazing Guides who truly do the clearing and healing work.

The Universe warns of the risk involved with doing some of this work. On occasion, we have been complacent in our spiritual protection practices, or have dealt with intensely negative situations, and have suffered painful consequences, both physically and emotionally. At times, we have picked up negative energies, much like catching a virus from a patient, that have caused us to feel drained, agitated, or even physically sick. In extreme situations, my consultants have experienced sudden onset of intense pain in their head, neck, back, or stomach from rogue spiritual entities.

We have learned to do this spiritual clearing together as a team so that one member stays grounded, keeping the others safe while they explore or tap into the unseen. We always call on the Guides of the Collective for protection and assistance in all situations.

If you are interested in some of the specific techniques my team uses for energy clearing and creating sacred space, please refer to the Resources section of this book. These tools and practices have made a huge difference in ensuring a positive outcome for personal and session work.

If you are interested in learning more about energy clearing, I invite you to join the online Inspiring Hope Community discussion group at www.ChroniclesOfHope.net/community to meet others with interest and expertise in this area. Community members ask questions, and have in-depth discussions with Team Hope members.

At the end of this session, as Gary was returning to full awareness, he tapped into the sound of the united prayer traversing the world that the Tibetan monks had begun. He fully experienced the power of cooperative prayer, hearing the murmur of a thousand voices chanting in unison. He also sensed the anguish of isolation that so many people feel on our planet. As I joined with Gary through the Reiki, we both felt the energy like an intense warm light shining through us. We experienced an unusually uplifting feeling like nothing we had ever experienced. We were inspired to do more of the same to help humanity.

As we collectively open our energy to join with others of similar positive intention, I'm confident our combined energy will glow like a bright beacon of light into the Universe, attracting both good and bad, beneficial and detrimental energies. If you choose to do this, you must learn discernment, and diligently practice protecting yourself from any negative interference.

As we merge with others who want to contribute to the positive shift for our planet, we may feel like a very small ripple in a very large pond. However, it is possible to make a difference as we come together with those of like mind to collectively share our spiritual energy. By uniting, we spread positive energy that can shift the morality on Earth, making a distinct difference in the favorable outcome of humanity.

We were truly astonished to have called on the Universe in prayer to begin this session and to have received the response "You spoke my name, and I am here." We are honored to have been granted audiences with the oldest spirits in the Universe, and now the Universe itself. We are grateful, and we appreciated the Universe's acknowledgment of us and for sharing such valuable insight.

"When a person responds to the joys and sorrows of others
as though they were his own,
he or she has attained the highest spiritual union."

—Krishna

Session 6 ~
I Am the Spirit of the Earth, Gaia, Your Mother

"I am the sum of the consciousness of all living things on the planet. All living things, not just humans."

—Gaia

Intention

In this session, Gary and I were joined by three new participants: Denise and Zeke, valued clearing consultants, and Linda, Gary's friend. Our intention this day was to communicate with the Spirit of Gaia, our Mother Earth. In past sessions, every spirit of the Collective had expressed great concern for Gaia, and this project had morphed into helping her and humanity. If possible, we wanted to hear from her directly to find out what she needed and how we could best assist her. Our new participants came with specific questions, and we discussed what would be appropriate to ask during the session.

In one of the early sessions in Book 1, the Collective showed Gary a vision of our beautiful blue-green Earth having turned brown and barren in the near future. We wanted clarification on what might cause this. Were the land and sea brown because of nuclear explosions and war, or from continued neglect?

Also, we wondered what was causing Gaia the most pain. Was there anything she could advise to best help her to prevent future harm? What could we do as humans to change our ways to create better outcomes? Was technology good or bad for our society? We had many questions and were excited to hear what Gaia might say.

Session 6 participants were: Lois, the hypnotist guiding the session; Denise and Zeke, the clearing consultants observing the session and protecting the energy; Linda, Gary's friend observing the session; Gary, the client channeling the High-Level Spirit; and Gaia, the Spirit of the Earth, being channeled through Gary.

Conversation

I guide Gary into a state of trance with the participants quietly observing. When he is noticeably relaxed, I begin the session.

Lois: We are asking Gaia to come through to share with us today. We wish to help alleviate your pain and suffering. We are here to receive your words, your message, your insight, and your inspiration. We are open to hearing what you would advise us to do.

Gary sits quietly for a time, then gently stretches his neck and slowly moves his hands. The spirit seems to take a moment to orient into Gary's body.

Lois: Hello?

Gaia: [Speaks in a soft, feminine, yet firm voice.] Hello.

Lois: Whom may I ask are we speaking with today?

Gaia: I am the Spirit of Earth, Gaia, your mother. [Rolls head and shrugs shoulders as she acclimates to the body.]

Lois: Hello, Mother Earth. Thank you so much for coming.

Gaia: There are things you want to know? [Opens eyes momentarily to look at Lois.]

Lois: Yes, there are many things we want to know. First, we're sorry for all the pain that humanity has brought to you, and we wish to know how we can best serve you. What can we do to help you?

Gaia: I know that there are humans among you who care. [Deep breath with a sigh and begins to speak painfully.] It is the *indifference* that hurts more than anything else. So many people . . . are so thoughtless. What can I tell you today? [Smiles gently at Lois.]

Lois: We've been shown that in some years to come, your beautiful body will be brown and the sky will be toxic.

Gaia: [Speaks softly.] Yes.

Lois: The marine life will die. Is that because of a nuclear war, or is it because the humans are not taking care? What is the main cause for that change? We are hoping to learn how to avoid this.

Gaia: That is just the lack of care, the lack of respect for the planet. There is no catastrophe that I foresee, except that which I may choose to bring.

Lois: When you choose to bring catastrophe, it is to specific people for their lack of care?

Gaia: I don't have the ability to target the individuals who are most responsible for the damage. [Deep breath with sigh.] It's just . . . it's just lashing out as any wounded creature would. [Speaks quietly, yet fluidly without much hesitation.] My consciousness is not an individual thing. *I am the sum of the consciousness of all living things on the planet.* All living things, not just humans. Everything that lives is part of me. My feelings, at any time, are the sum of the feelings of the living creatures on this planet. The more creatures who suffer, the more I suffer. That can produce a . . . a resonating effect. The more they suffer, the more I suffer, the more they feel it, and that can spiral out of control. And has many times. It's happening now.

Lois: The destruction of the rain forest, the extinction of animals . . . you're feeling all of that pain?

Gaia: Yes. [Takes deep breath.] Extinction is a natural event. More species have become extinct than have ever lived . . . than are living now. But . . . the rate of extinction is growing.

Lois: What can we do to stop that?

Gaia: That is a very complicated question. Or at least the answer is very complicated. I wish I could say that there was one simple thing that could be done. [Sighs.] But . . . the only . . . I'm sorry, this is very hard to put into words. The problem isn't just the destruction of the rain forests or the poisoning of the oceans or the execution of animals for sport. The problem isn't even the use and waste of resources. There are enough resources. The problem is the lack of . . . the lack of thought that people have for their actions in general. There is *no one action* to reverse the damage, other than pausing for a moment and considering the consequences of the actions you take.

It's a matter of raising the consciousness levels of the humans. Most life on Earth is aware of the complex web of life. Humans refer to a food chain, but that is an overly simplistic view. It is a web. Everything is connected to everything else. Anything you . . . change in one place will have more than one consequence. If humans were more aware of their own interconnectedness with everything else, and realized that *every action they take* has consequences far beyond those they could even foresee, and modified their actions to allow for the consequences they can foresee . . . that would be enough. There are those who realize that their actions are actively harmful . . . and do them anyway. There are those who witness this and do nothing to prevent it. That level of indifference is what causes more damage than anything else.

Some humans think that the task is simply too big . . . that to clean up the Earth is just not possible. For them, that is probably true. But I am capable of healing the Earth . . . provided that the level and rate of damage is reduced. If you think about the history of the planet and myself . . . it's hard for humans to comprehend time in billions of years. They don't realize how small their span is in the span of all things. I wonder sometimes how many have such an overinflated opinion of themselves, and at the same time realize that their span is an infinitesimal fraction of mine. I can heal the damage; they just have to *let me* do it. The rate at which they cause harm is greater than the rate at which I can heal. [Holds hands out in a shrug-like gesture with annoyance.]

But consider the things that have happened to Earth: the meteor strikes, the loss of the dinosaurs. [Shrugs again.] . . . I healed the planet enough for the human species to arise. In fact, the human species would not be here had the dinosaurs not been destroyed. [Explains emphatically.] That was not my doing. But . . . evolution is a punctuated process. It's not a smooth continuous event. It is a series of small events, each one triggered by either a natural or artificial occurrence. Sometimes it's a random mutation, sometimes it's an asteroid strike. Clearing away of one species makes room for another.

I would never extinguish humanity. However, I would not overextend myself to protect it either. Humans have to realize that they have a place on this world, and that they are no more superior to any other living creature than any other living creature is. Just because they have a bigger brain doesn't make them in control. And, in many ways, humans are not the most intelligent species on this planet. They need to understand their place and learn to live within it . . . and take only what they need.

Lois: One of the questions we have is related to our concern about the food chain and what we eat, as it's crucial to basic human existence. Is there anything we should be doing differently? For example, would it benefit us, as a culture, to limit our intake of flesh and eat more of a vegetarian existence?

Gaia: Again, that is a very complex question with a complex answer. [Deep breath.] It is not a food chain; it is a food web. There is no harm in eating land animals or aquatic animals, any more than there is harm in eating land plants or aquatic plants. It is only in excess that damage is done. These animals came about as a natural course of evolution. They weren't created for the purpose of human consumption. There is nothing wrong in humans consuming them, but again, not to excess.

If all humans suddenly became vegetarian, there would be a shortage of land on which to grow the vegetables and the plants that you would eat. Everything has to be taken in balance. That said, the animals which are raised for consumption, and in fact even the crops that are raised for consumption by humans or by animals . . . that process needs to be more carefully managed. It has sometimes been done in a wasteful fashion. When a cow, for example, is slaughtered, all of it *is* reused . . . even the parts that humans don't eat go into fertilizer, feed, and meal; the skin becomes leather. That is an acceptable use. There have been times when that was not the case. When an animal was killed, it was eaten for the parts that it was killed for, and the rest was just left. That is not an acceptable use.

But, the same is true of the crops that you grow. Some crops are very detrimental to the soil. Tobacco, for example, depletes the soil. Humans do understand crop rotation and the ability to naturally revitalize the soil, but it is easier and cheaper to dump chemicals onto the land. That is counterproductive because those chemicals wash away into the water, and the sea life that doesn't perish from it can become overabundant. You have red tides and algae blooms that are caused by the runoff of the chemicals you thought so beneficial to the land . . . into the water. These blooms can strip hundreds of cubic miles of oxygen from the ocean, and then everything else in the water in that area will die. The things that die degrade and add more fertilizer to the water, and it becomes a spiraling process. I don't need to tell you how to run farms. The knowledge is already there. It merely requires the desire to use it. It requires the desire to spend the extra amount of energy that it takes to do it properly.

Humans . . . humans have a lazy streak in them. They will do things in the simplest possible way to serve themselves without any thought of the consequence of their action. As I said before, *consequences have to be considered,* because they will catch up with you. There is no escaping it. It is a fundamental law of nature . . . a fundamental law of physics.

Lois: How can we inspire humans to do what is right when they know what is right?

Gaia: Most intelligent species respond most strongly to fear and to pain [sighs]. These are strong motivators. They come from part of the human brain that has not changed much in one hundred thousand years of evolution. Humans have added more layers to their brain and more complexity, but the reptilian brain is still there. When something hurts you, you learn not to do it. When you fear something, you learn not to do it. Fear of heights, for example, was built into most humans. There are exceptions . . . some Native Americans never developed a fear of heights, possibly because of the reverence they have for the land, and some are used to standing on high and looking around them.

But, if you can demonstrate to people what's going to happen to them in a way that is undeniable, then their natural preservation instinct will hopefully cause them to do things the right way. There are two problems with this. The first is, how do you make a demonstration in a way that is clear and undeniable? Even the wrath which I lay down periodically is all too frequently dismissed. It would not be my preference to be so blatant and obvious, and so destructive, as to make it inexplicable in any other way. I don't desire destruction. [Begins to choke up.] I cherish all life, as all life is my. . . is my charge.

Lois: The second problem?

Gaia: The second problem is more difficult to describe. [Long pause to consider.] How do you . . . hurt someone enough to let them know that doing it again will hurt, without hurting them so much that they don't get a second chance? That's the problem we face. [Looks at Lois.] Too many people look at things within their own lifespan. They say: "I have only a few years left, what difference does it make what I do to the world? It's not going to affect me." Some of them have children and don't even stop to think: "Is what I'm doing going to affect my children and their children?" They're so wrapped up in themselves, they don't even care about their own families.

I have no answer for how to overcome something that is so unique in life. Every other species has more care for their kin than they do for themselves. Humans are unique in their . . . self-centeredness and selfishness . . . that they don't even care about their own offspring's future. [Speaks sadly.] I have never faced that issue before. I have no solution to that problem.

Lois: Could modern technology that humanity is so preoccupied with be part of the problem?

Gaia: Manmade things are really no different than nature-made things. Anything can be used to a good purpose; anything can be abused to a bad purpose. Humans do tend to excess. Again, that is something that I don't see in any of my other children. Most animals, when they graze, know enough to not kill the plant they eat . . . to move on to another field so that the plants grow back. Migration patterns are caused by this. Humans must be aware of this, and don't seem to care. I find that inexplicable behavior.

It isn't that everyone needs to be convinced. *It only takes a few to make a big difference.* A very small snowball can turn into a very large avalanche given enough time. There are plenty of people who know these things, and who speak about them. But their voices are not heard, or worse, they're shouted down by the people who know they're doing damage but are doing it for profit.

There is a solution. If the people who misuse the resources do so because of profit, then the way to get them to change is to attack their profit. If that's all they care about, then that's how you have to strike them. This is an old philosophy, actually. But if the consumers don't buy things that are bad for them . . . and a lot of the food being sold today is very bad for them, either by deliberate act or by carelessness . . . then the producers will have to change their production. They'll have to change what they sell.

The tampering with nature using genetics is an example of things with unforeseen consequences. There are things that are going to begin to occur related to genetic modification that humans have done for which they had no foresight . . . no concept that this was going to happen. And it's not something that I'm going to do deliberately. It's a natural consequence of what they're doing, and it will hurt them. There's nothing wrong with hybridizing. I do that myself. [Speaks passionately, gestures with arm.] All of nature . . . the reason there's so many different things . . . is because of natural hybridization, a fair and reasonable process. But deliberate tampering is always going to produce a result that they don't expect. Unfortunately, those results are usually very long term.

Lois: One of the questions we're curious about is the melting of the glaciers and the resulting ice melt. Is the land going to change as part of this natural occurrence?

Gaia: Yes.

Lois: Do humans need to be aware of how soon that is going to happen, and how our coastlines are going to be affected?

Gaia: I think that most informed people or scientists do have a fair grasp of the timeframe involved. I think they underestimate how bad it ultimately will be. Nobody likes to foresee their own destruction. And again, it comes down to the fact that this is not going to happen within the lifespans of the people who are already on the Earth. It's the next generations that are going to start to see the side effects. However, man's impact on the environment isn't as great as they think it is, in terms of the climate. The climate will change; it will become warmer. Humans were very fortunate to have grown up in a time of very moderate climate at the end of a natural glaciation. *My* life is long. Humans can't see that sort of time span, and don't realize that had they come about now, rather than one hundred thousand years ago, their civilization would not have developed the way it did. The climate on this planet, by my standards, is normally much harsher than it currently is. Humans were *lucky* to have grown up when they did.

The climate at the time of the dinosaurs, for example, was one in which humans in their current form could not survive. However, evolution *does* work, and humans . . . intelligent creatures . . . would have come to pass, but they would not be recognized as what we would call human today. The problem is that the environmental change will outstrip the pace of evolution. However, there are events that could reintroduce glaciation: large volcanic eruptions, meteor strikes, anything that blocks the sun for any period of time.

You see, the history of glaciation is actually very interesting, and I don't think it's something that most of your scientists understand. When there was but one continent, the currents in the ocean, as there was only the one, were unrestricted. This meant that the water from the poles mixed more freely with the water from the equator, with the result that there were no icecaps. And icecaps can only form on land, not in mid-ocean. So, with no icecaps and with that circulation, the world was a much warmer place. Also, without icecaps reflecting the sun, there was more absorption of what little sun there was in the polar regions.

As the continents broke up and reached their current positions, they interfered with the circulation of the oceans. It became more difficult for the cold waters at the poles to move centrally, and for the warm water at the equator to move toward the poles. And as the land spread into the polar regions, it formed points upon which ice could form. So, the ice did form, which impacted the water's circulation, and reflected more solar heat, and that's what caused glaciers to move down almost to the tropics. Only where the sun was overhead most of the year did the ice not reach. As the oceans' currents stabilized, with the continents in the current position, the heat exchange increases and the ice melts, which reduces solar reflection, and so the ice continues to melt. That is a natural process.

If anything, the pollution that humans have pumped into the air is more likely to cool the Earth than it is to cause it to heat. That could bring back another glaciation. It is impossible to predict with certainty what will happen and when. There are too many . . . random variables. However, regardless of its impact on climate, pumping pollution into the air is self-defeating. Humans are literally poisoning themselves, the air, the land, the water . . . they *will* eventually extinct themselves, or enough of them that it won't make much difference . . . and then I start again.

Lois: One question that I know Gary wanted to ask is: "Are we going to suffer the same fate as Atlantis if we don't do what is being asked of us?"

Gaia: That's a slightly different case, because the Atlantean destruction was almost instantaneous. [Deep breath with a sigh.] They didn't heed the advice that they were given, and their destruction was almost immediate. In this case, it's going to be a much more prolonged period of time. There is . . . [Breathes in, shrugs shoulders.] . . . As powerful as Atlantis was, it was small compared to the Earth. There is nothing humans can do, short of an atomic war, that would cause such instantaneous change . . . for the good or for the ill.

When you're dealing with a planet, you're dealing with trends, not individual actions . . . barring large-scale events like meteor strikes, which could still happen. It's important that humans realize that just because things don't happen quickly, doesn't mean their effects aren't important. Starting a trend which is beneficial is worth doing, even if the results are not obvious until several generations later. Humans need to live for their own future, not for their current existence. They need to plan for their future, not their current existence. Things simply do not change that fast on a planetary scale, but that doesn't mean that every little bit doesn't help.

Lois: Thank you. There are some people here today that might wish to speak with you. Linda, Denise, and Zeke, do you have any questions?

Linda: I am honored to meet you, Gaia. I'm curious how much you intervene in our lives? You're aware of our thoughts as we're all connected . . . part of the oneness of the planet and the oneness with you. Are you the one who we consider the God of our Fathers? Are you the one who intervened with the Ten Plagues[1] and guided the Jewish people through the desert?

Gaia: [Turns to look at Linda.] My consciousness is the sum of the consciousness of every living thing on the planet, not just humans. I am not a guiding force; I am a reactive force. I respond to everything that happens on the planet. I do not dictate what happens to the planet. [Pauses to consider, sighs.] However, in moments of despair, I have lashed out. There are events that occur that might not have. There are events whose severity might be altered. But I am not the creator of things. In fact, I am created by things. I exist because my children exist. [Opens her hands.] If life on this world were to end, *so would I.*

The plagues are a natural occurrence that clever people wrote into a book and used as an example of what their God was capable of doing. If you look at the plagues and the order in which they occur, one event triggers the first plague. The result of that plague triggers the second. It was a natural occurrence of events, and these humans said, "We can take advantage of that, and use it as a lesson." Many of the things written into the Bible are natural events that were taken and written as examples of God or God's wrath. [Emphasizes with a pointed finger.]

However, ancient religions and ancient mythologies have done the same thing. The Greeks had the God of the sun,[2]

---

1. In the Old Testament, the Israelites escaped Egyptian oppression when God sent a series of plagues that caused the Pharaoh to release them from slavery.
2. Helios was the Titan God of the sun, while Apollo was the Olympian God of the sun. Apollo was also the Roman God of the sun.

and the God of the sea,[3] and the God of the land,[4] and the God of the underworld.[5] Anything that humans could not understand why it occurred was attributed to a God. There are many religions on Earth today . . . many polytheistic religions . . . that still attribute things to Gods. They're not completely wrong.

There are spirits that are non-physical . . . I wonder if you could define me as non-physical, as I am the spirit of a planet? But there are spirits who are non-physical that do interact and interject at critical moments, critical times. In some way, you could call them Gods. They are immortal, but they're not the all-knowing, all-powerful beings that are attributed to a God in a monotheistic religion. Taken as a whole, you could call the Collective group a God.

But still, creation is an accident, not an act of design. Creation comes about through a random, spontaneous event or through a process of evolution. But things are the way they are simply because they are. On other worlds, things probably come up in different ways. You have talked to spirits of the Collective who can speak to that better than I can. [Speaks to Lois.] My knowledge is limited to this world.

Linda: Thank you.

Lois: Our time is getting close. Are there any last questions we would ask of Gaia?

Denise: Are there any products or things that we use in our daily life that are harming you that you don't want us to use? Should we avoid anything specifically, or are there things that we can do to help you heal faster?

---

3. Oceanus was the Titan God of the ocean, while Poseidon was the Olympian God of the sea.
4. Gaia was the primordial deity that personifies Mother Earth. There was no single Olympian counterpart, but Demeter and Hestia come closest.
5. Hades was the Olympian God of the underworld. Tartarus and Styx represented the deepest, darkest part of the underworld and the River Styx, respectively.

Gaia: The littering of the surface of the world with *stuff* that doesn't go away for a long period of time impacts you more than it does me. The things that hurt me are the things that alter my very existence. The stuff on the surface is not an issue, but mercury and lead, and all of the horrible chemicals . . . they do leave a permanent scar. Although, eventually, I will process them and break them down and clean them up. My energy would be better spent elsewhere. As I mentioned before, the overuse of chemicals and fertilizers and genetic modifications, those are things I have more difficulty cleaning up. But remember, my consciousness is the sum of everyone else's. Everything I do is to help the life on the planet because I *am* the life of the planet. It would just simply be helpful to stop polluting. I can only clean up just so much, just so fast. Humans need to take a part in that cleanup. But, more importantly, they need to take a part in reducing the rate at which they do these things.

Take the rainforests, for example. I can bring them back to what they were provided humans leave them alone, but once they are destroyed, they're gone forever. There's no possibility of ever bringing them back because it's too interdependent. Humans don't realize that . . . the rainforests are a very delicately balanced organism unto itself and removing large chunks of it to make farmland won't work, because the ground in which rainforests live is not particularly fertile ground. It is ideally suited to the rainforest, but it is not suited to the growing of a single crop. And when the soil becomes depleted, the rainforest is gone. Adding chemicals will increase the productivity for some period of time, but ultimately will cause more damage than it started.

There is no one product. It's a matter of trying to live more naturally. That doesn't mean that you have to give up anything that you have. It just means that you should *use things in moderation.* Eating animals is okay, but fishing to the point of extinction is self-defeating and self-destructive. It only ever requires a little bit of care. Humans pride themselves on being so intelligent. Apply that intelligence . . . apply that reasoning to these very simple things. No major changes are required. A small change here, a small change there, and that's all it takes. When things start to get better, and people start to realize that these changes do have an effect, they'll be more willing to make more changes.

Denise: Thank you.

Lois: We appreciate you taking this time with us. Is there any last advice you have for us?

Gaia: All species with any level of intelligence and awareness have first and foremost a survival instinct. In most species, the instinct to survive is stronger than the instinct to even reproduce. There are exceptions, but humans simply don't think of their actions as ultimately going to harm them. They think that I am so large that I can absorb anything they do, and large as I am, that's not the case. There is a point at which I will not be able to protect them anymore. They just don't realize the consequences of their actions. The more care you take of me, the more care I will be able to take of you.

Lois: We understand.

Gaia: Use that to appeal to people's self-interests, since that seems to be what drives them. *By destroying me, they are only destroying themselves.*

Lois: Absolutely. Thank you, Gaia. We will each do our best to personally make a difference. And we will do our best to get your word out to others, and hopefully touch others' hearts.

Gaia: [Smiles, speaks very softly.] Thank you.

Lois: Thank you. We honor you.

I gently guide the spirit of Gary to reenter his body. I have him step into his aura, his energy field, by slowly and gently breathing himself back into full awareness. I asked the clearing consultants to check on his energy to be sure he was completely integrated. They replied that his energy was good.

Gary returned slowly and gently without any emotional reaction this time. He expressed feeling a little stiff, like in the sessions with the Anquietas. There was definitely a lot of energy coming through him, although he did not remember anything. He explained that sometimes there was an instant of overlap, as if whomever was coming through was reading his mind. There was not so much overlap this time, and he felt as if Gaia was gone before he came back. The consultants agreed that he lay completely limp for a brief moment before coming back to full awareness.

Reflection

As this was the first group setting for these sessions, to stay organized I prepared representative questions from those in attendance. I requested that the observers wait until the end for any additional questions they might have. Our intention was to ask for Gaia to speak with us. Since the Earth at this time was mostly devoid of storms, hurricanes, or other tempestuous activity, we had hoped this would be a good time to communicate with Gaia and that she would grant us an audience.

A few months before this session, when Hurricane Irma, a Category 5 storm, was headed straight for Miami with full force, Paul and I worked together to communicate with Gaia. At that time, we found her to be plenty angry. Paul was able to sense her energy, translating to me what he felt. This was different than Gaia's direct communication with me through Gary as a channel. At the time, many others were praying for her to shift course and lessen her fury. Paul and I implored Gaia to redirect the storm to sea or to another area that would be less damaging to vast numbers of people. Offering no guarantees, she said she would attempt to do something. We were amazed that within hours, the storm miraculously redirected its course to travel up the Gulf side of Florida, where it made landfall at a much lower intensity in an area that was less populated. Since we had experienced Gaia at a time of intense wrath, we were grateful to speak with her at this much calmer time.

Gaia was surprisingly quiet and gentle, yet strong and succinct in her demeanor. She didn't seem to struggle or hesitate with her words the way others of the Collective had. She spoke fluidly and confidently throughout the discussion. Although there were other people in the room, she rarely moved her head, with her attention focused solely on me during most of the conversation. She remained near motionless in the chair, expressing herself with a few movements of her hands. Even though this session was almost an hour in length, she held her energy strong until the end.

Although Gaia acknowledged there are humans who care and

want to make a difference, her attitude seemed to be one of annoyance, almost with a tone of resignation. Many times, she seemed to be admonishing people for their carelessness and neglect. I truly felt sorry for what humans had done, yet I experienced Gaia's presence as an incredibly powerful being who was intensely serious and a force to be reckoned with. The clearing consultants agreed that Gaia's energy was definitely one they had never experienced before and were impressed with what they saw and heard both physically and metaphysically. Linda was intrigued by the information from the session, and Denise stated it was one of the highlights of her life.

Gaia described herself as the sum of all consciousness on the planet. All living things are part of her; she is the life of the planet. As such, she feels and expresses what all other living creatures are feeling, from plants and animals to humans. She is the life force that lives in and around all of nature. We are all interconnected through her in a web of living energy. It was interesting that she does not consider herself to be a creative force, but rather a reactive force, responding to and reacting to the energy of her charges. When we pray in gratitude to Mother Nature, she senses it as we would when someone thanks us for something we have done. When we do something harmful to another, she feels that negative energy as well. I can relate this to coming home from a hard day's work to find your teenager has eaten you out of house and home, made a mess of the place, and is lounging on the couch watching TV, asking what's for supper. Relate this to those who are ungrateful and show disrespect for our homes, our families, and our lives. There are moments when Gaia gets angry with her humans, and justifiably so.

Gaia describes humans as being among the most intelligent beings on Earth, but also the most self-serving, often without consideration for the consequences of their actions. Many people come from a place of entitlement, so focused on themselves they rarely stop to notice how their choices and actions affect every living thing around them in a variety of unseen ways. It is a ripple effect. What one does affects another. Like a small wave from a pebble tossed into a pond, it eventually reaches across a wide expanse. When we come to understand that every action we take has consequences beyond our comprehension, and when we take inventory of our behaviors and make small changes, we will make a difference in our ultimate outcome.

Gaia was most concerned about the indifference of those who are thoughtless and self-serving, saying the lack of care or respect for our planet will be our own undoing. We had wondered if the devastation of Earth that others of the Collective had foretold would come through nuclear war or another catastrophe. We were surprised to discover that our own neglect could cause such extreme damage in a relatively short time. The fact that many people are not worried about the future for their own children is cause for alarm. This self-serving attitude contributes to separation, greed, and destruction. When we feel what we do matters for each other, we will come from a place of *what can I do to help* instead of *what's in it for me.*

The Iroquois culture embraces the concept of "Seventh Generation Principle," which urges the current generation to live and work for the benefit of the seventh generation into the future (approximately 140 years from the present). This Great Law urges people to consider whether the decisions they make today will benefit their children seven generations into the future. The modern concept of environmental stewardship or sustainability applies this practice toward conscientious decision-making for the benefit of our future.

Many teachings of native cultures are passed orally from generation to generation through stories and memories of tribal elders. The Ojibwe culture shares the story of the Seven Grandfather Teachings, a moral code of principles that guides their people with moral respect for all living things. The Seven Grandfathers are: humility, bravery, honesty, wisdom, truth, respect, and love. These teachings have also been adopted as a way of life among other cultures coast to coast. The similarity between these foundational principles and the Collective's messages is remarkable.

As I reflect on this session, it has been two years to the day since we experienced this visit from Gaia: two years of intense preparation and steadfast dedication to sharing these messages with the world in numerous ways. The coincidental timing of this chapter is astounding.

It is March 2020 and we are in the midst of a global pandemic caused by COVID-19. This minuscule killer virus is clearly demonstrating how interconnected humans are across all cultures, nationalities, and ethnicities worldwide. We have been brought to our knees by devastating sickness and halting economies. Humanity is becoming acutely aware of our commonality and vulnerability in a way that humans have never experienced in modern history.

Yes, people have lived through plagues, war, genocides, terrorism, hurricanes, fires, earthquakes, and more. All are tragedies that affect some people more directly than others. In this time of international connectedness, this microscopic virus has traversed the planet, disturbing individuals, families, communities, and countries on a worldwide scale, which is unprecedented. Even world wars were fought among certain nations, while others went about their normal daily lives. Yes, uninvolved nations experienced indirect impact and inconvenience. However, this viral bug is negatively impacting the life of every living human on the planet in some way and does not discriminate.

Gaia wishes humans could slow down the damage we are doing to our planet and become more thoughtful of our actions. She says one solution to stop people who are misusing resources for profit is to stop purchasing their goods. Cutting into their profit will cause them to change their practices. When we support those who are caring, we shift the energy to the positive and others will follow suit. As we shift from greed to conscientiousness, we allow Gaia to heal the wounds that have been inflicted on our Earth.

During the COVID-19 pandemic, our world economy has also taken a severe blow, with implications yet to be seen. Travel, events, restaurants, educational institutions, small businesses, and large corporations have been shut down due to this virus. It certainly seems as though Gaia is doing what she can to interfere with our routines and way of life so we will take notice. As we are pushed into making new choices, will these be of benefit for self or others?

As a result of people being forced into quarantine to avoid contact, blocking the spread of disease, we are already noticing shifts in nature. China was the first country affected by the virus, with thousands of deaths, exponential numbers of people still affected, and many still recovering as of this writing. Factories were closed and entire communities were ordered to shelter-in-place. The lack of pollution from several weeks' duration of this massive shutdown has caused a dramatic increase in the air quality of China. In neighboring India, locals are shocked to see the majestic Himalayan Mountains from their villages for the first time in thirty years.

In Italy, thousands are still suffering. While people in entire cities are forced to stay in their homes, businesses are shut down and cars remain parked. Each of these actions is contributing to alleviate pollution. For the first time in decades, animals are returning to their natural habitats. This virus has forced humanity into a brief pause. Gaia says she can heal the damage, we just have to let her do it. This crisis has caused us to observe just how quickly Mother Nature can heal her wounds as humans focus on healing theirs.

Gaia reminds us that we need to be good stewards of this beautiful planet we enjoy. If we take note of how chemicals destroy the quality of the air, land, and sea around us, we can become more cautious about what we are doing to consciously make changes to help instead of hinder. We have improved from the days when factories dumped their poisoned dyes, chemicals, and waste products into our rivers, yet we continue to spread poisonous chemicals on our land to kill bugs and weeds and stimulate crop growth. Though natural methods to accomplish the same goals may take more effort, they will yield healthier results.

The Old Testament of the Bible instructs farmers to let fields lie fallow every seven years. This process allows the soil to replenish itself so the crops will grow more vigorously. In the early 1900s, American farmers grew crops through the summer, harvested in the fall, and allowed the fields to rest in the winter. Now, with larger equipment, increased demand for product, and increased chemical use, farmers grow crops all year long (for example, summer wheat and winter wheat). Chemicals are sprayed to promote growth, eliminate weeds, and eradicate pests.

People wonder why so many are sensitive to gluten. Could it be we are actually reacting to the chemicals used to grow the wheat, barley, or rye? In one generation of change in the cultivation process, many people are reacting with food sensitivities. If this trend continues, in what way will it affect our children and grandchildren?

How is the use of chemicals to beautify our yards and gardens affecting us and our animals? My own cat developed an autoimmune reaction to chemicals used on our lawn. While humans may not actually ingest the chemicals, we do inhale them. Our animals get the residue on their paws and fur, and it is then absorbed into their skin and directly ingested when they groom themselves. Once we stop using these chemicals, our lawns may be less luxurious, but our pets and ourselves will be much healthier.

Gaia tells us genetic tampering is an example of human actions that cause unforeseen consequences. Some products related to genetic modification can produce unknown after-effects, creating great harm to humans over the long term. Could she also be describing vaccines, drugs, and other man-made substances such as biochemical agents, possibly even viruses?

She explains that genetic modification is part of her natural hybridization to stimulate growth and evolution of all species of life on our planet. Genetically-modified foods are created through changes introduced into the DNA of a plant via genetic engineering, as opposed to traditional cross-pollinating. These genetically engineered foods are designed to withstand herbicides and pesticides and increase yields and profits, but they can possibly cause health issues to sensitive consumers. Humans must be mindful of the reason for modifications they are creating and consider the long-term side effects and consequences of their tampering.

We know of the plight of the bees: how they are disappearing and being destroyed by the use of chemicals. These busy pollinators keep our crops, trees, and plant life growing. Without bees, our vegetation will not reproduce. A few years ago, I had a client who was passionate about helping the bees and wanted to communicate with them. While in trance, she spoke with the spirit of a drone bee, who told us the exposure to chemicals throws off their navigation system. They have a hard time finding the plants they need to locate, and chemicals interfere with their ability to return to the hives. In effect, if it doesn't kill them, the toxicity makes them confused, as if inebriated.

She also spoke with the spirit of a queen bee who was very annoyed with humans for several reasons. The queen didn't like the square hives that humans force bees into. The unnatural shape causes much stress in her hive, because it goes against the bees' natural inclination to create round or hexagonal hives. The natural shape allows for succinct communal rhythms and is far more efficient for her drones. The queen was happy to share some of her product with humans. However, her other annoyance was that humans take far more honey than they need, which is detrimental to the survival of her children. Human greed causes her hive to be vulnerable, as her bees require the honey as a source of food for the winter. It also provides necessary insulation against cooler weather. This was one of my more fascinating sessions and a testimony to how we can connect with all life on our wonderful planet, if only we listen and take heed.

Nature contains cycles of life. Most animals graze and move on, given the freedom to do so. Plants grow and die in natural rhythms and cycles. Sometimes fire is necessary to open certain seeds and clear the path for new growth. The fires die out through a natural process, and balance resumes. When humans interfere out of supposed wisdom or a desire for profit, it is often to the detriment of plant and animal life.

In the tropical islands of Hawaii, early seafarers inadvertently introduced rats that were aboard their ships. Since there are no snakes on these islands, the rats proliferated without any natural predators. Later, settlers introduced the mongoose to control the rat population, without considering that rats are nocturnal and the mongoose is not. So the mongoose fed on exotic bird eggs, leaving the islands devoid of their majestically colorful birds. Meanwhile, the rats continued to breed, as did the mongoose. In an attempt to control the growing mongoose population, a parasitic insect has now been introduced. Who knows where that will lead? People must truly understand the interconnectedness of life on our planet and how each different location is unique unto itself. One action affects outcomes in ways we must pay attention to.

In the early 1900s, gray wolves were deliberately eradicated from Yellowstone National Park,[6] resulting in a lack of natural predators for the elk, who then overpopulated and overgrazed the land. This ecological imbalance resulted in unforeseen destruction of the park's natural environment of trees and vegetation caused massive decline in small animals and birds, which created significant land erosion. Once wolves were systematically reintroduced in 1995, nature balanced herself, plants regrew, animals returned, and the ecosystem was restored.

These are a few examples of what Gaia tells us about how human interference affects the interconnectedness of nature. She can heal the land, if only we let her do what she has done to help the planet thrive for millennia. Clearing the rainforest for farming is another example of human indifference. On a global scale, we need the oxygen balance that the precious trees of the rainforest share with us. Gaia tells us specifically that soil in the forest is not meant to grow crops; it is intended to grow trees. Forcing a different use is detrimental to the soil, to the animals, and to humans as well. Humans' interference with nature has caused massive wildfires that are detrimental to all living things. We need to learn from these examples.

We are encouraged to use mindful consideration and to practice moderation instead of excess. Gaia is fine with us consuming animals, as long as we use all parts of the animal for benefit. Indigenous cultures have long honored animals, treating them with dignity and respect. Let's extend this to today's culture, and when it is necessary to take an animal's life, let's thank the animal, bless it, and treat it with reverence. Plants should be treated in the same manner. Native people share tobacco as an offering to Mother Earth when plants are harvested for food. Indigenous people demonstrate a natural sense of exchange and appreciation and are more aware of and sensitive to the energy of Gaia and all the abundance she offers.

---

6. Yellowstone National Park is an American national park located in parts of the western states of Wyoming, Montana, and Idaho.

In recent years, our international shipping practices have allowed us to have routine access to foods grown around the world. This is both a pleasure and a problem. In the past, we usually had access only to locally grown fruits and vegetables. Some food, like the pineapple, was considered extravagant in some regions, since it was available in limited quantities only at certain times of the year.

Natural health experts explain that food grown in the area we live in gives us exactly the nutrients we need to sustain ourselves in that season. Eating locally grown food gives us improved health and fortifies us for regional weather where we live. For instance, spinach is grown in the spring and helps to dry up dampness in our bodies from exposure to wet weather. Tomatoes are grown in the summer, providing needed moisture when we are dry. Squash and apples are prolific in the fall, giving us needed nutrients to sustain our health through winter months. The more seasonal and locally grown food we eat, the healthier our bodies will be. Shopping local is not only good for local growers but has major health benefits to consumers.

Gaia gives us an interesting history lesson on the formation of the continents and ocean currents, and how they affect glacial changes. She reminds us that we have been spoiled by growing up in a time of easy climate in a paradise-like land. We would have never survived the harsh weather at the time of dinosaurs.

Today, the climate is in a natural evolutionary process. We should take notice and do what we can to prepare for inevitable changes without pointing fingers of blame. We are going through a time of ice melting that will cause coastlines to change, yet our fertile lands will survive. The pollution we are introducing could actually cause a global freezing, resulting in a potential ice age. The actions we take affect our outcome. As good stewards of this land we are blessed to live in and on, we are responsible for what happens now and in the future.

If we take notice and do what's right, our future can be one of wonder, health, and peace. Or, if we continue with indifference and neglect, our future will be a slow bleed into barrenness, like a cancer eating away at our life. Unlike Atlantis, which experienced immediate annihilation when its people ignored the warnings, if we ignore the warnings of Gaia and the Collective, our destruction will progress over a long term. The difference is akin to dying quickly of a heart attack versus a slow, painful death through cancer or debilitating stroke.

The recent, unprecedented number of storms, fires, earthquakes, tornadoes, hurricanes, volcanoes, and global viruses are all symptoms of our Earth being out of balance. Although these are naturally occurring events, in recent years their frequency and intensity have accelerated disproportionately. Are these signs that the destruction of the world is coming faster? Gaia paints with a broad brush via localized catastrophes to get us to wake up, to take notice of what we can do to help her and each other.

In contrast, COVID-19 has caused a huge global shakeup. Was it natural? Was it caused by genetic tampering? Was it leaked to the public intentionally? Was it an accident? It is curious to consider. Regardless, the awareness created by this microscopic contagion right now is an important wake-up call to all of humanity. As I write the final chapter of this book, the timing is exceptionally applicable. If we pay attention and change our actions, our behaviors, and our attitudes, we can alter our current course to improve our ultimate outcome.

Many people are doing wonderful things to help the planet and need our encouragement to support their efforts. Yes, we need to stop using artificial products because they fill our lands with synthetic waste that does not break down and causes damage to animals that get caught in or ingest them. A machine to scoop the plastic from beaches has been invented; other organizations help remove tons of waste from our oceans. Did you know people have repurposed floating islands of discarded fishing nets to create strong carpets? When we alter our use of chemicals and discover how to use natural remedies to maintain balance, we can help Gaia to heal. As we develop methods to reuse our waste products in helpful ways, we all benefit.

Gaia is the life of our planet, the consciousness of every living thing. So let's step up and care for her and each other, as we are called to do. Although humans may be among those species with the largest brain, we are not necessarily the most intelligent species in the Universe. However, we have the awareness to know right from wrong, good from bad, and beneficial from detrimental. Our attitudes are what are most important.

Just as no two flowers are alike, no two snowflakes are alike, no two sunsets are alike, and no two humans are alike. We are each unique, with different skills, gifts, and talents. When we use our blessings for the benefit of mankind, we weave our thread into the fabric of humanity, we add our piece to the web of life, and we will make a difference.

How we handle our life experiences is most meaningful. When we come from a place of acceptance, togetherness, hope, and peace, the vibrational energy around us increases. The higher we vibrate, the more we are able to connect with and receive insight, knowing, and understanding from higher sources of wisdom. Then, communicating with our wise spiritual mind, Mother Gaia, and other Wise Ones of the Collective will become second nature, our sixth sense. If we individually and cumulatively raise our vibrational energy by being one with each other and all of nature, everything in and around our planet will thrive. What can you do to raise your energy to make even a small difference? As I told Gaia at the end of this captivating session, I promise to do my part.

"Humankind has not woven the web of life.
We are but one thread within it.
Whatever we do to the web, we do to ourselves.
All things are bound together.
All things connect.

All things share the same breath
The beast, the tree, the man.
The air shares its spirit with all the life it supports."
—Chief Seattle, Suquamish and Duwamish

Closing Thoughts

"The message is important, and you do have to get it out there,
and you have to get it out quickly.
Humanity doesn't realize how little time it has left."

—Aurora

Creating this *Chronicles of Hope* series has been an unprecedented learning journey for me, and I'm not done yet. The sense of urgency expressed by the Wise Ones of the Collective has caused me to put my personal life on hold. I have been driven to develop clarification of the conversations with personal insights to explain their messages for you. Although these ideas are not necessarily new, they are intended to reinforce what many people already know. These concepts are catalysts to help us remember who we are and why we are here. Their directives cause us to pause, reflect, and redirect our lives accordingly, for our highest good.

Incorporating the teachings from these Wise Ones has stimulated tremendous growth in my spiritual awareness, both personally and professionally. Integrating their sage advice into my daily life has given me the strength to navigate storms of intense negativity, while allowing me to bask in the sunshine of positive experiences. My client sessions have been more healing and fulfilling with the incredible assistance of the Collective and their teachings.

Personally, I have had extreme highs and lows on this path of bringing these messages to the world. Coming from a place of truth, honesty, and integrity has been particularly helpful to handle challenging people and difficult situations with resilience, faith, and hope. I have learned to trust the nudges from my spiritual muses as they awaken me in the middle of the night to capture their insightful messages. I can now fully sense their presence and feel their powerful encouragement in my daily life. I feel incredibly blessed, protected, and supported by them.

Incredible learning has happened for me by experiencing these amazing live sessions and through the writing and development of this book series. As I re-listened to the recordings and analyzed the words, I came to better know their meanings. It has been a process over time. No doubt, there will be more learning to come.

First, applying the principle that anger comes from deep in the troubled hearts of people affected by negative energy helped me to rise above a myriad of challenges. In trying times, I seriously considered giving up. However, I have been able to come from a place of understanding, often in a position to avoid taking situations personally. I learned to have patience with myself and others as I consistently asked for guidance from the Collective. Ultimately, I came to trust that everything works out for the highest good of all. Staying true to the Collective's insightful messages that resonate in my heart was ever the driving force behind my motivation to persist in spite of numerous odds.

At the same time, I am intrigued, in awe, and elated by the incredible members of Team Hope who steadfastly joined me on this journey. Many talented people have willingly taken the baton for stretches of this race. Countless circumstances that aligned to make it all possible can only be described as magical, if not miraculous. Navigating an often challenging road, I deeply appreciate those who have held me up, encouraged, and supported me.

Our dear clearing consultant team has gone above and beyond to keep my energy and that of all members of Team Hope cleared, strengthened, and protected. We experienced numerous negative encounters we have had to rise above. We also received incredible personal messages for direction and positive encouragement. I am ever grateful for their gifts, time, dedication, and friendship. I could have never gone so far down this uncharted path without their steadfast support.

The amazing editorial team has been with me through the

writing of both Book 1 and Book 2. Working with me each word of the way, they made sure what I wanted to say was captured with clarity, eloquence, and professionalism. They encouraged me to delve into the depths of my heart to write of my personal experiences so you may gain further insight into the messages. My ever-vigilant Team Hope reviewers offered insightful suggestions and asked questions on concepts that needed clearer explanation. As the reader, you have unknowingly gained much clarity from their involvement and gift of curiosity.

Keeping me on schedule through the process was my heartfelt publishing team, who provided valuable support and encouragement. Their guidance, along with our public relations team, led to a five-star rating from *Readers Favorite* and other amazing reviews for Book 1. I am also deeply grateful for the sincere testimonials from so many peers and professionals who took time to share their comments on both books.

The marketing team helped create a remarkably robust website, along with numerous supporting materials, and assisted in establishing an online media presence for the delivery of the messages to you. Another amazingly gifted team created the incredible audiobooks. As you listen, you truly feel as if you are secretly eavesdropping on the sessions as they unfolded, experiencing the conversations in an extremely personal way.

Team Hope established an online Inspiring Hope Community discussion group to support ourselves and others on this journey as we delve into the meaning of the messages. We meet remotely on a regular basis, sharing and learning new ways to apply the teachings in our everyday lives. All are welcome to join us as catalysts for positive change, individually and collectively.

Because of Jesus' message to speak the compliment out loud and amplify the voices of the good people, I started the good news radio show *Inspiring Hope with Lois Hermann.* I love shining light on many uplifting people who are making a positive difference in their own way.

Based on what I've learned about energy clearing over the years, compounded with insights from the Collective, I'm excited to have launched a didactic "Energy Clearing & Alignment" training program.

This online training is designed to help hypnotists, therapists, and mediums learn ways to readily clear negative energy from around themselves and their clients. If you know someone who may be interested, please let us know. We are open to doing whatever is necessary to raise the vibrational energy of humanity and bring the message of hope. We welcome your suggestions in our mission.

Finally, we have only started on this path to spread the enlightening messages of the Collective. I am ever dedicated to my commitment to the incredible Wise Ones, and am ever grateful to each of you, our readers, for your support. I hope you find these insights valuable for your own path toward enlightenment and that you will join the effort to share these messages any way you can. Thank you for joining me in helping to collectively shift humanity to be more positive. All will benefit from a world that is lighter, brighter, and healthier. Ultimately, we strive for our Mother Gaia's happiness, and all who dwell on her to live in peace as one civilization, our humanity.

Many Blessings,
Lois Hermann
Nashua, New Hampshire, USA

April 22, 2020 [4/22/20 = 4/4/4]
*In number sequences 444 means angels are around us.

> *"I alone cannot change the world.*
> *But I can cast a stone across the waters to create many ripples."*
> —Mother Teresa

"When it is from Divine intervention, it is willed to be heard.
It is necessary at this time for this information to be shared.
I am so proud of you for taking this journey, baby steps at a time,
in between the leaps of faith, to bring it into fruition.
It is very important, and this is the time.
The people involved in Team Hope,
it is part of their purpose, here and now.
This is what we are here for.
I could not give a lot of time directly into the process,
but I sure put a whole lot of prayer into it.
I honor every single person I have met who is connected to Team Hope.
They are exemplary humans walking on this planet,
fulfilling their spiritual quest
and being brought together through the creation of this series.
Part of their purpose of being here
is to give what they have that needs to be given.
Consider each person perhaps to be an instrument in the orchestra,
and you (Lois) are the conductor that has managed to bring it into form."

—Grandmother Blue Crow
Northern Cheyenne

Chronicles of Hope
The Archangels: Book 3

"The best thing you can do is to bring back
the beliefs of the Native Americans."
—Archangel Michael

Chronicles of Hope shares messages from the Collective in a three-book series. This tome has been designed such that the unique sessions with the High-Level Spirits who spoke with us are arranged into segments most meaningful and helpful for you. Sharing their insights over time allows you to digest the information more completely. You have the opportunity to practice integrating their advice and guidance into your life.

Coming next, in Book 3 you will hear from several Archangels with whom many spiritually-aware people communicate with regularly. These powerful Archangels have long been dedicated to assisting humanity in their many roles throughout the millennium.

Our beloved Archangel Michael, the great protector, is ever with me and my clearing consultant team on a regular basis to assist in our clearing sessions. He reveals even more secrets to facilitate clearing our Earth of negative energy and gives specific information to help keep your own energy clear and strong.

As the Archangel of transitions, Archangel Azrael emphasizes the importance of helping those near death come to a place of reconciliation in their lives, so they transition peacefully into the afterlife. He offers information on how humans can live more fully to enhance their ultimate transition toward enlightenment.

We again encounter Archangel Samael, but this time in the presence of several members of Team Hope who have their own questions. Samael provides answers and gives insight for managing challenge in the days to come. He also explains the nature of the energy involved in our names and tells us that parents are whispered the name of their child while the fetus is forming.

The incredible healer Archangel Raphael shares powerful insight on what we can do to heal our body, mind, emotions, and spirit on the journey to living a good and healthy life. He assures us we are all capable of healing ourselves, if we simply take the time to slow down and nurture ourselves more readily.

I am excited to bring this work to help you gain even greater insight into your life journey and communing with the great unseen. I look forward to passing on more wisdom from the Archangels that promises continued guidance for the next phase of your discovery voyage.

"Be content with what you have, rejoice in the way things are.
When you realize there is nothing lacking,
the whole world belongs to you."

—Lao Tzu

Chronicles of Hope: The Collective

Resources

Lakota Instructions for Living

Friend do it this way – that is, whatever you do in life,
do the very best you can with both your heart and mind.
And if you do it that way, the Power of the Universe
will come to your assistance
if your heart and mind are in Unity.

When one sits in the Hoop of the People,
one must be responsible because All of Creation is related.
And the hurt of one is the hurt of all.
And the honor of one is the honor of all.
And whatever we do effects everything in the universe.

If you do it that way – that is,
if you truly join your heart and mind as One,
whatever you ask for, that is the Way It's Going To Be.
— passed down from White Buffalo Calf Woman

Roadmap for Hope

"You have been granted audiences with the oldest spirits within me.
Listen to those words and pass them on.
Take them into your own heart and try to get others to do the same."
—Spirit of the Universe

The Anquietas tells us, "If you want to put the world in a positive, healing place, remember this: the act of wanting something generates a feeling of want, which is negative, adding to the problem. Believe positively that things are better or are on the road to improvement. This thinking creates positive energy. There is a difference between wanting, believing, and knowing. Knowing is the best, the strongest. Knowing how the world should be generates the strongest positive force. Do uplifting activities, simple things that create joy in your life, and think positive, grateful, and hopeful thoughts while doing them."

1. Honor our Earth—connect with nature.

2. Care for the body—make healthy choices.

3. Create with joy—do uplifting things.

4. Raise vibrational energy—smile and laugh.

5. Know that there is plenty—share what you can.

6. Respect each other—make personal connections.

7. Ask for assistance—reach for the Light.

8. Live with gratitude—appreciate what is.

Roadmaps have multiple sideroads you may take toward your destination. On the spiritual path, detours provide new vistas, awaken your awareness, and can elevate your consciousness.

"Be kind, for whenever kindness becomes part of something, it beautifies it."
—Muhammad

Guidelines for Living

"Gaia is the spirit of this planet and cares for all of you.
In some sense you are all her children."

—Jesus

Recurring themes throughout the *Chronicles of Hope* series:

1. Collective: High-level spirits who represent the collective energy of God.

2. Gaia: Spirit of our Earth, who is respected for providing everything we need.

3. Humanity: Civilization of man that is all one and interconnected with each other.

4. Vibrational Energy: Energy humans must shift to the positive for higher consciousness.

Essential practices to increase our vibrational energy:

1. Be respectful—encourage truth, honesty, and integrity. (Rae)

2. Be loving—choose kindness, compassion, and humility. (Jesus)

3. Be peaceful—embrace forgiveness, harmony, and wisdom. (Aurora)

4. Be strong—establish discernment, discipline, and protection. (Samael)

5. Be inspiring—share empathy, connection, and oneness with all. (Universe)

6. Be helpful—cultivate mindfulness, conscientiousness, and stewardship. (Gaia)

7. Be prayerful—practice asking, believing, and receiving with gratitude. (Collective)

8. Be grateful—express appreciation, acknowledgment, and share hope. (Anquietas)

Some specific steps to assist our Mother Gaia:

1. Honor all living things, everything.

2. Show respect for nature.

3. Use all parts of animals.

4. Conserve and reduce.

5. Limit chemical use.

6. Recycle and reuse.

7. Nurture our land.

8. Offer gratitude.

As we learn to embrace these essential guidelines and live our lives with intention, we can, will, and shall create a healthy, thriving civilization. We will begin to establish a foundation of hope for our future, our children's future, and our children's children's future.

"Alone we can do so little; together we can do so much."
—Helen Keller

Protective Bubble

"Ask for Protection, Healing, and Empowerment across all levels:
Physical, Mental, Emotional, Spiritual, Psychic, Social,
Professional, Financial, Relational, Environmental, and Technological.
That all beings come together as one for humanity."
—Archangel Michael

The best way to protect your energy is to create a protective bubble around yourself. Imagine yourself surrounded by a dynamic shield, one that is malleable and consistently replenishes itself.

1. Close your eyes and imagine, visualize, or think about your aura, the energy field in and around your body.

2. Imagine standing in a magical waterfall of rainbow light. Allow it to surround and fill you with any colors of light your body needs. Completely fill with positive energy.

3. Place a glowing ball of light inside you, wherever it feels Right. Allow this ball of light fill your entire being.

4. Create a dynamic shield on the outer surface of your aura, about three feet from your body. This thick-walled malleable bubble of light moves with you and expands as needed.

5. Fill this protective bubble with a warm, calming, and comforting fluid-like light.

6. Place a shiny coating over your aura, like a soap bubble, a silvery sheen, or reflective mirror to deflect anything negative.

7. You can place a high-pitched hum on the surface of your protective bubble to distract any low vibrational energies.

8. Imagine a violet flame surrounding your aura, enfolding you in a soft glowing light of protection.

Practice this spiritual self-care to keep your energy protected.

"I am peace, joy, and love . . . I rest in God."
—A Course In Miracles

Sacred Space

*"To make this world a better place,
find a way to emphasize the positive."*

—Rae

To receive messages from higher sources of wisdom, we are advised to clear our energy and raise our vibration. There are many ways to do this. Go outside to commune with nature; listen to music; be creative; change your thoughts, your clothes, or your environment. Analyze what is going on in your life and plan what you can do to make small changes. What are you feeding yourself: physically, mentally, emotionally, and spiritually? Are you making healthy choices? Reach out to a trusted friend to uplift you, be it a person, pet, or high-level spiritual being. Pray for guidance. Ask, believe, receive, and be grateful. If you are experiencing intense negativity, please reach out to a professional. Be sure to practice the Protective Bubble exercise daily.

We are advised to keep our space clear, protected, and sacred, whether at home, work, or when together in groups. Many use drumming, chanting, singing, smudging, dowsing, or praying to create sacred space. Here is one way to prepare your space whenever you gather.

1. Ask for protection, healing, and empowerment across all levels.

2. Imagine four columns of golden-white Light in the corners of your space.

3. Invite Divine Guides and masculine Light energies into the corners for protection.

4. Imagine walls of Light connecting the columns with a dome of Light over and under.

5. Fill the entire space with a stream of pure Light connecting Father Sky to Mother Earth.

6. Invite sacred feminine energy into the center of the space for intuitive, loving guidance.

7. Invoke the sacred violet flame to surround the space, removing any negative energy.

8. Thank the Collective for assisting with infinite guidance, wisdom, and protection.

9. Ask to lend courage, strength, and faith to speak with love and compassion.

10. Set the intention that this gathering be for the highest good of all.

When you begin every gathering by creating sacred space, you will feel the energy shift to be more uplifted, protected, and energized. Invite those of the Collective you wish to be present in your Sacred Space: Archangels, Guides, and Divine Energies of the Light. Adapt this process to fit your needs, beliefs, or culture. The intention can be different for each gathering, be it healing, strength, courage, clarity, or understanding. Ask for a higher, wiser perspective on the situation to assist with guidance for any question or challenge. Always end with heartfelt gratitude.

> *"Begin to see yourself as a soul with a body*
> *rather than a body with a soul."*
> —Wayne Dyer, PhD

Jesus' Top 40

*"People need to love each other.
It is a matter of simple compassion."*
—Jesus

Many profound messages and deep insights came through our communication with Jesus. He reminds us to stay true to his teachings, which have not changed in two thousand years. Jesus wants us to take these reminders into our hearts, reflect on them in our own way, and make our lives emulate them. Ask Jesus for help, and he will always be there.

1. First, do no harm.

2. Do unto others as you would have others do unto you.

3. Love each other. It is just a matter of simple compassion.

4. Do what you think is right.

5. It is not so much what you say; it is the belief in what you say that matters.

6. There is a reason why honesty has always been a most valued quality.

7. Gaia is the spirit of Earth and cares for all. We are all her children.

8. Gaia provides well for her children. There is no real scarcity on Earth.

9. There is no one, all-knowing, all-seeing, all-powerful being watching everything that everyone does.

10. There is no one judging everything you do. The only judge you ever have to face is yourself.

11. The only person you have to be better than is the person you are today.

12. Believe in yourself. You make reality exist.

13. My resurrection was one of spirit.

14. I can be anywhere, anytime, because I have no physical body to limit myself.

15. An "aura" is the result of the spiritual part of the body that resides without.

16. For every disease, there is a cure. For every individual, the cure is unique.

17. The Collective cannot predict the future. They see trends and probabilities. They don't know with certainty what will happen.

18. The Collective doesn't steer humanity one way or another because they don't know with absolute certainty which path ultimately will be best.

19. It is much more about the intent than anything else. All anyone can ever do is the best that they can do. If you intend no harm, you cannot do the wrong thing.

20. You will make mistakes. Don't let the fear of making a mistake stop you from doing what you believe is right.

21. If someone has picked up a bad habit, you can't give them a good habit. You have to get rid of the bad one first.

22. Even if the specific memories of past lives are not readily accessible, the ability to realize that there is more comes from having experienced more.

23. There is no external reward and punishment. There is no vengeful God. There is no devil.

24. You may deceive yourself in your corporeal existence into thinking that you've had such a wonderful life. When that life ends and your spirit reflects, it will see with much greater clarity what happened in your life.

25. The voices of the people who do more good than harm don't seem to attract the attention of the people in the middle. The

voices of the people who do more harm than good seem to be heard more clearly.

26. You need to make known the voice of the people who do good. They need to be heard.

27. Speak the compliment aloud. It is important to let people know when they have done well.

28. A system based entirely on punishment without reward can never work. Whenever you must say something to somebody to correct an action, try if you can to compliment them on a positive action at the same time.

29. So many deaths have been justified in the name of a God that doesn't even exist.

30. If humans need to pray to something more powerful than themselves, let that be Gaia. Gaia is more real and more powerful than one "imaginary" God.

31. Many religions on Earth have been and are connected with nature.

32. Some successful civilizations understand the existence of non-physical beings and beings greater than themselves without having to resort to calling them Gods, without attributing totally natural events to them.

33. Humanity is a single species. We are all the same.

34. Nothing remains the same. When you stagnate, you perish.

35. Difference and divergence are necessary for health and strength.

36. We are not alone in the Universe; there is something greater than ourselves.

37. The message has to be delivered in a way that humanity understands and in a way that they will accept.

38. It is the desire to enforce what you believe on someone else that generates the conflict.

39. There will always be people who believe, people who don't, and people who don't care.

40. I will always be here when you need me. I am never far away.

"Your task is not to seek for love,
but merely to seek and find all the barriers within yourself
that you have built against it."

—Rumi

Highlights

Highlights

"Starting a trend that is beneficial is worth doing,
even if the results are not obvious until several generations later."
—Gaia

These Highlights are a recap of the Conversation sessions in Book 2. They are organized by session and topics within each one. Some of the Highlights are paraphrased for clarity. Highlights that are in quotation marks are direct quotes from the Spirit who spoke them. These excerpts serve as a high-level review and easy reference, supporting the concepts shared in each session. We encourage you to use them as learning tools, and they can be shared with the public through social media channels.

"Just as no two flowers are alike, no two snowflakes are alike,
no two sunsets are alike, no two humans are alike.
We are each unique, with different skills, gifts, and talents.
When we use our blessings for the benefit of mankind,
we weave our thread into the fabric of humanity,
we add our piece to the web of life,
and we will make a difference."
—Lois Hermann

Highlights – Session 1 – Rae

The session with Rae offers many insights on the qualities that make a good civilization. He emphasizes being respectful and encourages truth, honesty, and integrity. All quotations in this section are attributed to Rae, Patron God of Atlantis.

Rae – Patron God of Atlantis

1. One of the Anquietas' Children, Rae's vibrational energy is so high that if he were to incorporate as a physical being, the amount of energy would be too great for the physical body, and it would be immediately destroyed.

2. The Anquietas' Children can only communicate directly through a human temporarily, and only under special circumstances.

3. It is difficult to consciously replicate the direct spiritual communion between Rae's level as an Archangel and a human. There are few bodies able to handle his presence.

4. As the Patron God of Atlantis, Rae's vibrational energy was too high to be matched to a human body. He communicated information through the High Priestess to balance the other governing sections of Atlantis.

5. The last time Rae communicated through a body on Earth was fourteen thousand years ago, when he channeled his energy through Lois in her past life as the High Priestess Arianya.

6. High Priestess Arianya belonged to a community of priestesses. She was seven feet tall with black hair and unusual golden eyes.

7. Rae felt it was an enormous honor to share Arianya's form with her for the short periods in the Atlantean time.

8. The situation where Rae was able to communicate through Gary was slightly different. Because Gary's body is closer in vibratory rate, Rae could more easily adapt to the body.

9. "Even if we could take human form more often, we would not. We want races to develop on their own."

10. Atlantis was Rae's favorite civilization, yet he feels he failed Atlantis, and the civilization died.

11. Some of the Collective have worlds they prefer to visit and civilizations that they prefer. They are concerned about our Earth right now.

Atlantean Realm

1. "The Atlantean culture was more advanced than anything Earth has today. There was no civilization then or now that rivals Atlantis' capabilities."

2. Atlantis dates back fourteen thousand years. Comprised of a confederation of states, it was made up of twelve islands and the Altiplano, a high mountain region of Peru.

3. The democracy of the Atlantean system of government preceded the creation of modern democracy by over ten thousand years.

4. The Atlantean Realm was ruled by a democracy consisting of four groups: the King and Queen, the Thirteen, the First Prime, and the High Priestess.

5. The hereditary King and Queen set the course for the Atlantean Realm.

6. The ruling body of the Thirteen ran the day-to-day business of the Atlantean Realm. These representatives were elected from each of the twelve islands and one from the capital city of Muir.

7. The First Prime of Atlantis was the leader of the military who came up through the ranks. The military comprised both the army and navy and was purely defensive.

8. The Atlantean High Priestess was chosen by Rae to maintain balance and keep the peace.

9. Atlantis was a peaceful civilization and was at peace with their neighbors. It was a simpler time with much fewer people.

10. Machu Picchu was a much later civilization than Atlantis, located in a similar region of Peru.

Destruction of Atlantis

1. Some technological improvements today could not have been conceived of by the Atlanteans. However, they controlled energy that our civilization today still does not truly understand.

2. Atlantis was destroyed by an overload to its crystal generators. The citizens wanted to control time by physically passing forward and backward through time. The overload caused the generators to explode in the capital city of Muir and on all of the islands.

3. The Universe only allows travel through time on a quantum level by using the power of the mind. It cannot be done at a macroscopic level.

4. Rae had told Arianya to warn the people what they were doing was dangerous. Although Arianya was one of the most respected citizens of the realm, the people didn't listen to her—even knowing her words came from Rae.

5. "I could have appeared before the Council without burning their eyes out and told them to stop. However, it probably wouldn't have helped."

6. The failure of the time travel experiment obliterated everything. All that was known of Atlantis was destroyed.

7. Only the few Atlanteans who were elsewhere in the world survived. What little culture they had was carefully preserved. When the Library at Alexandria was destroyed, that was truly the end of the Atlantean civilization.

8. The Atlantean genetic makeup has been lost by seven thousand generations. No trace of their race remains.

9. "The King and Queen were good people; they made a mistake. The Thirteen were good and just people; they made a mistake."

10. "It is the nature of all life to make mistakes. Even the Gods make mistakes; no one is perfect; we all make mistakes."

11. "Sometimes children can only learn from their mistakes. It doesn't mean that the parent has failed, but that makes it no less painful."

Bermuda Triangle

1. Several of the Atlantean islands were located in what is now called the Bermuda Triangle.

2. The confluence of forces caused by the explosion of the generators on the islands in the area of the Bermuda Triangle was so massive, it caused a rift or a tear in the ocean floor and the energetic boundaries of the area.

3. Rae and others of the Collective required much energy to repair the rift. However, it was too great to completely close.

4. Most of the rumors around disappearances in the Bermuda Triangle are simply accidents that occur because it is a heavily traveled area.

5. Some stories of the Bermuda Triangle are not rumors. If you are in the right space at the right time, with the planet in the

proper alignment, the rift opens and allows passage in both directions.

6. When the rift is open in the point near Bermuda, some things come through and some are lost.

7. A similar area exists on the opposite side of the Earth in the Sea of Japan. The Collective was able to repair that rift more completely, since it was less damaged than the one in the Bermuda area.

Early Life on Earth

1. Even though the original spark of life came from Mars, Earth was hospitable for life. Eventually the spark of life would have happened on Earth; life just got to Mars first. There is no cosmic significance to this.

2. There is an ideal balance between the amount of radiation that causes mutation and the amount of radiation that is dangerous. Earth's radiation level is just right to allow the mutation rate to spread life quickly.

3. Life on Earth spawned in three separate places at roughly the same time, in what are now known as Asia, Africa, and North America. Civilization grew in these areas and was prosperous.

4. Life was not quite the hardship modern people think it must have been. Earth provided everything that early man needed. Earth has always been an amazingly productive planet.

5. Some areas of the planet were less hospitable, but the climate was stable. Glaciations occurred over time, but between glaciations Earth was very fertile.

6. The Neanderthal were the first species truly recognizable as human. They were hunters and gatherers. The time of *Homo sapiens* Neanderthalensis predates Atlantis.

7. Modern scientists now believe that the Neanderthal, the Cro-Magnon, and modern man were not separate species. They were merely subspecies of *Homo sapiens,* much as two breeds of cat are the same species.

8. Humans evolve much more quickly than many other species, in part because they have a great capacity for imagination and creation.

Early Migration

1. The way in which early humans found each other has not been recorded in history, but it was simple migration. The Earth is as populated as it is because the Neanderthal were willing to travel, migrating far and wide.

2. While many humans migrated, others stayed in one place and fought over the limited resources. This is what happened in many of the early civilizations on Earth.

3. The Asian culture was the most isolated of the three for the longest period of time. The African culture met with the North American culture more quickly.

4. When the Earth was much younger, the African civilization migrated north, as did the North American civilization. These early civilizations met through what is now called the Bering Sea, which at the time was an ice bridge.

5. When the early civilizations contacted each other, it sometimes produced a conflict. Each civilization believed *they* were the center of the Universe and the only intelligent living beings.

6. It is a shock to the ego to discover you are not special, that there are others like you.

7. Some traveling groups were more willing to accept they would meet others. Those meetings were generally peaceful. As they formed communities of their own, they created civilizations that were different from their original parent group.

8. At times these early groups fought. Humanity survived those early conflicts, and some of the small civilizations learned to live together.

9. As populations grew, these groups hesitated to spread out any farther, for fear they might meet more people. So they stayed as one group in common areas. Groups that decided to stay in one place sometimes overstayed the land's ability to provide.

10. Staying in one place leads to a reduction in the sustenance that humans need. You can over-live an area of your world to the point there is not enough food. Some groups traveled on; others stayed and fought over food.

11. "It is a curious piece of human nature that the capacity for love and the capacity for war are equally great. It's difficult to explain why this happens, even for those who have watched humanity grow for fourteen thousand years."

Mother Gaia

1. "People's spirits grow rapidly on Earth, partly because it is Gaia's nature; she is alive and not all planets are."

2. "The spirit of the Earth is suffering in modern times, yet still strives to spur evolution. Gaia is a good mother who has only love for her children, only the best intentions for them."

3. "Humans seem to have lost the ability to hear Gaia. This is the most important piece of information that can help humanity. We must reconnect with the spirit of our Earth."

4. "This world is infamous among the Universe because it attracts new spirits that seek to learn by doing. Spirits can do so much more on this world than on most others, therefore, Earth is often the first choice for new spirits."

5. When a human body dies, even in its first incarnation, and the spirit is released, it will have grown more than older spirits who are leaving an incorporation as another species.

6. Too many new souls or spirits can destabilize a world. However, enough old souls are here to make Earth the paradise it once was.

7. The Anquietas' Children are more involved than the Anquietas are because they have the ability to interact with the physical world. They have learned to have emotion and feel the suffering of the races who suffer.

8. Humanity almost seems to enjoy suffering, which in some ways may not a bad thing. Suffering and conflict promote growth and strength, but that growth can take many paths.

9. "People need to choose a path that promotes harmony, as opposed to a path that promotes conflict."

10. On Earth there has always been somewhat of a balance, yet that balance may swing like a pendulum. It has been pinned too far to the wrong side for too long on Earth.

11. "If some sort of balance does not begin to restore itself, Earth will reach a point where it will not be possible to achieve balance anymore. The spirits that Earth will attract won't even permit the balance to happen."

Evolved Civilizations

1. Humans today do not give humans of the past sufficient credit for their abilities. They tend to think of everything as having been learned by their civilization for the first time.

2. Many mysteries of ancient artifacts or unexplained events are not alien projections or creations. Ancient humans knew much, and much of that knowledge was forgotten or destroyed by conflict and competition.

3. "That is why there are other races that have evolved higher. There are many other worlds with corporeal life. Some are more evolved, with older civilizations that progressed in such a way that they never went through a competitive stage."

4. If you're on a world that easily provides for everything you need, there is no need for conflict, and you wind up with a very different type of civilization.

5. "Even though most corporeal races have existed for the same length of time, the differences between the races are caused by how the race developed, not by how long they have been a race."

6. In a sense, there is one civilization on Earth, yet there is still tribalism.

7. The Collective would like to see humans outgrow this need for competition, yet it is a deeply engrained piece of humanity.

Alien Visitation

1. There are countless species on many worlds that develop into intelligent life; however, it is not as large a number as some human scientists think.

2. "The physical distances are so vast that it is almost impossible to travel between worlds populated by intelligent species."

3. "The ability to cross greater distances at what would be perceived as faster than light is possible. However, very, very few species develop this ability."

4. "The ability to travel faster than light is rare, partly because it is a difficult process, but mostly because species who develop that level of technology tend to destroy themselves."

5. Usually, what is perceived as alien visitation is not a physical visitation, but a spiritual one.

6. Typically, what is seen by the observer is a projection into the minds of others. It is a function of how the mind processes the information.

7. If you introduce a vision into someone's mind, they will think they see it. It is possible to make yourself appear to really be there. This is what alien encounters typically are.

8. Sometimes the projection can appear as solid form. While extremely difficult, it is possible to take local material and form a temporary body held together by the energy.

9. Few races have evolved to the point of projecting solid form. Humans are not there yet.

10. "There are races who do share their information. They want to see other races evolve to their level and want to be visited in return."

11. The aliens whom some think to have helped humanity grow over the millennia were truly the Wise Ones of the Collective, including mythological Gods and unseen Archangels.

Astral Projection

1. "While you cannot physically move freely through time, mentally it is possible. Humans have that ability. The process is known as astral projection."

2. It is possible to project a part of your spirit and part of your consciousness to any point. Enough of your spirit is always left behind to keep the body going.

3. "You can project within your own physical dimension and you can project into the astral plane. There is no speed-of-light limitation on that process."

4. You can be anywhere at any time. Spiritual travel in present time, travel to the past and to the future, *is* sometimes possible with the right thought, the right control, and the right reason.

5. Why you want to do a thing is always more important than what you are actually doing.

6. A hologram is a trick of the light. It is something seen by the eye and occurs entirely within the brain. There is literally nothing there, yet multiple people can see it at the same time.

7. In astral projection, someone projects an image into another's mind to see something. While looking at the same space, one person would see something, and the other person would not.

8. It would be difficult for an alien to project their spirit into a human body.

9. When a physical body is born, a spirit is either chosen or created to take that body. They are matched at birth. Rae says this union that occurs at birth is magical.

10. It is almost impossible for another spirit to enter another human's body. Partly because the body can only barely contain the spirit it holds, and also because the vibrational match won't be precise enough.

11. The spiritual and physical match exists for the life of the combination. When the physical body dies, the bond is broken.

Afterlife Beliefs

1. The Collective cannot intervene; they can recommend.

2. The Collective recognizes that humans, more than most intelligent species, need to believe in something greater than themselves.

3. "It doesn't get much greater than to be human, if you're corporeal."

4. It may be that people need to return to the beliefs the Ancient Ones wanted humans to have: "We are your Gods, we make thunder, we make lightning, we make it rain."

5. The reason humans were encouraged to believe in Gods was to have them follow a path that was less self-destructive.

6. Making people think there was reward and punishment in an afterlife helped them behave, especially if they weren't so inclined to do so on their own.

7. Upon your passing, you experience no reward or punishment, except what your spirit carries with you. When you pass from a mortal form, you bring all memories of the actions that occurred when you were in physical form. There is no "good" and "bad." Everything is entirely relative.

8. Once your life ends, you see your life with much more clarity than you possibly could when you were *in* physical form. All rationalizations disappear, and you see everything for what it truly was.

9. Many spirits who pass on linger within the physical dimension while they sort through their lives and determine what will they will do next.

10. Some spirits may want to atone for things they've done when they were in corporeal form and might immediately reincarnate to start again. Other spirits who believe they led a just life will move on or come back because they enjoyed themselves. It is entirely up to the spirit what happens to it.

11. "Those spirits who realize their life had been hurtful to others lose so much energy through negative thought, that they sink down to a lower vibrational dimension from which they cannot reincarnate. It can take time to bring themselves back. Some never recover."

Angels and Demons

1. Lois and her team work with the Collective to help low-level energies into the Light, where there is an opportunity for healing. Rae acknowledges that several of his kin do this sort of work, particularly for this planet.

2. As Lois' team assists spirits into the Light, they identify many low-level energies; most are lost human souls, while others are more malevolent.

3. Some extremely negative, almost evil energies tend to manipulate people and make them suffer. These nasties or demons are identified as being from another dimensional level.

4. Jesus, Archangel Michael, and his Legions of Light are called on to take care of these more destructive energies.

5. "It is the balance of energies within a vibrational dimension that defines the dimension."

6. As the balance changes and the vibrational energy lowers, it becomes harder for higher-vibrational beings—what we think of as angels—to come in to assist, because their vibrational difference is too great.

7. "As the vibrational energy of Earth lowers, it becomes easier for the lower-vibrational energies, what are called demons, to get in."

8. Most of the spirits people consider to be angels are Rae's children. Many of the spirits people consider to be demons are also his children.

9. The imposition of good and evil is a corporeal thing. When you agree with something, you think of it as good. When you disagree with something, you think of it as evil.

10. "Good and evil are not absolutes; they are relative. Something can only be good in comparison to something that isn't."

11. "Make no mistake. There are spirits which do not have the best interests of corporeal life in mind, and a lot of times it's hard to tell the difference."

The Collective

1. The Collective are individuals and they share a joint consciousness. They each know what the other does and are a part of what the other does.

2. Archangel Michael is one of Rae's kin who helps humans. Lois and her team have a great deal of respect for all he does to assist.

3. The name "Archangel Michael" takes credit for a lot of the work the Collective does. Each of the Archangels has been associated with different activities, yet they are all equal; any one of them can do any of those things.

4. "It is in human nature to want to apply labels, such as Archangel Michael, on things. When you ask for Archangel Michael, you're asking for an image of a being that has a certain task that it can perform."

5. The Collective's spirits all exist in a higher-dimensional plain, and some can lower their energies to enter the physical.

6. It is easier for the Children's Children, like Jesus, to lower their energy to enter the physical. Rae was part of the creation of Jesus, whom he calls his Child.

7. "Jesus is capable of incorporating in physical form, as all of his siblings are. When not in corporeal form, Jesus is in the vibrational realm as an angel."

8. "When not in physical form, any one of Jesus' 32,786 siblings can at any time be 'Jesus' to somebody who seeks his name."

9. Those of the Collective who do incorporate try to help from a quiet distance.

10. "Jesus got a larger reputation than they (the Children's Children) generally like to get when they appear on worlds. Jesus appeared at a time of great discord. He's not the first and he won't be the last."

11. Rae reminds us what Jesus said two thousand years ago: "I am not God. Don't follow me. You are the Gods. Follow each other. Learn to love each other. That will solve all your problems."

The Tipping Point

1. The Collective has lost some worlds where races evolved such that their technology outstripped the evolution of their wisdom.

2. The Collective can't see the future. They predict based on what they see happen and what they have seen happen. They know the time is close.

3. Many of Rae's kin spend more time here on Earth than on other worlds. No world is at such a tipping point right now as Earth. Earth is on an accelerating curve, but it hasn't reached the point that it cannot be corrected. *That point is very near.*

4. Humanity needs to hear the message Jesus delivered two thousand years ago: "You must cooperate. You must harmonize."

5. Those who have too much need to give. Those who have too little must be willing to accept. The balance has to be brought back before it's too late.

6. Greed comes from a belief that there isn't enough; it comes from insufficiency. If you believe there isn't enough for everyone, then you will hoard things, and greed becomes a self-fulfilling prophecy. Then there isn't enough for everyone.

7. Given Earth's population, there is still enough for everyone. Nothing needs to be hoarded.

8. Humans have the technology to fix even the problems that Gaia cannot fix. Some places are arid; they could be watered. Trees can be replanted.

9. The rainforests *are not gone yet.* They can be brought back, but once they are gone, they cannot be brought back.

10. "It's not simply a matter of planned genetics; the system has a hysteretic ability. You can bend a piece of wood, but if you bend it too far it breaks. You can't put it back together again."

11. The system is such that it needs the proper environment in which to grow. Once the environment has been destroyed, you *cannot* bring it back.

Message of Hope

1. The world holds a lot of despair today. A message of hope is all that most people need to hear and act on.

2. There are those whose intent is questionable, as is their idea of hope.

3. "There are so many people in need of hope, they will believe the wrong message as well as the right message. You have to reach them first."

4. "The people who put the greatest good for the greatest number ahead of themselves are the people you can trust. There are a lot of them on Earth."

5. It's what is in people's hearts that defines their spirit, not what comes out of their mouths.

6. Positive activities go largely unnoticed. It is much easier to attract attention when you do something perceived as being wrong, than it is when you do something perceived as being right.

7. If we can find a way to emphasize the positive, we'll go a long way towards making this world a much better place.

8. Lois wants to share these messages and teach people how to balance their energy. She is concerned about reaching enough people. Rae tells her: "If you teach two people, and they teach two people, it doesn't take very long to reach everyone."

9. "The reason that Hitler was able to create the most powerful and efficient civilization in modern history was because hope was stripped from Germany after World War I."

10. What most people never stop to realize is the first country the Nazis took over was Germany. That can still happen today.

The Book

1. "This book you are writing is good."

2. The book is sufficiently controversial that it will attract attention. Many people will speak out against it, and that will drive more people to it.

3. "Let opposition strengthen you. Publish your thoughts; say what you want to say. Do not be afraid; don't back down. The Collective is behind you."

4. It would be nice if Rae could simply appear and tell people this message of hope. Unfortunately, it doesn't work that way.

5. "The words that we have given you are good words. Make them your own, and you will succeed."

6. The Collective is giving us the messages they want communicated. They depend on us to take these words and put them out where everyone can see, hear, and read them.

7. "Some will believe; some will not. Some will follow; some will not."

8. We must do our best to spread the message of hope.

"Oneness of God,
oneness of man's relation,
oneness of force, oneness of time,
oneness of purpose, ONENESS in every effort."
—Edgar Cayce

Highlights – Session 2 – Jesus

The entire context of the conversation with Jesus is captured in these highlights for review and reflection. An additional list of Jesus' Top 40 quotes is included in the Resources section. Jesus tells us to be loving, and to choose kindness, compassion, and humility. All quotations in this section are attributed to Jesus.

Jesus' Spirit

1. One of the Anquietas' Children's Children, Jesus has a fondness for Earth and is never far away, although he is not in physical form.

2. Jesus' generation, the Children's Children, identify very closely with the physical world. They interact with it constantly and can incorporate to become part of it.

3. Jesus might not have taken a physical form again, but he wanted to be here through Gary because he was asked, and he knew we would share his words.

4. The work Lois and her team does to shift the energy to the positive is very important, especially now.

5. "A turning point is coming to the Earth."

6. The Collective would not be here speaking with us if they did not believe we had the ability to carry out the task they hope we will carry out.

7. "It is the same message I gave two thousand years ago. That message has been distorted through time and distorted through people."

8. The messages Jesus gave us are the same ones that have been given throughout time, and not just in his previous incarnation.

Suffering and Compassion

1. Because Jesus' energy is close enough to humans, he feels emotion. His older kin of the Collective, the Anquietas, do not share the same level of emotion.

2. The God Rae felt a strong connection with Lois in her Atlantean life as Arianya. Feeling that level of emotion was unusual for the Children.

3. It pains the Collective greatly when people suffer needlessly.

4. "Some suffering is necessary. You cannot enjoy pleasure unless you experience pain."

5. Those who willfully harm others bring great pain to the Collective.

6. "People need to love each other. It's just a matter of simple compassion."

7. "Compassion is a human quality that is rare in the Universe."

8. Not all intelligent races have emotion; some have a limited set. It saddens the Collective to see emotions wasted so often.

Civilizations and Beliefs

1. Not all worlds have their own spirit. Jesus tells us: "Gaia is the spirit of this planet and cares for all of you. In some sense you are all her children. We are all made of her bones while in physical form."

2. Some humans are Earth spirits and are intimately tied to Gaia, yet are not restricted to Earth. Once a spirit reaches a certain age of maturity, it can go anywhere in the Universe.

3. "Gaia provides well for her children. There is no real scarcity on Earth. There is enough. It hurts Gaia when her resources are wasted."

4. "There is too much greed in the world. There is enough to go around. It is not necessary for people to take more than they need."

5. The Roman Empire was one of the physically strongest civilizations, although they lacked in morality towards the end of their civilization.

6. "What ultimately brought down the Roman Empire was not attack from the outside, it was decay from within, to the point that they no longer had the will to defend themselves."

7. The spiritual Anasazi people of the American Southwest were a civilization that literally evolved out of the need for corporeal existence.

8. "The Incan civilization was destroyed from outside attack. They had practices which modern man might question, but they had their moral code and they stuck with it."

9. "It's not so much what you say, it's the belief in what you say that matters. As long as you do no harm, pick your frame of reference and stay with it."

10. If you can be true to your beliefs, as long as you do no harm, that essentially makes you a good person. Too many people don't live this way. They lack belief in what they say.

11. "There's a reason why honesty has always been a most valued quality. If you cannot be true to your own beliefs, how can you possibly be true to anything?"

High-Level Spiritual Beings

1. Buddha, Muhammad, and many of the other great prophets are Jesus' brothers.

2. "Most of the Gods who have been worshipped have been my parents."

3. Jesus finds English to be a difficult language. He says words have definitions and connotations, and it's difficult to speak literally without being misinterpreted.

4. "There have been civilizations that have recognized there are planes of existence beyond the physical."

5. Other civilizations recognize the existence of wise spiritual beings without believing they are Gods, like the spirit of Jesus, who live in higher realms of existence.

6. "There are spiritual beings who have natural superior abilities, just as there are different abilities among humans. It is a bell curve that exists everywhere, even among my kin."

7. There are those in the Collective who believe that some level of competition is necessary. Others, such as Jesus, believe there is always a peaceful answer.

8. "We are not the one true God that many human religions believe. There is not one, all-knowing, all-seeing, all-powerful being."

9. As a group, the Collective comes close to being what we consider Gods. Given all of their years of existence, the Collective has vast knowledge.

10. "There's no one being watching everything that everyone does, and certainly there's no one judging everything you do."

11. "The only judge you ever have to face is yourself. The only person you have to be better than is the person you are today."

Corporeal Spirits

1. "Do what you believe is right."

2. Hippocrates said it best: "First, do no harm."

3. Jesus wonders why we would even need to tell people his simple message that seems so self-evident: "Do unto others as you would have others do unto you."

4. "Believe in yourself. You are the only ones that make reality exist." Jesus says our scientists are only beginning to understand what this actually means.

5. When not in physical form, the Children's Children are everywhere and nowhere. They are wherever they focus their conscience.

6. Our spirits are everywhere and nowhere until we choose the physical body into which we will reside as a human. Then we become incarnated as corporeal spirits.

7. The body is our point of focus when we are in corporeal form until it's time for our spirits to move on. The physical body can limit the spiritual travels we take.

8. "I can be anywhere, anytime, because I have no body that I need to worry about."

9. The spirit cannot wholly exist within the body. The physical body cannot contain all the spiritual energy.

10. "Our spirits reside within and without our bodies. What you call an *aura* is the result of the spiritual part of the body that resides outside the body."

11. As we looked around Gary during this communication with Jesus, we could see the merger of their spirits outside his body.

Physical Existence

1. "For every disease there is a cure, and the cure is unique for every individual."

2. While in physical form, the spirit usually does not retain memory of previous lives or knowledge that there is anything other than the current life.

3. The memory of past lives is usually blocked until the person is ready to understand.

4. "The human brain is the pinnacle of corporeal development. Remarkable as it is, the human brain can only handle so much information."

5. Jesus encourages us to use our brain to expand our consciousness.

6. Some healers who are older spirits are less willing to help themselves. They feel they are here to assist others and put the greater good before themselves.

7. "Every corporeal existence, even the newest spirits, make changes in every life that is touched. Every person we touch sends them in a direction they might not have taken on their own."

8. Our spirit is eternal. Our current physical incarnation is only one piece of existence.

9. "When the corporeal body passes away, it is only the physical body that dies; our eternal spirit lives on."

10. "When our spirits depart our body, the physical body dies. It doesn't hurt our spirit, but we can't come back to that physical body."

11. In our session, when Jesus departs Gary's body, Gary's spirit returns, and his body continues. They are close enough in energy that Gary's spirit did not completely leave.

The Future

1. The Collective is happy to share pearls of wisdom with us.

2. "We are not all-knowing; we cannot predict the future. We see trends and probabilities. We do not know with certainty what will happen."

3. The Anquietas can explain the history of the Universe, but does not make recommendations. Jesus explains their reticence is because when they have interfered in the past, the result was not what they intended.

4. The Anquietas' Children also do not make recommendations yet will answer most any question. If we were to ask Jesus'

father, Rae, how to build an Atlantean crystal generator, he would not tell us, because he saw what happened once before.

5. "We do not interfere with corporeal beings' development. We do not steer humanity one way or another because we do not know with absolute certainty which path ultimately will be best."

6. Knowledge of the future makes the Collective unwilling to share it. "If you knew the precise date and time of your death, what would you do with that information? Would you try and avoid it? By avoiding it, you may cause it. By avoiding it, you may bring it nearer."

7. Jesus' generation (Children's Children) can take physical form; the very act represents change. His visitation with us creates incalculable changes in the probability timeline.

8. Based on their experience with other civilizations, the Collective shares general messages, hoping to steer civilizations in a positive direction. They know certain actions will almost always produce certain results. It's the *almost* that makes the Collective hesitate to share with us.

9. The messages Jesus gave us two thousand years ago endure and are applicable to this day.

10. General messages are really all Jesus can offer us. Some things he cannot share, and he even declined to answer certain questions.

11. The Earth's tipping point is coming faster than the Collective had predicted.

Messages and Mistakes

1. Jesus knew we wanted to speak with him the moment Gary's consciousness slipped aside. Because time works differently in the spirit realm, it was a long period of time for him to decide if he wanted to come through Gary's physical form.

2. It had been two thousand years since Jesus had taken physical form, as opposed to how we hear his voice in our hearts and minds when we pray.

3. "Seeing what humanity has done with the messages that I left has made me hesitant to return."

4. Jesus hopes these messages are kept true. He trusts us or he would not be here. He cautions that some will try to use these words for their own purposes.

5. Jesus knows that we will defend the words, and that it will not be easy. No one who has ever brought a world-changing message, on any world, has it easy. There is a limit as to what the Collective can do to assist us.

6. The Collective tells us they will understand if we choose not to proceed with sharing these messages; they have given us the choice. However, they know we will choose to share their messages with humanity, or they wouldn't be using their energy here.

7. If we are helping others by removing the negative energy around them, we are not interfering with their destiny or karma.

8. "If you intend no harm, you cannot do the wrong thing. You will make mistakes. I make mistakes. It's much more about the intent than anything else."

9. "Atlantis was destroyed because its citizens attempted to challenge time travel, which was a mistake. Many civilizations have fallen because of mistakes. All anyone can ever do is the best that they can do."

10. "We all have our strengths, we all have our weaknesses, we all have our blind spots. That's normal, even for us."

11. "Don't let fear of making a mistake stop you from doing what you believe to be right."

Listen and Learn

1. It is important to get people to listen and act on these messages. We are encouraged to deliver them in a way that humanity will understand and accept.

2. The Collective prefers to use the word "spirit" instead of "soul" for the nonphysical part of our being. They are one and the same. The word "soul" carries more religious implications.

3. Even though the memory of previous lives is blocked in an existence, the *elasticity of thought* stays with us. The more lives you have experienced, the more your spirit has learned. The memory of these lives can be accessed through intention or past-life regression.

4. "Even if the specific memories are not accessible, the ability to realize that there is more comes from having experienced more, even if the experiences themselves are lost."

5. "The newer the spirit, the more limited its frame of reference, because it has had fewer lives."

6. "The high percentage of very new spirits on Earth is causing disturbance. The newer spirits do not have the elasticity of knowing, they lack maturity."

7. "When given a small box, it is difficult to add something new to the box without emptying some of the contents first."

8. "If someone has picked up a bad habit, you can't give them a good habit. You have to get rid of the old one first."

9. "This is what you have to do on a global level. People have got to unlearn before they can relearn."

10. Jesus says many people accept and know his good messages. While most understand the message of being good to each other, many are hesitant to be vocal about it for fear of repercussion.

11. As he did two thousand years ago, Jesus delivered his messages to us. This time, instead of allowing them to be misinterpreted or lost, we are determined to protect them and keep them alive.

Reward and Punishment

1. The Collective knows that physical existence is fleeting. Upon death, spirits are released from the physical body.

2. "There are a limited number of beings in the Collective and a great many worlds. We are never bored."

3. "The concept of reward and punishment after death was introduced as a way to control people. If you're good now, it will be good for you later."

4. The concept of karma is not wrong. The payback for your actions exists, but it comes from within yourself.

5. "There is no external judgment to what you do. There is no external reward and punishment. There is no vengeful God. There is no devil."

6. "Reward and punishment come from within. You may deceive yourself into thinking that you've lived a wonderful life. But when that life ends and your spirit reflects, it will see that life with greater clarity."

7. Jesus wonders how people can believe in reward and punishment and still do the kinds of things they do. He tells us it does happen on other worlds, yet is more prevalent on Earth.

8. In your life, if you have done more harm than good, your spirit will punish itself. Some spirits have done so much harm they have dissociated themselves, terminated their own spirits, and released their energy back to the Universe. They will never return.

9. When an individual terminates their consciousness, nothing is ever lost, as parts of the terminated spirits are reused.

10. The Collective questions why things are so negative on the Earth. In billions of years, this human conundrum of negative competition is one the Collective has not resolved. It is unsure what they would do if they knew since their traditions prevent intervention.

Speak the Compliment Out Loud

1. Jesus explains that a system based entirely on punishment without reward will not work. Whenever you must correct an action, try to compliment on a positive action at the same time. It can be used as a teaching moment without reducing the importance of the message.

2. It seems easier to point out a wrong than to congratulate someone when something is right. We complain when something goes wrong. Yet when someone does something good, it is often easy to think to yourself, "That was nice," and move on without acknowledgment.

3. "A good message to remember is to speak the compliment aloud. It's important to let people know when they've done well."

4. In a bell curve, there are always be a few at each end of the positive and negative curve, with hope for an even balance. On Earth, the bell curve is skewed more to the positive; more people do good than do harm.

5. "The voices of the people who do more good than harm don't seem to attract the attention of the people in the middle, and the voices of the people who do more harm than good seem to be heard more clearly."

6. "You need to make the voice of the people who do more good known. They need to be heard."

7. Jesus didn't know how the message "Do unto others . . ." got lost, as it was such a simple message. It became a tenet of

the early church. He is concerned that when people say good things, sometimes their actions do not follow.

8. Jesus explains that the bell curve is not static, since it moves when each new life comes in and when each old life goes out. With every interaction, the curve moves one way or the other.

9. When Jesus was on Earth, the curve was moving in the negative direction. He thinks his timing was off because there was so much turmoil at that time.

10. Jesus wonders if he should have come sooner or waited until the pendulum had swung as far as it was going to. Maybe then, he could have given it more energy in the direction it needed to go.

11. "I came, and I pushed when the pendulum was still moving the wrong way, and I wasn't able to apply enough force to make any difference, and the message was simply forgotten. I'm sorry, it wasn't really forgotten. People still know that message, don't they?"

Gaia Is Real

1. When Jesus was here in physical form two thousand years ago, some treated him with cruelty and brutality.

2. "Sadly, that is the fate of many a prophet. I can't help but think of those who inspired followers with unhealthy messages, but their fate was never any better."

3. We wonder how to deliver Jesus' messages so they are interpreted correctly this time.

4. The Collective and most corporeal beings understand the challenge of change. Even when change is for good, it can be painful.

5. Change is constant at some level. One of the basic laws written into the fabric of the Universe is, "Nothing remains the same. You stagnate, and you perish."

6. It is possible to try to change too much too quickly. When you challenge a person's beliefs, whatever they are, the result is always going to be negative.

7. "You cannot force people to change. Even if you give them something that they know is right, even if you give them something that they know is better to do, if you force them to do it, they're going to resent it."

8. Jesus advises us to present these messages as reminders, including the fact that there is enough for everyone.

9. "Gaia is alive and cares for humanity. If humans need to pray to something more powerful than themselves, let that be Gaia. Gaia is more real than an imaginary God. Gaia is more powerful than an imaginary God."

10. Jesus tells us there have been many religions on Earth that are based on honoring nature.

11. At Jesus' death, there was a solar eclipse, and three days later he appeared to his followers. Coincidentally, the day of Jesus' visit with us was exactly three days after a solar eclipse that occurred in North America for the first time in many years.

Keep the Message Alive

1. "When my physical body died two thousand years ago, it died. When they took me down off the cross, I died in the arms of the woman I loved."

2. "My resurrection was one of spirit. I had followers with whom I was very close. Having been corporeal only days before, part of my spirit was still within them. I was able to appear in their mind's eye. I told them to keep the message alive."

3. Similarly, because the spiritual energy of Arianya (Lois) and the God Rae were very close, he could appear in her mind while she was alive. Rae was also able to reconstruct her spirit after the Atlantean explosion.

4. Jesus realized that his timing had been off, and his message was going to be lost. He relied on his followers to help keep the message alive and try to bring peace to the world.

5. Sadly, Jesus feels that his message was changed over time. Instead of following the simple message, leaders tried to force people to obey. His message was never meant as a command.

6. Religions were created based on the message that Jesus was trying to give. However, people tried to force others to follow, and even executed those who didn't follow their rules in Jesus' name.

7. Jesus was disturbed by the number of deaths that have occurred in his name. It wasn't what he intended.

8. "So many deaths have been justified in the name of a God that doesn't even exist. Death in my father's name, who isn't the father people think."

9. "These are those moments that hurt us. These are the moments that at some level we regret having gotten involved. That's why we try not to get involved."

10. "What saddens me most is not the death itself, because I know that these spirits continue on and are reborn. What saddens me most is the harm to the people that are doing the killing. So many of them do not recover."

11. "I don't understand how anyone can profess a belief in any God, and then knowingly do something that is contrary to anything that any God has ever said. What do they think will happen?"

Enforced Beliefs Generate Conflict

1. It is the negative that seems to be amplified. There are many more good people than bad, and much good came out of Jesus' message. Lois' team intends to perpetuate the good and to keep the positive messages alive as best they can.

2. When Lois asks if negative energies can externally influence humans by causing them disturbances, Jesus replies they do exist, but that doesn't really explain what occurs with most humans.

3. Jesus feels it is part of human existence and part of civilization on this world to encounter and experience the negative.

4. On some worlds, life begins in a single place, spreads, and remains essentially as one civilization. On worlds where there were sufficient resources, people were willing to expand in such a way as to not crowd each other, and conflict never developed.

5. Although some conflict that occurs on Earth is over physical things, most conflict is over beliefs and ideals.

6. "Difference and divergence are necessary for health and strength. It is normal that people grow up being taught different things with a variety of beliefs."

7. "It's the desire to enforce what you believe on someone else that generates the conflict."

8. "Perhaps it is because my kin are of one kind, we don't have that conflict. Which is not to say we don't have differences of opinion, but the fundamental conflict is not there."

9. It is important to remember: "Humanity is a single species. You are all the same." Jesus reminds us it is not the case of us versus them, e.g., *Homo sapiens* versus Cro-Magnon.

10. Jesus tells us we are not fighting aliens. We are all one people; it doesn't matter where we were born or what we were taught. We are all the same.

Believe What Is Real

1. "The Ten Commandments were simple messages written by good men who wanted people to be good to each other."

2. Some of the Collective thought the belief in a single God might unify people.

3. "However, even the major religions that believe in a single God have gone astray and don't realize that it is *one God* they all believe in. They seem to think that their God is somehow different than the next person's."

4. Polytheistic religions have *multiple* Gods. These Gods are the Children of the Anquietas, the wise spiritual beings of the Collective.

5. Polytheistic religions don't seem to have belief conflicts among one another. Many people with different religions live adjacent to each other without fighting over their Gods.

6. Conflict gets more intense when it's *one God* versus another's *one God.* Some people cannot accept that someone else might believe in something different.

7. "Within Christianity, conflict is even sillier, because the differences between God in the different sects are so minuscule. How could you fight over this?"

8. "There are civilizations who understand the existence of non-physical beings and beings greater than themselves without having to resort to calling them Gods, without attributing totally natural things to them."

9. The Greek, Romans, and Norse believed in high-level spiritual beings. For instance, thunder came from Thor, one of the ancient Gods.

10. "Perhaps we could get humans to believe in what is real in the Universe, and not what they would like to be real."

11. Jesus admits that he made mistakes. He won't tell us what to do, because he knows doing so is not the right thing to do. "We all do the best we can do."

God-like Beings

1. "Get people to understand that they aren't alone in the Universe. Get them to understand that there is something greater than themselves."

2. "There are God-like beings who assist us from the Collective, yet they are not *the One God* people have been taught to believe."

3. Those who believe in ghosts are not wrong. Humans often sense ghosts as Earth-bound spirits of those who have passed. The words "ghost" and "spirit" are often interchangeable.

4. High-level Wise Beings of the Collective will assist when asked.

5. If we can get people to understand that the High-Level Spirits of the Collective are God-like beings who exist to help everyone, maybe people won't fight over it.

6. Jesus expresses concern: "You're likely to cause a fight between the people that will believe you and the people who won't. I don't see how to not create two sides."

7. "There will always be people who believe, and people who don't, and people who don't care." Jesus says those with apathy are the safe ones and are needed for balance.

8. Jesus tells us most people are satisfied with their lives. The vast majority of the population on this planet is that way.

9. "It's always the people who care that cause the trouble. It's only the few who rattle the cage."

I Will Always Be Here

1. Jesus tells us we can speak to any member of the Collective on any topic, at any time.

2. Jesus and the Collective have great faith in our ability to do the right thing, especially with this information.

3. The Collective recognizes these messages will cause unrest and does not envy Lois her task. They appreciate that she is willing to take the task on and says it will not be easy for her.

4. Jesus has faith in our team to choose the right way to pass his messages on to humanity.

5. When asked if he would be willing to speak to an audience through Gary, Jesus was uncomfortable with this request.

6. Jesus says in his incarnation as Jesus, he became more famous than usual. He had his time in the spotlight and prefers to encourage others from the spiritual realm.

7. Jesus reminds us: "I will always be here when you need me. I am never far away. I am always in your heart."

"Balance, peace, and joy are the fruits of a successful life.
It starts with recognizing your talents
and finding ways to serve others by using them."
—Thomas Kinkade

Highlights – Session 3 – Aurora

Aurora gives us many valuable messages. She advises us to be peaceful, to embrace forgiveness, harmony, and wisdom. All quotations in this section are attributed to Aurora.

Names of the Collective

1. Aurora is a sisterly spirit of the Collective.

2. Aurora has been known in the past as Goddess of the dawn.

3. Aurora says she chose the name for us to call her because it was on Gary's mind when she came through.

4. Spirits of the Collective have no names we could speak of and do not communicate in a way we would understand because they have no bodies.

5. Aurora says the Collective are all one and are also individuals with different predilections and avocations.

6. Aurora's main role is to watch out for her siblings while they are in corporeal form.

7. Some of Aurora's siblings are very passionate about their avocations and can be very stubborn.

Two Outcomes

1. Aurora tells us there are two likely outcomes for the future of humanity. They are only probabilities and are not cast in stone.

2. "Humanity has a choice and it is a very simple choice. Either they learn to live together, or face extinction."

3. "It is very dangerous for someone to know too much of their own personal future, and it can be even more dangerous for a civilization."

4. "All that is certain is that the world as we know it is heading for an end. The path that humanity is currently on, if it makes no changes, will invariably lead to its own end."

5. "Civilization will fall first. Civilization is very fragile, especially on Earth."

6. "Humanity as a species will most likely survive, but it is hard to see the future."

7. "Some humans will survive to start again. The ultimate future of the species depends largely on who the survivors are."

8. The people who cause the most trouble and are leading civilization down the path of destruction are the ones who will make the strongest effort to protect themselves. However, they likely won't succeed.

New Civilization

1. Two thousand years ago, Aurora's brother, Jesus, said: "The meek shall inherit the Earth." That is still the probable future, the most likely outcome for civilization.

2. "There is too much inequality in the world today. There will be a new civilization based on equality and respect for each other."

3. Civilization on this planet seems to be based on the premise that there isn't enough to go around. But greed is unnecessary. There is more than enough of everything.

4. It seems obvious that there is enough, but there are people who have no food, no clothing, no shelter: people whom civilization ignores.

5. Some people need help and have no voice. This isn't necessary; there is more than enough for everyone. There is no scarcity. Gaia provides people with all they need.

∞

6. The only other path civilization can take would be to make changes that support one another. It is necessary to share resources for everyone to heal and contribute.

7. "Sadly, the people who need to make the decisions to support others are the people who decided to send humanity down this path in the first place."

Gaia Loves Her Children

1. "Gaia doesn't like the way that people treat each other and likes even less the way they treat her."

2. "Gaia's reactions to civilization will become much worse in a very short period of time."

3. "Gaia cannot target the people whom she realizes are responsible. She can only paint with a very broad brush, and weeps for the innocent who suffer because of her actions."

4. "Gaia loves all the children she creates, but sometimes one species must be lost to allow another to develop."

5. Mass extinctions have happened five times in Earth's past. Several of the apocalyptic events were beyond Gaia's control, but some of them were of her own doing.

6. "Gaia weeps for the species that are lost, and for every life that is lost. But sometimes it comes down to the greatest good for the greatest number."

7. Gaia takes the only actions she can and is with the Collective in their desire to find a less violent way to evoke the change that is *so* necessary.

Many Messengers

1. "We have sent many messengers; many of my siblings have been on Earth before. They have all said the same thing, and the *message has been lost every time.*"

2. "It is sad that our messages are so often twisted, or forgotten, or buried."

3. We had asked to speak with Muhammad and were told his spirit is incorporated in physical form on another world in a galaxy unknown to us. He is helping a species similar to humans that are some twenty thousand years younger.

4. "Jesus has not returned to Earth in the last two thousand years for fear of producing another revolution that might be even more harmful. It was never his intention to create friction between groups of people."

5. Jesus taught that people should be as one. "In a sense, you are all one. You are all children of the Earth; you are all one species."

6. Prophets and other advanced spirits are around us in spiritual form. If we ask them to speak with us, they will. But all they can do is repeat the same messages Jesus gave us.

7. "The Collective has no recommendation on what to do other than to speak out. There is no force they can bring to bear to help."

8. The Collective will not interfere: "Even if we could, we would not. It is not our place. We can only advise. That is what my siblings have done, for countless millennia."

Earth's Tipping Point

1. "Earth is at a tipping point right now, several hundred years sooner than predicted."

2. Aurora can't tell us how long we have left, and she wouldn't if she could.

3. Reviewing the history of our species, the Collective has trouble determining where this need for conflict originated among humans. Although not unique, it is a peculiar trait of humans to thrive on conflict.

4. "There are many species on many worlds who do not have the internal conflict that seems so pervasive on Earth."

5. Conflict is necessary to strengthen a new species. It weeds out those who are too weak to survive. Beyond a certain point, conflict becomes excessive and leads to class disparities that exist on Earth now.

6. "Humans believed that without the promise of reward or the threat of punishment, the physically strong would simply dominate everyone else."

7. If you examine civilization today, you will see the strong still dominate, except the definition of *strong* has changed. It is no longer the biggest and the physically strongest.

8. Those who have managed to gather more than they need are modern civilization's definition of strong.

9. "Considering most of the resources of the world are controlled by a very small handful of people, what you have is *not* a stable civilization."

10. "It is a minority of people who cause the majority of problems."

One True God

1. "The concept of one true God was created by men in order to motivate people to behave in a way that they believed was righteous or right."

2. "For two thousand years, humanity has believed in the *one true God*. It would be best not to dispel them of this idea."

3. "It is difficult for humans to have their faith shaken. Most of the information that you have been given in these sessions is potentially very destabilizing."

4. Aurora advises it is best to avoid targeting any religious group or belief, since humans do not react well to having their beliefs challenged. Our history is written in blood.

Chronicles of Hope: The Collective   ∞

5. Aurora suggests we reiterate the messages in a generic way. "The message has to be delivered in a way that the people are going to be willing to accept."

6. The Collective hopes that simply reminding people that we are all one people would be enough. While it is doubtful this will help, it is the only recommendation they know how to make.

7. "We almost wish there was an omnipotence in the Universe incapable of error, but there is none such. We make mistakes. We have before. We will again."

8. "When Jesus spoke two thousand years ago, the words were simple enough. But somehow, they were not accepted."

9. "The knowledge of what Jesus truly is, is in your hands right now."

10. "That Jesus was more than simply human is understood, but he wasn't the son of God. You could say he was the son of Gods."

11. The Collective has no desire to be worshiped. They would be happy to have humans simply take their advice.

Love Thy Neighbor

1. Jesus' simple message can be delivered as it originally was, without religion: "Love thy neighbor; do unto others as you would have others do unto you."

2. Humans have evolved beyond the need to believe in Gods. We have science now and don't need to think that when it thunders, a God is angry.

3. "If humans want to attribute something beyond them-selves to what they see around them, they should be more respectful of Gaia. By any human definition, Gaia is a God, a Goddess."

4. Many cultures, such as the Native Americans and the Druids, respect nature.

5. "Humanity is also worthy of respect."

6. "Present the message of peace, of restoring balance."

7. "If Jesus' message 'Turn the other cheek' were one of the basic tenets by which people lived, most of the problems would go away."

8. "Pause to reflect before taking an action. It is very simple to give in to a reflex. It takes maturity to stop and consider your response."

9. Any struggle can be stopped by only one side if they simply choose not to fight. Aurora says it really is as simple as that.

10. "It is not necessary to give in to hatred so easily. It only takes a simple effort of will."

11. "People need to be reminded that they are better than they think they are."

Humanity Will Destroy Itself

1. "People need to be reminded in a secular way of the basic messages that all religions have. It is the religious trappings that cause difficulty."

2. The Collective finds it hard to understand how some religions that seem so similar on the surface could *hate each other* so much. Other religions that are vastly different do not possess that level of hatred.

3. Even though the Collective knows the history of the world, they do not know where that hatred comes from. They do not know how hatred became so ingrained in humanity.

4. The Collective understands that love and hate cannot exist independently, any more than dark and light can exist independently.

5. Some ancient civilizations on Earth were peaceful and were able to interact with others while remaining peaceful.

6. Humanity is unique in having evolved to the point of having civilization, then devolved back into conflict. The Collective has never seen that on another world.

7. The Collective has seen conflict in younger species, but once they grow out of conflict, they leave it behind.

8. "Humanity has not only carried conflict with them, they wear it like a badge of honor. It is very self-destructive, and that destruction is coming."

9. "Humanity will destroy itself if it does not learn to live with itself. Those are the only two outcomes."

How Spirits Develop

1. Aurora tells us that humans have four parts. The physical part is the receptacle in which the etheric parts reside.

2. The etheric consists of three parts: the mental-intellectual, the emotional, and the spiritual.

3. "When a human is conceived, the physical body begins to develop and develops throughout its entire life."

4. "At some point during the physical development, the intellectual and emotional bodies are created. The timing is different for each individual."

5. "The spiritual body is fully formed and developed when it enters. At a point before birth, the spiritual body synchronizes and joins with the other parts and a whole person is created."

6. "Most of the spiritual changes occur at the end of life, when the physical body is broken."

7. In our life review, as the spiritual part of our being reviews the mental and emotional parts of the life it just lived, it keeps the parts it wants. This is how our spirits develop.

8. A brand-new spirit is complete when it enters, just less developed. It will learn quickly as the human body develops.

9. The Collective is discouraging new spirits from being born as humans right now. They are allowing older spirits a chance to bring Earth back into balance.

10. The Collective makes suggestions to send new spirits elsewhere in the Universe, yet it cannot stop a spirit from being born where it wants to be born.

All You Have Left

1. It is unusual for beings of the Collective to speak directly through a physical species, partly because it is so difficult, but mostly because their efforts often backfire.

2. The reason they are talking with us is because we are human. They hope we will recognize flaws that the Collective cannot see from their higher perspective.

3. The Collective hopes that coming from native humans, their messages might be better accepted, even though people won't fully understand where the messages come from.

4. Of the three Children's Children on Earth at the start of this communication, one has returned to the spirit world, leaving only two of them alive on Earth. In a very short time, another will return.

5. The spirit that motivates Gary's body will be the last of their kind to incorporate on Earth until humanity makes its choice.

6. "The reason that I chose to come here today is in the hope that you can do something that might relieve some of the human struggle."

7. "The message is important, and you do have to get it out there, and you have to get it out quickly. Humanity doesn't realize how little time it has left."

8. "If there is any hope for humanity at all, it is in the work that you are all doing."

9. "These messages will be all that you have left. We wish you the best. We hope you succeed."

"I've learned that people will forget what you said,
people will forget what you did,
but people will never forget how you made them feel."
—Maya Angelou

Highlights – Session 4 – Samael

Archangel Samael advises us to be strong, to establish discernment, discipline, and protection. All quotations in this section are attributed to Archangel Samael.

A Very Old Story

1. "Two kinds of people call on me: children playing with fire, and souls so badly damaged that they wouldn't understand my response."

2. Samael tells us his is a very old story. At the dawn of humanity, he took on a role of the God of the underworld.

3. "You might know me as Osiris, Nergal, or Hades . . . oddly enough, one of my names is Samael, the Bringer of Light."

4. It wasn't until certain religious belief systems that Lucifer was painted in a negative light. Organized religion viewed the creation of Lucifer as a dark force as a necessary counterpoint to the creation of an all-powerful, all-positive force.

5. At the same time, religious leaders were trying to convince people of a reward in the afterlife, so they had to convince them of punishment in the afterlife. That sort of control over individuals can be understood.

6. "What I have trouble forgiving is the need for organized religious leaders to force their belief on others. This is still going on today."

7. "It disturbs me greatly to be remembered as I am being remembered. At some level, humanity is still my children."

8. "All of my kin are beyond such mortal conceptions as good and evil. I do not desire to be remembered as evil. Even if I were capable of such, it was never my intent."

9. When asked how he would choose to be remembered, Samael replied: "The Mesopotamians described me well as Nergal,

and the Norse described me as Loki, and even the Egyptian Osiris was a reasonable form for me to take."

10. Samael brought much knowledge to humanity and to evolving intelligent life on many worlds.

Strong Civilizations

1. "I want humanity to survive, but I want it to survive with strength."

2. Those of the Collective are individuals and are also one together. Any of them can respond to offer information, which is the same regardless of who delivers it.

3. The Collective is judicious in what they teach, and humanity is not ready for some knowledge.

4. "Were I in a generous mood, I would say that humanity is still in its infancy. As of the moment, I am not in such a generous mood, I would say that humanity is being infantile."

5. "Throughout time and throughout the Universe, evolution is along a single path. Civilizations can end in failure where they simply die, obliterate themselves, succumb to some external force, or they can end in enlightenment."

6. "The Anasazi and the Lemurians evolved beyond the need for a physical form. The Atlanteans and the Incas were destroyed. These cultures represented peaks of evolution on this planet."

7. The current state of civilization is considerably less evolved than what some earlier civilizations on Earth enjoyed.

8. "Do not let the fact that you have technology delude you into thinking that you are evolved."

9. "I bring knowledge, but I bring discord as well. I am one of my kindred who believes that conflict is essential to the

survival of any civilization, even if that conflict can bring about the end of the civilization."

10. "If a civilization cannot survive the challenge, it does not deserve to live. This is not a popular message, even among my own kin."

11. "It is my desire to see humanity survive, but only if it can be a strong civilization. I have no desire to promote survival of the weak, because that is not survival, that is existence."

One Species

1. "The knowledge that has been passed on to you over these last few months needs to be disseminated across the world. Here is an area where modern technology will help you."

2. "When there was less technology on Earth, there was less struggle. Civilization has become too technocratic. It has forgotten its roots in nature."

3. "Civilization has forgotten that all humans are humans. You are *one* species. The fact that you grew up in a different place, and your ancestors came from a different continent, does not make you any less related."

4. "Every living human, every living *creature* on this planet can be traced back to an original common ancestor, primitive as that ancestor may be. Remember that you are *all* brothers and sisters to each other."

5. "Taking on the role of God of the underworld in so many ancient civilizations has never been a pleasant task. No one looks forward to meeting what I represent. I believe you are the first two humans ever to address me directly."

6. "Remember that your spirits, the young ones and the old ones, are immortal spirits. You need have no fear of death."

7. When asked if he sends entities to harm people, Samael tells us most of them are not *sent* at all, and certainly not by him. He has no desire to bring harm.

8. Samael has never sent entities. Had he wanted to hurt someone, he is more than capable of doing that on his own.

Damaged Spirits

1. Most of the entities we encounter in our clearing sessions are of two categories.

2. The first are simple non-physical beings, creatures of a lower order of energy that seek to feed. Every living thing must feed; the fact that they have no body makes them no less living. They never give us any trouble when we ask them to leave.

3. Other forms we encounter are spirits who had physical lives, but the eternal spiritual part of them is damaged.

4. In some cases, these damaged spirits cling to a life form even if it isn't their own. In others, they are looking to regain the energy they need to resume incorporating.

5. We have the most trouble getting rid of these damaged spirits because there is conscious will behind them.

6. "The number of humans on Earth right now with souls so badly damaged that they will *not* reincorporate, or some so extremely damaged that they will dissolve, is considerable."

7. "When the body dies, the spirit lives on, but if the spirit realizes that it has led a life that has been so harmful and hurtful and hateful to others that it can no longer tolerate its own existence, that spirit simply dissociates, it evaporates."

8. "The energy of a terminated spirit is not lost. It will be used to create a new spirit, but that original spirit is gone."

9. "It is sad that the number of people on Earth right now with badly damaged spirits has never been higher."

10. "Having this many damaged spirits is not a uniquely human condition, but it does occur on this planet in a great amount and more regularity than it does on most others."

Individual Development

1. It is difficult for the Collective to understand how so much hate can be brought about. Having never taken corporeal form before, Samael could not answer the question with certainty about why there is so much hate among humans.

2. Samael tells us his version of the four parts of the individual: the physical body, and the unseen etheric, which is comprised of the mental, the emotional, and the spiritual parts.

3. The spiritual part is eternal, is fully formed when it enters, and is what motivates the physical body.

4. "Be that spirit new, in its first incarnation, or be it as old as one of my Children, the mental and emotional etheric parts of an individual are new for each incorporation."

5. "The etheric parts develop as the physical body develops, as the individual develops, independently of the spiritual body."

6. "It is possible that the conditions that an individual developed under in a particular incarnation will result in mental or emotional bodies that are damaged or poisoned."

7. "For individuals with well-developed spirits, this presents an almost inescapable conflict between the nature of their spiritual self and the nature of the individual self."

8. "Many humans that are thought of as insane suffer from this internal conflict. This condition has never occurred in so many people as it has *right now* on this planet."

9. The environment in which new individuals, not new spirits, develop produces discord between essential parts of their own individuality, which results in undirected anger.

10. People do not know why they hate, and any convenient target is suitable for the subject of their hatred. Usually, the focus of someone's hatred is undeserving of it.

Strengthen Humanity

1. "There have been many dictators in the history of Earth who have used the principle of hatred to build power for themselves, by channeling the unfocused hatred of people who become their followers."

2. "Hitler was elected chancellor before he became dictator. We see that in several individuals on Earth right now."

3. "Remember that the citizens of Germany were the first to fall to the power of the Nazi regime."

4. Many of the people in power today have their power only because it was given to them.

5. Samael seeks to strengthen humanity to prevent harmful leaders from being able to gather a large enough number of people who are angry.

6. "If people had more self-determination, and if the individuals did not have unfocused hatred and anger, it would not be so simple for a dictator to gather them up into an army."

7. It's difficult to strengthen a herd without culling the weak individuals, yet the Collective prefers that selection be natural.

8. We are advised to focus on the vulnerable people with the work we are doing to seek a way to bring hope back to humanity.

Dissonance to Empowerment

1. Nothing forbids us from clearing others of negative energy. Doing this will not interfere with another's destiny or karma.

2. To a large extent, clearing their negative energy is something that people must do for themselves. We need to teach this. It is something everyone needs to learn.

3. "It will be much more difficult for you to remove internal negative influences. Partly because it is a literal part of that individual, and partly because those forces will have been there for so long and have become more entrenched."

4. "The problem is that most people don't realize why they have the anger and the hatred."

5. "People don't understand the true nature of their own selves, and therefore cannot see the dissonance between pieces of themselves that they are unaware they even have."

6. It is not possible to completely remove the dissonance between a spirit that is naturally positive and emotional and intellectual bodies that are essentially negative, but the effects of that dissonance can be minimized.

7. When people clear the path of dissociation between their essentially positive spirit and the parts of their etheric selves that have developed negatively, they become empowered.

8. When people believe in their own internal power and do not seek to place it in the hands of another, we hope that most of humanity's issues will resolve.

9. "I understand that this work you do is to bring hope to the world, which is a laudable goal. It must contain some instruction."

10. "Even if they don't dismiss it, even if they want to believe, even if they want to follow, they won't be able to. They need to understand their own true natures."

11. "Individuals must heal themselves before you can heal the world. If the people do not understand their own natures, let alone the nature of the Universe, then nothing else you present will make any sense to them."

Gaia's Frustration

1. "You have no idea how upset Gaia is with her humans. She is, by right, frustrated right now."

2. "Do not mistake Gaia's frustration and anger for a lack of love for her children."

3. "Children require discipline. Discipline is something else lacking in modern civilization."

4. "In the very near future you will begin to see a drop-off in population growth. That will be in part Gaia's work."

5. It isn't that Gaia cannot support more people, but she can do so only if the people become more thoughtful.

6. If people do not understand their own true nature, you cannot expect them to understand a living planet.

7. Not all planets have a spirit like Gaia. Not all planets have a spirit. All planets with intelligent life do have a spirit; it is probably a necessary factor.

8. "Yes, Gaia requires healing as well. When there are a sufficient number of people who understand, there will be a sufficient number of people to help."

9. "Right now, all of the energy that the people who do understand could muster would not be enough to even mollify her, let alone heal her."

10. "Gaia hears your words. What she decides to do with them is up to her."

Helpful Groups

1. "If you can be the voice that rallies them, rather than somebody who would use them for ill, you will have accomplished your goal."

2. "It is very easy to make that statement. It will not be easy for you to do it. Do not fall into the trap that my son Jesus fell

into two thousand years ago. Do not become the objects of adoration."

3. "There are only a handful of people on the world right now who can do what you two are trying to do."

4. "There is only one other like Gary on this world right now, and she will not be here much longer. When Gary passes, and his spirit is freed, he will be the last of the Collective to take corporeal form until the world decides one way or another what its fate is going to be."

5. "If this work does not succeed, it is not the end of all hope for Earth, but it is Earth's best hope right now. No one else is in possession of the knowledge we have given you. If we did not think you were perfect for this task, you would never have heard from us."

6. "The material we have given you speaks for itself and is the same message given two thousand years ago."

7. "Humanity is in worse shape now than it was two thousand years ago. You have an upward struggle."

8. "There have been many who have said, 'My way is the only way.' Nothing could ever be further from the truth. Humanity is too complex to believe that there is ever one course of action."

9. Others, in their own way, are trying to bring about positive change for the planet. They are doing similar work and, of necessity, are on different paths.

10. Groups with similar goals have not had the benefit of communication with the Collective. We must vet carefully anyone who seeks to join us.

11. "We try to make your path as smooth and straight as possible."

"*Each man is questioned by life.*
He can only answer to life by answering for his own life.
To life, he can only respond by being responsible."
—Victor Frankl

Highlights – Session 5 – Universe

The Spirit of the Universe urges us to be inspiring, to share empathy, connection, and oneness with all. All quotations in this section are attributed to the Spirit of the Universe.

The Universe Is the Sum of All Consciousness

1. The Universe's consciousness is a representation of all conscious living things. You might say the Universe is the sum of all the consciousness that exists within the Universe.

2. "The Anquietas came from my energy but, prior to their creation, I *was only energy*; there was no conscious thought."

3. "In a sense, the Anquietas came of my energy. My consciousness came about at the same time. In a sense, we are more brethren than children."

4. "I am the sum of the first 8 (the Anquietas), and the sum of that 8 plus the next 512 (the Children). My consciousness grew again with the next 32,768 (the Children's Children)."

5. "Once planets began to form, with spirits of their own that were similar in that they were the sum of the consciousness of the creations on those worlds, my consciousness expanded again."

6. "Terra's conscious spirit is Gaia, the name by which you know her. Her consciousness is then part of me. She is sister to *many worlds* that have their own conscious spirits. Not all worlds have conscious spirits like Gaia."

7. "Still today, parts of my energy go to produce new spirits. Over time, those spirits gain consciousness and again become part of my own."

8. "That is *why* all living things are kin to each other. Because all living things are part of me, as I am part of all living things."

Chronicles of Hope: The Collective ∞

9. "I do not exist independently. I am the sum of all parts of the Universe."

10. "There are many belief systems on Terra that are mutually exclusive. Yet Terrans never seem to notice that all of their descriptions of what they think the Universe truly is cannot possibly be right."

11. "Most beliefs humans have about the Universe are quite far from the true reality. It would not be possible for a human mind to truly conceive of the infinite."

Terrans Are All the Same

1. "*You are all the same.* Not only do you share a common physical ancestor, all life on any planet shares common physical ancestry."

2. "All life in the Universe is tied together. All life in the Universe are brother and sister to each other."

3. "When conflict arises, it is as though family were fighting within itself."

4. Humans exist as individuals and as parts of collectives. We exist as part of the consciousness of our own world.

5. Terrans have not yet realized that life exists throughout the whole fabric of the Universe.

6. The Universe is aware of some of the issues associated with Terra. These issues are common throughout the fabric of the Universe.

7. "Terrans need to understand that you are not alone. You need to know you are part of a greater family. You need to use that information to help bring humanity together."

8. "Terrans are very isolated as individuals. The immortal parts of humans do not coalesce with other individuals, as happens on worlds without conflict."

9. "Terrans view themselves as being isolated and alone. This is not the case. Humans need to learn to share themselves with others."

The Origin of Hate

1. "It is the isolation that Terrans feel that causes the hatred."

2. "Hate comes from isolation, from separation, from the thought that Terrans are alone."

3. "Hate is a symptom, a cause. It, in turn, becomes a cause for the actions that occur."

4. Much hatred is based on the belief of difference: that another individual is deserving of hatred because they believe differently.

5. When someone is unable to experience what others around them experience, believing that others somehow have more, promotes feelings of jealousy and greed that can ultimately lead to hatred.

6. Humans believe their actions occur in isolation. That is not the case. Humans need to learn that every action and thought they take affects all those around them.

7. "Terrans never truly realize how each of their lives affects each other, because they do not feel what each other feels."

8. Many conflicts on Terra begin with a group of individuals being painted as different, providing a focus for hatred. By removing the belief in that dissimilarity, you remove the focus of the hatred.

9. Closer individuals believe themselves to be brothers. Not only does that reduce the cause of hatred, it also makes it more difficult for the individual to hate.

10. "When individuals learn to feel what their neighbors feel, when they experience the pain they cause others, the natural

desire will be to avoid inflicting pain. *That is the true path to peace.*"

Remove the Barriers

1. "Terrans need to learn to share, not only the physical world around you, but your feelings and emotions, even your thoughts."

2. The spiritual part of each person strives to communicate directly with the spiritual part of all the people around them.

3. "The environment in which most Terrans are brought up discourages this spiritual communication from birth. The result is that Terrans as individuals are, in fact, more isolated than individuals need to be."

4. With true communication comes the realization the differences are not so great between us, and our hatred thus dissipates. It is difficult to hate someone whom you view as similar to you.

5. "By breaking down the barriers between individuals, by allowing Terran minds to share information directly, by striving toward the common consciousness, it would help each individual see that the people around them are not so very different."

6. "Breaking down the barriers between individuals, allowing them to experience each other's thoughts and feelings. That is the cure."

7. "Someone has to be the first to be willing to drop the barriers isolating themselves from another."

Coming Together

1. "Coming together is the solution. Remove your own feelings of isolation."

2. "When you see into the spirit of the people with and around you, then you will know without any shadow of a doubt, without any conscious thought, with whom you may share whatever you wish."

3. When we are well matched, and we trust and love one another enough, we don't need barriers between us.

4. None of us actually realize or understand the method by which we can allow the spiritual parts of ourselves to truly become one with another.

5. The Children's Children have the knowledge of how to do this, because they have existed in both corporeal and non-corporeal form. They know how to drop their barriers when they leave the body and exist more closely to Universal consciousnesses.

6. Any of the Children's Children can teach us how to remove barriers to blend together while we remain in physical form.

7. "It is a process not without risk, not without discomfort. You will be opening yourselves up primarily to each other, but also to any free spirit near you."

8. "You will need to protect yourselves against unwanted intrusion. When you open yourselves up, our light will shine more brightly and will be visible across dimensions."

9. Our light will show brightly to those who desire the same change we seek, who will respond to a feeling of openness. If we are open to them, they will without conscious thought become open to us.

10. "You will be the first ripple in a very large pond. But any ripple, no matter how small, will eventually reach all the way to the borders of that pond."

11. As more and more people around us become open, *it will spread*. We have the opportunity and the ability to make the

moral change on Gaia. It's up to us to decide whether we want to do it.

You Will Become A Beacon

1. "You will become a beacon. Those around you who want to experience the positive energy, will."

2. "However, you will attract non-physical beings that seek out any source of energy. You have the skills to protect yourselves. But you must be vigilant with exercising these skills or you will become burdened."

3. In Book 1, the Anquietas gave us explanations about non-physical beings, such as low-level entities that are from other dimensions and are attracted to both positive and negative energies as food sources.

4. The Anquietas also gave us information about the Protective Bubble to use for protection. It is detailed at the end of both books.

5. It would help make our process easier to clear the negative first.

6. "It would help make your process easier . . . if other Terrans had some conscious desire to want to experience what you are going to show them. It is possible to make your path clearer by removing some of the hatred."

7. "There are lessons that you can teach to help people, to be more thoughtful of their own thoughts and actions and to not to be so reactive and defensive."

8. "Clearing your path in the physical dimension will help clear our path in the non-physical dimension. You can simplify your task in that way."

9. What the Universe sees within us is that we have all we need to succeed.

10. "You have been granted audiences with the oldest spirits within me. Listen to those words and pass them on. Take them into your own heart and try to get others to do the same."

11. "Most importantly, your instincts are good. You need to trust them. You have no need to doubt yourselves in any way."

"There is a force in the Universe, which, if we permit it,
will flow through us and create miraculous results."
—Mahatma Gandhi

Highlights – Session 6 – Gaia

Gaia gives great insight into how we can be better stewards of this Earth and shift the planet toward long-term vitality. She desires that we be more helpful, to cultivate mindfulness, conscientiousness, and stewardship. All quotations in this section are attributed to Gaia.

Spirit of Earth

1. "I am the Spirit of Earth, Gaia, your mother."

2. "I know that there are humans among you who care. It is the indifference that hurts more than anything else. So many people are so thoughtless."

3. The future vision with the Earth being brown originates from the lack of care or respect humans have shown for our planet.

4. "There is no catastrophe that I foresee, except that which I may choose to bring."

5. Gaia doesn't have the ability to target individuals who are most responsible for the damage. However, she does lash out as any wounded creature would.

6. "My consciousness is not an individual thing. I am the sum of the consciousness of all living things on the planet. All living things, not just humans. Everything that lives is part of me."

7. "My feelings are the sum of the feelings of the living creatures on this planet."

8. The more creatures who suffer, the more Gaia suffers, and the more they feel it. Many times, that feeling can spiral out of control. It is happening now.

9. "Extinction is a natural event. More species have become extinct than have ever lived . . . than are living now. But the rate of extinction is growing."

The Problem

1. "I wish I could say that there was one simple thing that could be done to help the Earth."

2. "The problem isn't just the destruction of the rainforests or the poisoning of the oceans or the execution of animals for sport. The problem isn't even the use and waste of resources. There are enough resources."

3. "The problem is the lack of thought that people have for their actions in general."

4. There is not one specific action humans can take to reverse the damage to our Earth, other than to pause to consider the consequences of our actions.

5. "It's a matter of raising the consciousness levels of the humans."

6. "Everything is connected to everything else. Anything you change in one place will have more than one consequence."

7. "If humans were more aware of their own interconnectedness with everything else, and realized that every action they take has consequences far beyond those they could even foresee, and modified their actions to allow for the consequences they can foresee, that would be enough."

8. "There are those who realize that their actions are actively harmful and do them anyway. There are those who witness this and do nothing to prevent it. That level of indifference is what causes more damage than anything else."

9. Most humans think the task to clean up the Earth is too big and is just not possible. That is probably true for humans.

10. "I am capable of healing the Earth provided that the level and rate of damage is reduced."

Gaia Can Heal the Damage

1. When you think about the history of our planet and Gaia, it's hard for humans to comprehend time in billions of years. We don't realize how small our life span is in the span of all things.

2. Many humans have such an overinflated opinion of themselves. At the same time, they need to realize their span of life is an infinitesimal fraction of Gaia's.

3. "I can heal the damage; humans just have to let me do it. The rate at which they cause harm is greater than the rate at which I can heal."

4. "Consider the things that have happened to Earth: the meteor strikes, the loss of the dinosaurs, I healed the planet enough for the human species to arise."

5. "The human species would not be here had the dinosaurs not been destroyed. That was not my doing."

6. "Evolution is a punctuated process, not a smooth continuous event. It is a series of small events, each one triggered by either a natural or artificial occurrence. Sometimes it's a random mutation, sometimes it's an asteroid strike."

7. "Clearing away of one species makes room for another."

8. "I would never extinguish humanity. However, I would not overextend myself to protect it either."

9. "Humans have to realize that they have a place on this world, and that they are no more superior to any other living creature than any other living creature is. Just because they have a bigger brain doesn't make them in control."

10. "In many ways, humans are not the most intelligent species on this planet. They need to understand their place, and learn to live within it and take only what they need."

Our Food Web

1. Most humans are aware of the complex web of life, often referring to it as a food chain. This is an overly simplistic view. It is an interconnected web.

2. "We need to consider it a food web instead of a food chain. Everything is interconnected."

3. "There is no harm in eating land animals or aquatic animals, any more than there is harm in eating land plants or aquatic plants. It is only in excess that damage is done."

4. "If all humans suddenly became vegetarian, there would be a shortage of land on which to grow the vegetables and the plants that you would eat. Everything has to be taken in balance."

5. Animals came about as a natural course of evolution and were not created for the purpose of human consumption. There is nothing wrong in humans consuming them.

6. The process involved with raising animals and crops for human and animal consumption needs to be more carefully managed. It must not be done in a wasteful fashion.

7. "When an animal is killed and eaten only for the parts that it was killed for, and the rest is just left, that is not an acceptable use."

8. When a cow is slaughtered, and all of it *is* reused, that is an acceptable use. The parts humans don't eat should go into fertilizer, feed, or meal, and the skin used for leather.

9. "Eating animals is okay, but fishing to the point of extinction is self-defeating and self-destructive. It only ever requires a little bit of care."

Care for Our Land

1. "The littering of the surface of the world with stuff that doesn't go away for a long period of time impacts you more than it does me."

2. "The things that hurt me are the things that alter my very existence. The stuff on the surface is not an issue, but mercury, and lead, and all of the horrible chemicals do leave a permanent scar."

3. "The overuse of chemicals and fertilizers and genetic modifications, those are things I have more difficulty cleaning up. Although, eventually, I will process them and break them down and clean them up. My energy would be better spent elsewhere."

4. "Some crops are very detrimental to the soil. Tobacco, for example, depletes the soil. Humans do understand crop rotation and the ability to naturally revitalize the soil, but it is easier and cheaper to dump chemicals onto the land."

5. Using chemicals is counterproductive because the chemicals wash into the water. The sea life that doesn't perish from it can become overabundant.

6. Chemicals thought beneficial to the land run off into the water and cause red tides and algae blooms. These blooms can strip hundreds of cubic miles of oxygen from the ocean, causing everything in that area of water to die. When the things that die degrade, they add imbalance to the water, and it becomes a spiraling process.

7. Humans have the knowledge to run farms properly. However, it requires the desire to use that knowledge and the desire to spend the extra amount of energy it takes.

8. "It would just simply be helpful to stop polluting. I can only clean up just so much, just so fast. Humans need to take a part in that cleanup. But, more importantly, they

need to take a part in reducing the rate at which they do
these things."

9. "Humans don't realize that the rainforests are a very delicately balanced organism unto itself and removing large
chunks of it to make farmland won't work, because the
ground in which rainforests live is not particularly fertile
ground."

10. The ground in the rainforest is ideally suited to the rainforest but is not suited to the growing of a single crop. When
the soil becomes depleted and the rainforest is gone, adding
chemicals will increase crop productivity for some period of
time, but ultimately will cause more damage than it started.

11. Gaia can bring back the rainforests to what they were,
provided humans leave them alone. Once they are destroyed,
they're gone forever. There would be no possibility of ever
bringing them back because their life is too interdependent.

Consider the Consequences

1. "Humans have a lazy streak in them. They will do things in
the simplest possible way to serve themselves, without any
thought of the consequence of their actions."

2. "Consequences have to be considered because they will catch
up with you. There is no escaping it. It is a fundamental law
of nature, a fundamental law of physics."

3. "Most intelligent species respond most strongly to fear and
to pain. They are strong motivators."

4. "Fear comes from part of the human brain that has not
changed much in a hundred thousand years of evolution.
Humans have added more layers to their brain and more
complexity, but the reptilian brain is still there."

5. "When something hurts you, you learn not to do it. When
you fear something, you learn not to do it."

6. Fear of heights was built into most humans, with some exceptions. Many Native Americans never developed a fear of heights, possibly because of the reverence they have for the land, and because some were used to standing on high to look around.

7. "If you can demonstrate to people what's going to happen to them in a way that is undeniable, then their natural preservation instinct will hopefully cause them to do things the right way."

8. The problem is, how do you demonstrate the consequences in a way that is clear and undeniable?

9. "Even the wrath which I lay down periodically is all too frequently dismissed. It would not be my preference to be so blatant and obvious and so destructive as to make it inexplicable in any other way."

10. "How do you hurt someone enough to let them know that doing it again will hurt, without hurting them so much that they don't get a second chance?"

11. "I don't desire destruction; I cherish all life, as all life is my charge."

Survival Instincts

1. "All species with any level of intelligence and awareness have first and foremost a survival instinct."

2. "Humans are unique in their self-centeredness and selfishness, that they don't even care about their own offspring's future. I have never faced that issue before. I have no solution to that problem."

3. Too many people look at things within their own lifespan and say, "I have only a few years left, what difference does it make what I do to the world? It's not going to affect me."

4. Some people have children and don't even stop to think: "Is what I'm doing going to affect my children and their children?" They're so wrapped up in themselves, they don't even care about their own families.

5. "I have no answer for how to overcome something that is so unique in life. Every other species has more care for their kin than they do for themselves."

6. "In most species, the instinct to survive is stronger than the instinct to even reproduce. There are exceptions, but humans simply don't think of their actions as ultimately going to harm them."

7. "Humans think that I am so large that I can absorb anything they do, and large as I am, that's not the case. There is a point at which I will not be able to protect them anymore."

8. "Humans just don't realize the consequences of their actions. The more care you take of me, the more care I will be able to take of you."

9. "Appeal to people's self-interests, since that seems to be what drives them. By destroying me, they are only destroying themselves."

Make Small Changes

1. "Humans do tend to excess. Again, that is something that I don't see in any of my other children."

2. "Most animals, when they graze, know enough to not kill the plant they eat, to move on to another field so that the plants grow back. Migration patterns are caused by this."

3. "Humans must be aware of the effects of overuse, and don't seem to care. I find that inexplicable behavior."

4. "It isn't that everyone needs to be convinced. It only takes a few to make a big difference. A very small snowball can turn into a very large avalanche given enough time."

5. "There are plenty of people who know these things, and who speak about them. But their voices are not heard, or worse, they're shouted down by the people who know they're doing damage but doing it for profit."

6. "If the people who misuse the resources do so because of profit, then the way to get them to change is to attack their profit."

7. "If the consumers don't buy things that are bad for them, and a lot of the food being sold today is very bad for them either by deliberate act or by carelessness, then the producers will have to change their production. They'll have to change what they sell."

8. "Manmade things are really no different than nature-made things. Anything can be used to a good purpose; anything can be abused to a bad purpose."

9. "There is no one product that is detrimental; it's a matter of trying to live more naturally. That doesn't mean that you have to give up anything that you have. It just means that you should use things in moderation."

10. "No major changes are required. A small change here, a small change there, and that's all it takes. When things start to get better, and people start to realize that these changes do have an effect, they'll be more willing to make more changes."

11. "Humans pride themselves on being so intelligent. Apply that intelligence, apply that reason to these very simple things."

Genetic Modification

1. "There's nothing wrong with hybridizing. I do that myself."

2. "In all of nature, the reason there are so many different things is because of natural hybridization, a fair and reasonable process."

3. "The tampering with nature using genetics is an example of things with unforeseen consequences."

4. "There are things that are going to begin to occur related to genetic modification that humans have done for which they had no foresight and no concept that this was going to happen."

5. "Consequences of genetic modification is not something that Gaia is going to do deliberately. It's a natural consequence of what humans are doing, and it will hurt humanity."

6. "Deliberate tampering is always going to produce a result that humans don't expect. Unfortunately, those results are usually very long term."

Earth's Climate

1. Gaia's lifespan is so long humans can't perceive that sort of time span. We don't realize that had humans started evolving now, rather than a hundred thousand years ago, our civilization would not have developed the way it did.

2. "The climate on this planet is normally much harsher than it currently is. Humans were very fortunate to have grown up in a time of very moderate climate at the end of a natural glaciation."

3. "The climate at the time of the dinosaurs, for example, was one in which humans in their current form, could not survive."

4. "Evolution does work and humans, intelligent creatures, would have come to pass, but they would not be recognized as what we would call human today."

5. "The problem is that the environmental change will outstrip the pace of evolution."

6. "Man's impact on the environment isn't as great as they think it is, in terms of the climate. The climate will change; it will become warmer."

7. "Most informed people or scientists do have a fair grasp of the timeframe involved with coastal changes. However, they underestimate how bad it ultimately will be. Nobody likes to foresee their own destruction."

8. "It comes down to the fact that this is not going to happen within the lifespans of the people who are already on the Earth. It's the next generations that are going to start to see the side effects."

9. "There are events that could re-introduce glaciation: large volcanic eruptions, meteor strikes, anything that blocks the sun for any period of time."

Glaciations and Pollution

1. "The history of glaciation is actually very interesting, and I don't think it's something that most of your scientists understand."

2. "When there was but one continent, the currents in the one ocean were unrestricted. This meant that the water from the poles mixed more freely with the water from the equator with the result that there were no icecaps."

3. "Icecaps can only form on land, not in mid-ocean. So, with no icecaps and with the ocean waters circulating, the world was a much warmer place."

4. "Without icecaps reflecting the sun, there was more absorption of what little sun there was in the polar regions."

5. "As the continents broke up and reached their current positions, the land interfered with the circulation in the oceans. It became more difficult for the cold waters at the poles to move, and for the warm water at the equator to move toward the poles."

6. "As the land spread into the polar regions, it formed points upon which ice could form. When the ice formed, it impacted the circulation, which reflected more solar heat, and that's what caused glaciers to move down almost to the tropics. The only place the ice did not reach was where the sun was overhead most of the year."

7. "As the oceans' currents stabilized with the continents in the current position, the heat exchange increases and the ice melts, which reduces solar reflection, and so the ice continues to melt. That is a natural process."

8. "It is impossible to predict with certainty what will happen and when. There are too many random variables."

9. "If anything, the pollution that humans have pumped into the air is more likely to cool the Earth than it is to cause it to heat. That could bring back another glaciation."

10. "Regardless of its impact on climate, pumping pollution into the air is self-defeating. Humans are literally poisoning themselves, the air, the land, the water."

11. "Humans will eventually extinct themselves, or enough of them that it won't make much difference. And then I start again."

Start a Trend

1. Atlantis was a slightly different case than what we may expect for humanity today. They didn't heed the advice they were given, and their destruction was almost immediate. As powerful as Atlantis was, it was small compared to modern civilization on Earth.

2. In the case of humanity, the destruction is going to be over a more prolonged period of time.

3. "There is nothing humans can do, short of an atomic war, that would cause such instantaneous change for the good or for the ill."

4. "When you're dealing with a planet, you're dealing with trends, not individual actions, barring large-scale events like meteor strikes, which could still happen."

5. "Starting a trend which is beneficial is worth doing, even if the results are not obvious until several generations later."

6. "Humans need to live for their own future, not for their current existence. They need to plan for their future, not their current existence."

7. "It's important that humans realize that just because things don't happen quickly, doesn't mean their effects aren't important."

8. "Things simply do not change that fast on a planetary scale, but that doesn't mean that every little bit doesn't help."

Immortal Spirits

1. "Many of the things written into the Bible are natural events that were taken and written in as examples of God or God's wrath."

2. "The plagues of Egypt were a natural occurrence that clever people wrote into a book and used as an example of what their God was capable of doing."

3. If you look at the plagues and the order in which they occur, one event triggers the first plague. The result of that plague triggers the second. It was a natural occurrence of events, and humans said: "We can take advantage of that and use it as a lesson."

4. Ancient religions and ancient mythologies attributed things the people didn't understand to a God. The Greeks had the God of the sun, and the God of the sea, and the God of the land, and the God of the underworld.

5. "There are many religions on Earth today, many polytheistic religions, that still attribute things to Gods. They're not completely wrong."

6. "There are spirits that are non-physical. I wonder if you could define me as non-physical, as I am the spirit of a planet?"

7. "There are spirits that are non-physical that do interact and interject at critical moments, critical times. In some way, you could call them Gods."

8. "These helping spirits are immortal, but they're not the all-knowing, all-powerful beings that are attributed to a God in a monotheistic religion. Taken as a whole, you could call the Collective group a God."

9. "Things are the way they are, simply because they are. On other worlds, things probably come up in different ways. You have talked to spirits of the Collective who can speak to that better than I can. My knowledge is limited to this world."

I Am the Life of the Planet

1. "My consciousness is the sum of the consciousness of every living thing on the planet, not just humans."

2. "My consciousness is the sum of everyone else's. Everything I do is to help the life on the planet because I am the life of the planet."

3. "I am not a guiding force; I am a reactive force. I respond to everything that happens on the planet. I do not dictate what happens to the planet."

4. "In moments of despair, I have lashed out. There are events that occur that might not have. There are events whose severity might be altered."

5. "Creation is an accident, not an act of design. Creation comes about through a random, spontaneous event or through a process of evolution."

6. "I am not the creator of things. In fact, I am created by things. I exist because my children exist."

7. "If life on this world were to end, so would I."

"The best remedy for those who are afraid, lonely,
or unhappy is to go outside,
somewhere where they can be quiet,
alone with the heavens, nature, and God.
Because only then does one feel that all is as it should be."

—Anne Frank

Oh, Great Spirit,
Whose voice I hear in the winds,
And whose breath gives life to all the world,
Hear me, I am small and weak, I need your strength and wisdom.

Let me walk in beauty and
make my eyes ever behold the red and purple sunset.
Make my hands respect the things you have made
and my ears sharp to hear your voice.

Make me wise so that
I may understand the things you have taught my people.
Let me learn the lessons you have hidden in every leaf and rock.
I seek strength, not to be greater than my brother,
but to fight my greatest enemy—myself.

Make me always ready to come to you with clean hands and straight eyes.
So when life fades, as the fading sunset,
my Spirit may come to you without shame.
—Lakota Sioux Chief Yellow Lark

Glossary

"If there is any hope for humanity at all,
it is in the work that you are all doing."

—Aurora

32,768: The number of Anquietas' Children's Children, which is 8 to the fifth power. Rae states that about half are incorporated on a planet, and the other half are in spirit form across the Universe. Interestingly, when added together and distilled to a single digit, this number equals 8 (3+2+7+6+8=26, 2+6=8).

A Course In Miracles: (ACIM) A book written in 1976 with a curriculum that aims to assist its readers in achieving spiritual transformation. One of the main goals of ACIM is to heal our relationships through the inspired practice of forgiveness.

Altiplano: (al-tuh-plah-noh) Spanish for "high plain," refers to a region in west-central South America, where the Andes Mountains are at their widest. It is the most extensive area of high plateau outside of Tibet. Most of the Altiplano lies in Bolivia, but its northernmost part is in Peru, and its southernmost parts are in Chile and Argentina.

Anasazi: (ah-nuh-sah-zee) Also known as the Ancestral Puebloans, the Anasazi were an ancient Native American culture. Their territory included what is now the southwest region of the United States.

Ancient Ones: The Anquietas in "the Collective" of spirits that we meet in this series, these are the "First Ones." They were coalesced out of Universal Energy when the Universe was formed. They are the closest thing to what humans would call God, yet there are eight of them and they act as one. They bring knowledge and retain history based on what they have been told.

Angel: Any spirit who is dedicated to helping others. These beings may be found in the physical and spiritual realms.

Anquietas: (ohn-kwee-A-tus) This word comes from the ancient Greek, meaning Ancient Ones. In *Chronicles of Hope: The Anquietas: Book 1,* they are the First Ones, the First Consciousness who say they are eight and they are one. They express concern for the state of humanity and our planet Earth. They want us to come together as one before it is too late.

Apocalypse: (uh-pok-uh-lips) Often refers to a revelation. Its literal meaning, from the Greek ἀποκάλυψις (apokálypsis), is an uncovering. In this context, it could mean a lifting of veils or it could refer to a catastrophic event or chain of events detrimental to humanity or nature.

Archangel: An angel of high rank, usually associated with Abrahamic religions. Derived from the Greek ἀρχάγγελος, the word literally means "chief angel." The number of Archangels and their names differs by religion. The Archangels' vibrational energy is too vast to take on corporeal form. However, they have helped humanity throughout the ages as Gods and other celestial beings. Though they assist in many ways, in this series the named Archangels are: Archangel Michael, who is the great protector; Archangel Raphael, who assists with healing; and Archangel Jophiel, who illuminates the creative light within.

Ascended Master: Powerful spiritual Guides who help humans live their life to the fullest. Many have lived a physical existence on the Earth plane as a wise prophet, teacher, or helper.

Astral Projection: An intentional out-of-body experience in which the astral body or spiritual consciousness of a person travels outside of the physical body. It has been documented in many ancient cultures. In modern times, astral travel is associated with dreams, meditation, or hypnotic trance states.

Astral Plane: Comprises the entire existence of spiritual life. Describes where all spirits go to live out their non-physical life and where all consciousness resides across all existences, encompassing all worlds.

Atlantis: An ancient land believed to have been the home of a great civilization circa 12,000 BC. Its capital city, Muir, was located in the Altiplano region in South America.

Atlantean Realm: Referring to the mainland and twelve islands that comprised the civilization of Atlantis.

Aura: The energy field that surrounds all living things. It is the spiritual part of the body that doesn't fit completely into the physical body. The older the spirit, the larger the aura, so there is more of it that extends beyond the physical body. The aura can change color based on emotions and external influences at any given time.

Aurora: The Roman Goddess of the dawn, who announced the coming of the sun by painting the night sky with beautiful colors. Ancient Greek poets used the name Aurora in reference to dawn's play of colors across the dark sky.

Aurora Borealis: Referred to as northern lights, auroras are natural displays of multicolored lights in the Earth's sky. They are seen in the extreme northern (borealis) or southern (australis) magnetic poles of the Earth.

Aztecs: A Mesoamerican culture that thrived in central Mexico from the fourteenth to sixteenth century.

Bering Sea: Connects the continents of America and Asia at the area of Alaska. On a world map, the Africans would have traveled up through Asia to get to this location.

Bermuda Triangle: Also known as the Devil's Triangle or Hurricane Alley, it is a location in the western part of the North Atlantic Ocean where many ships and aircraft have disappeared under mysterious circumstances.

Buddha: (Gautama) A religious leader who is the primary figure in Buddhism. Gautama lived in ancient India between the sixth and fourth centuries BC and taught the Middle Way between indulgence and severe asceticism. He is believed to be an enlightened teacher who shared insights to help humans end suffering.

Channel: One who channels or allows the energy of a spiritual being to actively communicate through them to speak with a human being.

Channeling: A situation where one channels or allows the energy of a spiritual being to actively communicate through their body to speak directly with an incarnated person.

Children: The Children of the Anquietas have closer contact with worlds, with energetic frequency, or "vibrational energy" too high to incarnate or take physical form. Of their 512 Children, which is 8 to the third power, many were ancient Gods of mythology, some are Gods in polytheistic religions, and we call them Archangels.

Children's Children: There are 32,768 of the Anquietas' Children's Children, which is 8 to the fifth power. The Children's Children have vibrational levels that allow them to incarnate, often as prophets of history such as Jesus, Buddha, Muhammad, Lao Tzu, and Quan Yin. In between incarnations, they assist as angels and Guides.

Chronicles of Hope: The Anquietas: Book 1: Published 8/8/2019, the book is the first in the *Chronicles of Hope*™ series, in which the Ancient Ones who call themselves the Anquietas share their concerns about what is happening on planet Earth and give warnings for humanity.

Clearing Consultants: Spiritually-aware individuals who have developed the skill of seeing, sensing, or feeling another's energy while in a guided trance state. They assist in clearing the negative energies in person or remotely from around clients.

The Collective: The group of spirits vibrating at extremely high levels that communicate in the sessions of this book. They consist of the Anquietas (the Ancient Ones), their Children, and their Children's Children.

Corporeal: (kor-por-ee-uhl) Having, consisting of, or relating to a physical, material body; having a physical, material existence. The Ancient Ones often refer to physical life forms (including humans) in this way.

The Council: Atlantean governing body comprised of the Thirteen Representatives, the King and Queen, the First Prime of the military, and the High Priestess.

COVID-19: Pandemic of coronavirus disease that originated in 2019 and swept the world in 2020.

Darshan: Darshan, from the Sanskrit दरशन (darśana), which means sight or vision. It can refer to the seeing of the image of a holy person or deity. It can also refer to the ease with which people can learn a concept once a "first" person has worked to acquire that knowledge.

Demons: A supernatural being or spirit with divine power that historically did not carry negative connotations. In some religions, they are considered harmful entities that can take possession of humans.

Druids: Members of a professional class in ancient Celtic cultures. While best known as religious leaders, they were also legal authorities, lorists (all of their knowledge was passed down orally), and medical practitioners. They possessed a great respect for and connection to the natural world.

Easter Island: An island in the southeastern Pacific Ocean famous for nearly a thousand enormous statues called *Moai*. It was settled around 1200 AD by Polynesian travelers, who created a thriving culture. Land clearing for cultivation led to gradual deforestation, with subsequent diseases that depleted the population. It is now a barren wasteland.

Emotional Energy Feeders: (EEFs) These are described in *Chronicles of Hope: The Anquietas* as simple, draining Earth energies that feed off the negative energy that is given off with human emotion. Much as an algae eater feeds, these EEFs serve to neutralize the negative energy, allowing the opportunity for positive change.

Empath: A person who is sensitive to all types of energy. They are capable of sensing and feeling the emotions of others. Empaths need to learn ways to handle the energy they detect and protect themselves from taking on too much.

Extinction Event: See Mass Extinction.

First Prime: The military leader of Atlantis who rose through the ranks and governed the army and navy.

Gabriel: The Archangel whose name means "God is my strength" is one of the guardians of Israel. An interpreter, revealer, and communicator, Gabriel interpreted the dreams of Daniel and appeared to Zechariah and Mary to foretell the births of John the Baptist and Jesus. He is believed to be the one who communicated with Muhammad.

Gaia: (gai-eh) From the Greek Γαῖα, the primordial Goddess, Mother Earth, from whom all life springs. During the dialogues in this book, Gaia refers to the living spirit of Earth, while Terra refers to the physical Earth itself.

Ganesh: (gah-nes) The Hindu God of new beginnings, the remover of obstacles, and the God of wisdom and intelligence.

Gnosticism: (Gnostics) A system of religious concepts among early Christian and Jewish groups that emphasized personal spiritual knowledge over orthodox teachings. Many Gnostic texts focused on enlightenment with mystical and esoteric insight based on direct communication with the divine.

Great Library of Alexandria: Located in Alexandria, Egypt, it was one of the largest and most significant libraries of the ancient world. It contained massive amounts of papyrus scrolls and was considered the greatest source of literary knowledge. It declined over time and was finally destroyed around 390 AD. Metaphysically, some consider the ancient information from the Alexandrian libraries to exist in etheric form in what is known as the Akashic Records.

Greek God of Sun: Helios was the Titan God of the sun, while Apollo was the Olympian God of the sun. Apollo was also the Roman God of the sun.

Greek God of the Sea: Oceanus was the Titan God of the ocean, while Poseidon was the Olympian God of the sea.

Greek God of the Land: Gaia is the primordial deity that personifies Mother Earth. There is no single Olympian counterpart, but Demeter and Hestia come closest.

Greek God of the Underworld: Hades is the Olympian God of the underworld. Tartarus and Styx represent the deepest, darkest part of the underworld and the River Styx, respectively.

Guardian Angel: An angel that acts as a protector or Guide for a person, group, or place (including a planet).

Guide: In the metaphysical sense, this indicates a wise spiritual energy that assists an incarnated human when called upon. This can be a wise master such as Jesus, a passed-over relative, a guardian angel, or even a helpful Earth energy that provides guidance when asked.

Hades: Greek God of the underworld, often portrayed as stern, yet passive rather than evil. His role was to maintain relative balance and hold his subjects accountable to his laws.

High Priestess: The spiritual leader of Atlantis who received messages from the Patron God, Rae. She brought peace and balance to the realm.

Hippocrates of Kos: (460–370 BC) Ancient Greek physician considered to be one of the most remarkable figures in the history of medicine. He revolutionized medicine, establishing it as a distinct intellectual discipline and profession. He founded the Hippocratic School of Medicine, which is the basis of Western medicine.

Hitler: Adolf Hitler was a German politician and leader of the Nazi Party who rose to power as the chancellor of Germany in 1933. His aggressive policies were considered the primary cause of World War II. His Nazi regime was responsible for the genocide of millions of Jews and others who were considered socially undesirable.

Hologram: A three-dimensional image created by a system of light diffraction that can appear to be real.

Homo sapiens: The name for primitive man. The Collective says we are all descendants of the same ancestor; we are all one species with different subsets.

Hypernova: Also called a super-luminous supernova, it is an exploding star that produces at least ten times the brilliance of an average supernova, which itself is a more massive explosion than a nova. Only extremely large and fast-burning suns, most of which were produced in the early Universe, can end their lives as a hypernova.

Hypnosis: A state of human consciousness involving relaxation, reduced distraction, focused attention, and an openness to connect with all states of the mind.

Hypnotist: A person trained in the art of hypnosis. A hypnotist assists others on their journey of self-discovery to change patterns, habits, and attitudes. They guide others to connect with the power of the subconscious and superconscious mind to empower infinite possibilities for positive change.

Hysteretic: (hysteresis) A lag in response based on change.

Incans: Originally a pastoral tribe in the twelfth century, the Incans became the peoples of the largest pre-Colombian empire in South America, which existed from the fifteenth to sixteenth century.

Incarnation: Literally meaning "embodied in flesh," it refers to a corporeal existence of a spirit. When a body is born, the spirit that motivates that body is living out an incarnation.

Inspiring Hope with Lois Hermann: Good news radio show on WSMN1590.com, WSMN 1590 AM or WSMN 95.3 FM featuring everyday people who are doing inspiring things to help each other and our world.

Isis: Egyptian goddess who represents feminine strength and power. She assists with balance in family and career. She is said to help spirits transition into the afterlife and restore spirits of the departed.

Jesus: One of the Anquietas' Children's Children, the eternal spirit of Jesus is always willing to assist when called on. A beloved prophet, teacher, and healer, Jesus of Nazareth was a human incarnation of this spirit. He brought, and still brings, the message of love for one another.

Jophiel: The Archangel associated with illumination and wisdom. Jophiel is often pictured holding a flame of light. The Statue of Liberty may have been modeled after this Archangel.

Karma: The spiritual principle of cause and effect in which intent and actions of an individual (cause) influence the future of that individual (effect). Karma in the present affects one's future in the current and future lives.

Kumo'a: The Collective's term for direct communion between a high-level being and an incorporated human, where the human allows the high-level being to physically use their body to communicate through.

Lakshmi: Goddess of abundance, good fortune, and beauty among both Hindu and Buddhist followers. As the mother goddess and wife to Vishnu, she transforms money worries into prosperity and financial flow.

Lao Tzu: (Laozi) Ancient Chinese sage who created the *Tao Te Ching*, translated as *The Book of the Way and of Virtue.* Believed to date to the late fourth century BC, this fundamental text is the basis of the philosophical religions of Taoism, Confucianism, and many others. This inspirational text is one of the most translated works in world literature.

Legions of Light: Angelic helpers who assist the Archangels, especially Archangel Michael.

Lemuria/Lemurians: (le-moo-ree-uh) In ancient mythology, a hypothetical lost civilization. In our channeled sessions, we were told the Lemurian civilization pre-dated and possibly spawned the Atlantean civilization. The Lemurians were highly spiritual beings who evolved beyond the need for physical form. Their spirits may still be found within Mount Shasta in California, United States.

Life-Between-Lives: The place in between physical incarnations where the spirit of the person decides what they want to do or experience next.

Light: A human understanding of the higher vibrational and greater energy level that exists between corporeal existences. Some consider the Light to be what is called "heaven." The human mind interprets it as the Light having no other reference for that type of energy.

Loki: Norse God of mischief who sometimes assists the Gods and sometimes behaves in a malicious manner toward them. A shapeshifter, he appears in many different guises and is associated with knots, loops, and webs.

Low-Level Entities: These dark spirits have a low vibrational energy and come from a dimension that has a lower vibrational energy level than our physical dimension. When the veil between the dimensions becomes weak, they cross over and seek out people with a higher vibrational energy, or those with a lower vibrational energy to feed on their energy. They often resist leaving their energetic food source and require assistance from higher-energy spirits to move on.

Lost Spirits: The spiritual part of a deceased human who was confused or damaged and did not go into the Light. They are stuck in the Earth's plane and often attach to incarnated humans.

Lucifer: The Archangel considered the Bringer of light, who has mistakenly been associated with the devil based on historic lore. He is a Greek and Roman mythologic God referred to as "shining one" and "morning star," is associated with the planet Venus, and is thought to be the son of Aurora, bringer of the dawn. Lucifer brings intelligence and enlightenment and was not associated with the devil in the early versions of the Bible.

Machu Picchu: (1438–1472) An Incan citadel located on a mountain ridge in southern Peru.

Mars: In Book 1, we learned the first bit of life arrived on a meteor from Mars. Conditions on Earth were excellent for life, but the first spark of life originated on Mars.

Mayans: A millennia-old group of people indigenous to Mesoamerica, who still exist to this day in Central America. While the term "Mayan" encompasses people of different cultures and ethnic groups, they all share some common cultural traits and linguistic origins.

Mass Extinction: An event during which the preponderance of life (all life—not just human) dies off. There have been five recorded mass extinction events on Earth: the Ordovician–Silurian, the Late Devonian, the Permian–Triassic, the Triassic–Jurassic, and the famous Cretaceous–Paleogene (also known as the Cretaceous–Tertiary) that ended the reign of the dinosaurs.

Michael: The Archangel sometimes referred to as Saint Michael. This Archangel is considered the great protector. He is often called on to protect from evil and help lost souls find their way into the Light.

Mother Mary: Beloved mother of Jesus known for her compassion and gentle love. She is venerated in many Abrahamic religions as one who helps mothers and children.

Mother Teresa: (Mary Teresa Bojaxhiu) Venerated modern-day Saint Teresa of Calcutta was granted a Nobel Peace Prize in 1979 for her tireless charitable work helping the poor, sick, and infirm in India.

Muhammad: (570–632 AD) Arab religious, social, and political leader, and founder of Islam. In Islam, he is considered a prophet sent to confirm monotheistic teachings as preached by Adam, Abraham, Moses, Jesus, and others. Muhammad united Arabia with the Quran as the center of his teachings.

Muir: In this book, it is the capital city of Atlantis, located in the Altiplano region of Peru.

Nag Hammadi Library: (second century AD) A collection of early Christian and Gnostic texts discovered buried in a jar near the town of Nag Hammadi, Egypt, in 1945. These thirteen leather-bound papyrus codices comprise fifty-two writings, including several gospels from early Christians.

Nazis: (1920–1945) The National Socialist German Workers' Party was a German political party under Adolf Hitler that established the ideology of National Socialism. They wanted to protect the supposed purity of the Aryan race by exterminating people of other nationalities, races, religious beliefs, sexual orientations, or those with compromised health. In what was called the Final Solution, the Nazis implemented a system of genocide, murdering millions of people in what is now referred to as the Holocaust.

Neoteny: (nee-ot-n-ee) The slowing or delaying of physical development, resulting in features that are a combination of traits from early- and late-stage development. If this combination breeds true, it can result in a new subspecies that coexists with the original.

Nergal: Mesopotamian God of war and pestilence who represents the noontime sun and the summer solstice. Also called "the king of sunset," who over time developed to God of the underworld.

Non-Corporeal Beings: Beings that exist entirely as energy (spirits) and have no physical bodies. Some of these spirits can take on physical form (become incarnations) for the life of that body, then return to noncorporeal form when the body dies. Other spirits never (by choice or limitation) take on physical form.

Odin: The Norse supreme deity and God of war, wisdom, death, and poetry. Considered to be the wisest of all deities, other Gods sought advice from him. Odin is considered to have created all living things, including the first mortals.

Osiris: The Egyptian God of fertility, agriculture, the afterlife, and the dead. He is brother to Isis. Often depicted as a green-skinned god with mummy-wrapped legs, Osiris was judge of the underworld and the Kings of Egypt were associated with him.

Pandora: In Greek mythology, Pandora was the first woman. Her body was fashioned by Hephaestus, into which Zeus then breathed life. The story of Pandora's Box is a precursor to the Biblical story of Eve and the apple.

Polytheistic Religions: The worship of or belief in multiple Gods and Goddesses as Guides for a civilization.

Power Vs. Force: The Hidden Determinants of Human Behavior: 1995 book by David R. Hawkins, MD, PhD, that details the study of the vibrational energy of emotions.

Prometheus: Greek Titan who defied the Gods by stealing fire and giving it to humanity. He was known for intelligence and considered a champion of humankind.

Protective Bubble: A spiritual technique designed to protect one's energy from external interference. It was outlined in detail in Book 1. You can use this spiritual hygiene to keep your energy strong and protected.

Quantum Entanglement: A phenomenon that occurs when a group of particles is created in a way that each cannot be described independently, but only as a group. The effect is that measurement of one particle will instantaneously produce a known countervalue in the other(s), regardless of the distance between them. Thus entangled particles communicate with no propagation delay (i.e., faster than light).

Quantum Level: In physics, a term describing a system of particles that are confined spatially and can only take on certain specific energy levels.

Quan Yin: (Guanyin) The beloved Buddhist Goddess of compassion and mercy. Guanyin hears all prayers and assists those who ask for her help. She represents forgiveness, compassion, peace, gentleness, and love.

Reincarnation: The rebirth of a spirit or soul into a physical life form, such as a body.

Raphael: The Archangel attributed to healing in most Abrahamic religious traditions. Raphael is associated with the angel in the Bible who stirs the water at the healing pool. Also known as Israfil, he is often pictured with a trumpet to bring the news of God.

Reiki: (ra-key) A form of energy balancing and healing that involves a Reiki practitioner placing their hands on or over parts of the receiver's body. It can be sent energetically by advanced students and is passed by a Reiki Master-Teacher to a student through a series of attunements.

Reiki Master-Teacher: The highest-level practitioner who practices, sends, and teaches Reiki, a form of energy balancing and healing. Reiki is passed from a Master-Teacher to a student through a series of attunements.

Rift: Geologically, a linear tearing apart of the Earth's crust. Esoterically, a tear in the energetic layers surrounding the earth.

Roman Empire: (27 BC–286 AD) Period in ancient Rome consisting of large territories around Europe, North Africa, West Asia, and the Mediterranean Sea. The principalities were ruled by emperors, with Italy as the metropole and Rome as the capital city.

Samael: The Archangel who brings discord and challenge. One of the seven Archangels in the Old Testament, Samael is considered the angel of death. With grim and destructive duties such as destroying sinners, he is one of God's servants and is not evil, as his functions resulted in balance. He is associated with bringing the tree of knowledge to man. He is noted as the Archangel who communicated with Muhammad in the Quran.

Shirodhara: (she-row-dar-ah) A sacred form of Ayurvedic therapy that involves gently pouring warm oils onto the forehead.

Shiva: (shee-vuh) The Supreme God in the Hindu religion. He is one of the Hindu Trinity, along with Brahma and Vishnu. Shiva is the Supreme Destroyer of Evil and the God of arts, meditation, and yoga.

Sleeping Beauty: A Disney story that is based on a 1344 AD folk tale later adapted by the Brothers Grimm, in which a princess was placed under a spell and slept for one hundred years, only to be awakened by true love.

Soul: The concepts of a person's spirit and soul are actually the same. The term "soul" carries more of a religious connotation. This is the immortal part of the being that survives bodily death.

Spirit: The immortal part of a living being that continues on when the physical body expires. Sometimes defined as a supernatural being, or a nonphysical entity such as a ghost, fairy, or angel. A ghost usually relates to a manifestation of the spirit of a deceased person who is stuck or still Earthbound. A spirit is often referred to as the essence of a deceased person who is in a good place and appears to some in order to assist the living.

Spiritual Guides: Spiritual beings who help humanity to evolve. The Wise Ones of the Collective are considered spiritual Guides.

***Spirits of Amoskeag: The Wounded Heroes of the Manchester Mills*:** Published in 2016, author Lois Hermann wrote this book in answer to a promise given to a group of spirits who died in the days of child labor in Manchester, New Hampshire, USA. Hermann shares their heartfelt stories in this poignant book.

Stonehenge: An ancient structure consisting of a ring of standing stones topped with lintels, surrounding five trilithons (pairs of stones each topped with a lintel). It was constructed in phases from 3100 to 1600 BC. The alignment of the stones is such that it serves as an astronomical calendar, indicating the solstices and equinoxes.

Subconscious: The deep internal part of the mind that drives the autonomic system and is the storehouse of every memory. The subconscious is the inner driver for choices, habits, and emotions.

Superconscious: The infinite part of the mind that communicates with higher sources of wisdom in different ways. It could be referred to as the wise mind, divine wisdom, or higher power. The superconscious is the part that connects with angelic beings, ascended masters, loved ones, or other spiritual Guides.

Sumeria: (2000 BC) The first literate civilization of ancient Mesopotamia, which scribed writings on stone tablets and regarded deities as responsible for all matters pertaining to the natural and social order.

Team Hope: The team of talented, dedicated, and determined individuals (spiritual and corporeal) who assist with the *Chronicles of Hope* journey.

Ten Plagues: In the Old Testament, the Israelites escaped Egyptian oppression when God sent a series of plagues that caused the Pharaoh to release them from slavery. During the tenth plague, the Israelites were instructed by God to mark their doorposts with the blood of a lamb. Their home was passed over from the death of their firstborn, hence the term and event "Passover."

Terra: Latin for "Earth." It is also the common name for the primordial Roman Goddess, Terra Mater, Mother Earth. In this series, Terra refers to the physical earth itself, while Gaia refers to the living spirit of Earth.

Terrans: Inhabitants of the planet Earth.

The Thirteen: The elected representatives from each of the islands and mainland of the Atlantean Realm who ran the day-to-day business of the realm.

Toltec: (tohl-tek) A Mesoamerican culture that thrived in the Tula, Hidalgo region of Mexico from the tenth to the thirteenth century. They were a predecessor to the Aztec culture, which considered the Toltec to be an intellectual civilization. Their name in Nahuatl, "Tōltēcatl," later came to mean artisan.

Turn the Other Cheek: A passage from Jesus' Sermon on the Mount that refers to responding to injury or insult without revenge. This passage has many interpretations, one being an expectation of nonresistance and pacifism on part of the victim.

"But I say to you who hear, love your enemies, do good to those who hate you, bless those who curse you, pray for those who abuse you. To one who strikes you on the cheek, offer the other also, and from one who takes away your cloak do not withhold your tunic either. Give to everyone who begs from you, and from one who takes away your goods do not demand them back. And as you wish that others would do to you, do so to them." — Jesus Christ, *English Standard Version* (Luke 6:27–31)

Universe: The expansive cosmos that comprises space and time including planets, stars, galaxies, and all other forms of matter and energy.

Veil: A boundary between different vibrational energy levels. It represents a shift-point between different dimensions and responds to vibrational energy changes.

Vibrational Energy Level: All things living and inanimate have a natural frequency at which they vibrate. Living things possess a spirit, which also vibrates at a certain energy level. Spirits that were created early in the Universe's development possess a high vibrational rate, corresponding to the high energy level of the Universe itself. Spirits that were created as the Universe became cooler possess a correspondingly lower vibrational level.

Vibrational Energy: Beings across the Universe are made of energy. Living things vibrate at different energy levels based on how old the spirit is, the number of lives they have had, and the type of spirit, i.e. animal or human.

White Buffalo Calf Woman: A prophetess who appeared to the Lakota people during a time of famine. She brought sacred rites to honor the Earth and a sacred pipe to use for prayers that might connect Earth to heaven. As she was leaving, she turned into a buffalo of many colors to symbolize the unity of all people. She helps with peace in relationships and our world.

Wise Mind: The part of the human mind that connects with higher sources of wisdom. It is most often the source of positive influence or guidance.

Wise Ones: Infinitely wise spiritual beings who willingly assist humanity when asked.

World War I: (1914–1918) Also known as the First World War or the Great War. This global war originated in Europe and was one of the largest wars in history.

Zeus: From the Greek Ζεύς, the God of the sky and thunder, and king of the Olympian Gods. He was born of Chronos, the king of the Titan Gods, and Rhea, Titaness daughter of Gaia. He is considered the eldest of the Olympian Gods.

Glossary

"Faith is taking the first step
even when we don't see the whole staircase."
—Martin Luther King, Jr.

About the Author

"If you can be the voice that rallies them,
rather than somebody who would use them for ill,
you will have accomplished your goal."
—Archangel Samael

A seasoned spiritual and metaphysical teacher, Lois Hermann is a Board-Certified Hypnotist (BCH), Certified Hypnosis Instructor (CHI), and a Neuro-Linguistic Programming Trainer (NLP-T). Lois has decades of experience in advanced hypnosis techniques, is an Energy Clearing & Alignment Master (ECAM) and specializes in Emotional Freedom Technique (EFT Tapping). She is also a Reiki Master-Teacher (RMT) and a multi-registered ultrasound medical professional (RDMS, RDCS, RVT).

For many years, Lois has conducted highly effective spiritual, energy-based, and success coaching programs to help clients discover ways to achieve success using the power of their mind, body, and spirit. She has guided professionals to the next level via individual or group sessions and is a frequent speaker on rapport building, organization, confidence, motivation, powerful public speaking, attitude of gratitude, energy clearing and alignment, inspiring hope, and more.

For decades, Lois has assisted clients, both children and adults, in person and remotely via video. She helps with issues related to stress, fears, worries, weight, sleep, nightmares, relationships, energy clearing, and more. Her clients learn to empower themselves and connect with their amazing mind to establish new mindsets, positive patterns, and healthy habits, as they develop enhanced personal and professional practices.

As a leading Certified Hypnosis Instructor, Lois has trained many individuals on a personal level to use hypnosis to empower themselves and their families. She teaches holistic practitioners to expand their practices through specialty training programs. Lois is passionate about sharing her skills, techniques, and tools to help individuals achieve success and wellness, as well as helping professionals to better assist their clients and patients. With her diverse background and experience, her trainings are always organized, engaging, and interesting.

For forty years, Lois enjoyed an extensive career as an award-winning pioneer in the field of diagnostic ultrasound. This background has helped her more fully understand and relate to how vibrational frequencies affect our bodies, minds, and spirits. As an international corporate trainer, clinical director, and systems designer, she holds several patents for ultrasound system design.

Lois is a frequent speaker at industry events and conferences, including the National Guild of Hypnotists annual convention, the Heartland Hypnosis Conference, and other professional conferences. She serves on the board of directors for the National Association for Transpersonal Hypnotherapists, where she was granted a prestigious award in 2019 for her contributions to transpersonal hypnotherapy.

In addition to the *Chronicles of Hope* series, Lois has published numerous works, including the historic mystery *The Spirits of Amoskeag: The Wounded Heroes of the Manchester Mills*, as well as many articles and blogs.

Her radio show *Inspiring Hope with Lois Hermann* was motivated by the channeled messages from Jesus to highlight the good people on Earth. Her show shines the light on positive people in our world who are making an inspiring difference.

Lois has dedicated her life to the mission of sharing the messages given to her by the Collective. With the information revealed in the *Chronicles of Hope* book series, she helps people shift their energy to be more positive, uplifted, and empowered so each can make a difference for humanity and our planet.

The Lord is my shepherd; I shall not want.
He maketh me to lie down in green pastures.
He leadeth me beside the still waters. He restoreth my soul.
He leadeth me in the paths of righteousness for his name's sake.
Yea, though I walk through the valley of the shadow of death,
I will fear no evil; for thou art with me

Thy rod and thy staff they comfort me.
Thou preparest a table before me in the presence of mine enemies.
Thou anointest my head with oil. My cup runneth over.
Surely goodness and mercy shall follow me all the days of my life.
And I will dwell in the house of the Lord forever.
—Psalm 23, *King James Bible*

Praise for Chronicles of Hope

"The book you are writing is good."

—Rae

"*Chronicles of Hope: The Anquietas* rattled my psychic being and queried my spiritual awareness. It was a game changer. *Chronicles of Hope: The Collective* brought unity to my psychic consciousness and was a spiritual transformation. It not only changed the game; it altered the outcome of the entire championship. The book describes how the Ancient Ones desire to bring wisdom, sustainability, and unity to our beloved planet and its inhabitants. Regrettably, they are seeing ignorance, environmental decline, and large inequities in the makeup of our societies—largely due to greed, hoarding, and injustice. However, we can all do something to bring about positive change. Read this book. Join the Collective."

—Neil Helm, PhD
Scholar in Residence (Ret.), Atlantic University, Virginia
Beach, Virginia

"In this volume, as each of the Energies responded to the call, my awareness of questions which had emerged throughout my lifelong spiritual journey was sharpened! Many questions have been answered, in addition to information validating my Spiritual Knowing. Their primary message is the key to recreating our world in harmony amongst all beings. This encapsulation in kindness can pave the pathway to preserving our world. Gaia is suffering, and we must consciously honor her spirit and her body. We cannot exist without her. We will perish, as other cultures have done. The profound importance of these messages is an example of the urgency to which we must respond. We are here at this time to do this work in joy and harmony."

—Grandmother Blue Crow
Northern Cheyenne

"Lois Hermann joins a divinely inspired empathic community of changemakers enlisted by Spirit to usher humanity to a higher vibration of cooperation and harmony for healing personal wounds through the infinite wisdom of the Universal Collective Mind. You will be guided to transform yourself and our conflicted world by these sacred messages that guide us to enlightenment and an improved human condition. So fascinating as Ms. Hermann offers details on ancient Atlantis and a past life as a priestess. Find power, calmness, and truth within this creative offering. Resonate with every new connection to the eternal stream of creation. A masterful book to awaken the sleeping soul. A must read in this lifetime!"

—Sheryl Glick, RMT
Author, Host of *Healing from Within*

"This is a profound, graceful, and loving book which brings forth the possibilities for all humanity. Here you'll find the work of a highly skilled professional, Lois Hermann, who helps to gather information to share with humanity. She works with sensitivity and precision in unveiling and explaining powerfully channeled information, as well as through other great experts who reveal the mysteries of the Universe and civilizations from Earth and beyond. This opens us to ancient truths buried in the inner being. A book of revelations."

—Marilyn Gordon, Board-Certified Hypnotherapist
Instructor, Author, Owner of Life Transformation Company

"The spirits that shared their communications in Book 2 will move you to tears, give you hope, and reset your intentions. The insights speak to every cell of your body. Be prepared at times to have your beliefs challenged while other times feel validated by truths you've experienced but were afraid to share. Open your heart to receive the urgent beckoning for us to wake up, respect our Earth, its species, and each other. Be a part of the profound shift that must occur on this planet and choose to be a voice for Gaia. Future generations will honor

and thank you. I absolutely loved this book! By far, it is the only book that has loved me back!"
—Denise McCalvey, CHT, RM
Transpersonal Hypnotist

"Suspend your biases as you read this book. It will deliver a message that moves your spirit. We are facing a serious threat to our planet and humankind. It is not a virus. It is not just a figment of our imaginations. We all come from somewhere and something extraordinary. If these words are true, our world is careening toward a point of no return. This book is for those who care about humanity and dare to hope. This is our Collective call to action. Thank you, ALL!"
—Heather Tallman Ruhm, MD
Integrative Medicine

"I love a book that stirs a resonance within; one that not only increases awareness but enhances that enlightenment beyond expectation. For me, this book was cause for many pauses for reflection and deep introspection. This book moves through enlightenment to awaken who we truly are and who we truly must be. The message is clear: we must change. We must embrace the narrative of these ancient spiritual beings to raise the vibrational energy of humanity and bring their message of hope. It is a once in a lifetime read, in the hope of saving our planet and the people on her."
—Brian Hill, PT, CH
Hill Rehab & Manual Therapy

"In this time of chaos, emotional confusion, and spiritual discord, *Chronicles of Hope: The Collective* is your port in the storm. Reality is multidimensional. Our problems cannot be solved with a three-dimensional mentality. This book delivers intellectual insights in a clear format to reverse humanity's negative emotional and spiritual decline. It offers ancient time-tested messages in a factual, intellectual structure and shows how negative emotional issues historically have destroyed

people, countries, and even whole civilizations. *Chronicles* offers a solid format for fantastic intellectual, spiritual, and emotional growth to benefit all. The structure is brilliant. It is simple, not simplistic! I hopefully await your next book in the series."
—Albert Marotta, MA, CHT
Transpersonal Hypnotist

"Lois offers amazing channeled information from many ancient societies and Guides from outside of our normal reach. Their views on our society are stated with such purpose. Lois mentions many times about the importance of clearing energy. I especially enjoyed learning about the Protective Bubble because it reminded me of having to protect myself from lower energies. I was fascinated with the details she shares about Gaia, Mother Earth, the planet, and its inhabitants. Especially helpful is that the Highlights are all consolidated in one place."
—Catherine M. Laub
The Celestial Spoon Podcast Host, Author

"This book is an incredible gift to anyone who reads it! It is partly a call-to-action and partly a roadmap for living a conscious life. I was able to see Jesus and his teachings from the depth of his perspective. New understandings were created while old misunderstandings were corrected. Lois helps bring insight about our origins from the perspective of our creators through the eyes of their Children's Children. The resonating truths are palpable, and the information is uplifting. The presentation is so engaging that at times I felt like I attended the session in person."
—Kathleen Kubacki, LMT, CHT
Transpersonal Hypnotist

"With the world in such a state of disarray, this book is right on time. The messages speak truth to our true nature as human beings. The messages are profound and inspiring, encouraging every one of us to explore ourselves deeper. We must truly ask who we are and what is

our purpose here as a human collective. It was wonderfully written and keeps you engaged and wanting more with each chapter. I am already craving insights from Book 3."
    —Justin Etling, Recovery and Spiritual Teacher
      Author, Founder of Ascend Video Virtual Communities

"I am deeply moved by the *Chronicle of Hope* books. Personally, I appreciate how Book 2 gives a plan of how to live in a deeply spiritual way to begin repairing the damage on our Earth so our children and grandchildren have a place to live. Growing up in church, I was told to first ask God for direction and wait. Now, I understand to seek first my own spirit's path and then partner with my Creator. Professionally, I share these ideas with my psychotherapy clients as they seek to manage depression and anxiety. This book gives them a framework to follow that boosts their joy and allows them to let go of negative memories and emotions."
    —Laurel Kramer, PhD
      Psychologist

"I have followed hypnosis colleague, Lois Hermann, with fascination through her books. *Chronicles of Hope* addresses the serious concerns many of us feel about the direction our country and the world is heading. As the Spirits attest, we are almost at the tipping point. In this atmosphere of looming doom, hope is very much needed. It will come as we step into our own power with each person doing whatever is theirs to do, seeking and following their own inner guidance. I sincerely hope those reading this book take the warnings seriously and do something now."
    —Roxanne Louise, Hypnotherapist
      Former President of the American Society of Dowsers,
      National Speaker, Author

"This book places the reader in the front row, amplifying the most important and compelling messages of our time and for our generations to come. The invitation is palpable: pause, reflect, consider, and act. Each of us has the power to change the world for the better and this insightful and inspired book provides a recipe for hope and success. If you have been confused by biblical parables and conflicting messages about right and wrong, this book can allay your misperceptions, giving you real hope. It is easy to read, reference, and remember its teachings. Be blessed as you read each page or consult the last pages for daily reminders and inspiration."

   —Melinda Tourangeau
     Author, Motivational Speaker

"I have the utmost respect for the courage it took to write such a powerful, insightful, awe-inspiring, and life-altering book. The Collective shares such insight and guidance for humanity at a critical tipping point of our existence. We are left with clear choices to save humanity, restore our planet, and live with hope, peace, and love. I invite readers to set aside personal prism and formed perspective. With childlike innocence, allow your spirit to be open to all the possibilities of the Collective's messages. If you bring these insights into your own life, you will vibrate at a higher frequency filled with light and hope, having a rippling affect for others you touch."

   —Christine Peck, CH
     Transpersonal Hypnotist

"Three loves of my life are words, music, and nature. *Chronicles of Hope* speaks to all three. Of words: the Collective, a group of Divine Spirits and Angels, kindles my hope that incites and lights my path toward positive thought and action, raising my vibrational energy. Of music: the messages in this book reverberate and ring the bell of awakening deep within, and my wellspring of spirit is renewed and responds with joy and expression. Of nature: I hear Gaia, the living Spirit of the Earth, singing the refrain of life that is the drumbeat of all hope."

   —Lizzie Fleenor
     Writer, Reader, Spiritual Seeker

Additional reviews and contact information can be found at
www.ChroniclesOfHope.net

"Go placidly amid the noise and the haste,
and remember what peace there may be in silence.
As far as possible, without surrender,
be on good terms with all persons.
Speak your truth quietly and clearly,
and listen to others..."
—Max Ehrmann, from the *Desiderata*

Connect with Team Hope

Blessed are the peacemakers,
for they shall be called children of God.
—Jesus

Inspiring Hope Community: ChroniclesOfHope.net/Community

Inspiring Hope with Lois Hermann Radio Show:
WSMN1590.com / WSMN 1590 AM / WSMN 95.3 FM

Insights Newsletter: LoisHermann.com/Insights

Facebook.com/ChroniclesOfHopeTheMessages
Facebook.com/LoisHermannSuccessCoach
Linkedin.com/in/loishermann
Twitter.com/lois_hermann
Instagram.com/loishermann_
YouTube: Lois Hermann & Associates

www.ChroniclesOfHope.net
www.LoisHermann.com

"Yesterday is but a dream, tomorrow is only a vision.
But today, well lived, makes every yesterday a dream of happiness,
and every tomorrow a vision of hope.
Look well, therefore, to this day,
for it is very life of life."
— Sanskrit Proverb